Python in Practice

Developer's Library Series

Visit **developers-library.com** for a complete list of available products

---

The **Developer's Library Series** from Addison-Wesley provides practicing programmers with unique, high-quality references and tutorials on the latest programming languages and technologies they use in their daily work. All books in the Developer's Library are written by expert technology practitioners who are exceptionally skilled at organizing and presenting information in a way that's useful for other programmers.

Developer's Library books cover a wide range of topics, from open-source programming languages and databases, Linux programming, Microsoft, and Java, to Web development, social networking platforms, Mac/iPhone programming, and Android programming.

✦Addison-Wesley **Cisco Press** EXAM/**CRAM** **IBM** Press. QUE¯ ░░ PRENTICE HALL **S/\MS** | Safari¯

Python in Practice

Create Better Programs Using Concurrency, Libraries, and Patterns

Mark Summerfield

✦▾Addison-Wesley

Upper Saddle River, NJ · Boston · Indianapolis · San Francisco
New York · Toronto · Montreal · London · Munich · Paris · Madrid
Capetown · Sydney · Tokyo · Singapore · Mexico City

Library of Congress Control Number: 2013942956

ISBN-13: 978-0-321-90563-5
ISBN-10:   0-321-90563-6

Text printed in the United States on recycled paper at RR Donnelley in Crawfordsville, Indiana.
First printing, August 2013

*This book is dedicated to
free and open-source software contributors
everywhere—your generosity benefits us all.*

Contents at a Glance

www.qtrac.eu/pipbook.html

Contents

Foreword

I have been building software with Python for 15 years in various application areas. Over that time I have seen our community mature and grow considerably. We are long past the days of having to "sell" Python to our managers in order to be able to use it in work-related projects. Today's job market for Python programmers is strong. Attendance at Python-related conferences is at an all time high, for regional conferences as well as the big national and international events. Projects like OpenStack are pushing the language into new arenas and attracting new talent to the community at the same time. As a result of the robust and expanding community, we have more and better options for books about Python than ever before.

Mark Summerfield is well known in the Python community for his technical writing about Qt and Python. Another of Mark's books, *Programming in Python 3*, is at the top of my short list of recommendations for learning Python, a question I am asked frequently as the organizer of the user group in Atlanta, Georgia. This new book will also go on my list, but for a somewhat different audience.

Most programming books fall at either end of a spectrum that ranges from basic introductions to a language (or programming in general) to more advanced books on very focused topics like web development, GUI applications, or bioinformatics. As I was writing *The Python Standard Library by Example*, I wanted to appeal to readers who fall into the gap between those extremes—established programmers and generalists, both familiar with the language but who want to enhance their skills by going beyond the basics without being restricted to a specific application area. When my editor asked me to review the proposal for Mark's book, I was pleased to see that *Python in Practice* is designed for the same types of readers.

It has been a long time since I have encountered an idea in a book that was immediately applicable to one of my own projects, without it being tied to a specific framework or library. For the past year I have been working on a system for metering OpenStack cloud services. Along the way, the team realized that the data we are collecting for billing could be useful for other purposes, like reporting and monitoring, so we designed the system to send it to multiple consumers by passing the samples through a pipeline of reusable transformations and publishers. At about the same time that the code for the pipeline was being finalized, I was also involved in the technical review for this book. After reading the first few sections of the draft for Chapter 3, it became clear that our pipeline implementation was much more complicated than necessary. The coroutine chaining technique Mark demonstrates is so much more elegant and easy to understand that

I immediately added a task to our roadmap to change the design during the next release cycle.

Python in Practice is full of similarly useful advice and examples to help you improve your craft. Generalists like me will find introductions to several interesting tools that may not have been encountered before. And whether you are already an experienced programmer or are making the transition out of the beginner phase of your career, this book will help you think about problems from different perspectives and give you techniques to create more effective solutions.

Doug Hellmann
Senior Developer, DreamHost
May 2013

Introduction

This book is aimed at Python programmers who want to broaden and deepen their Python knowledge so that they can improve the quality, reliability, speed, maintainability, and usability of their Python programs. The book presents numerous practical examples and ideas for improved Python programming.

The book has four key themes: design patterns for coding elegance, improved processing speeds using concurrency and compiled Python (*Cython*), high-level networking, and graphics.

The book *Design Patterns: Elements of Reusable Object-Oriented Software* (see the Selected Bibliography for details; ➤ 285) was published way back in 1995, yet still exerts a powerful influence over object-oriented programming practices. *Python in Practice* looks at all of the design patterns in the context of Python, providing Python examples of those that are useful, as well as explaining why some are irrelevant to Python programmers. These patterns are covered in Chapter 1, Chapter 2, and Chapter 3.

Python's GIL (Global Interpreter Lock) prevents Python code from executing on more than one processor core at a time.★ This has led to the myth that Python can't do threading or take advantage of multi-core hardware. For CPU-bound processing, concurrency can be done using the multiprocessing module, which is not limited by the GIL and can take full advantage of all the available cores. This can easily achieve the speedups we would expect (i.e., roughly proportional to the number of cores). For I/O-bound processing we can also use the multiprocessing module—or we can use the threading module or the concurrent.futures module. If we use threading for I/O-bound concurrency, the GIL's overhead is usually dominated by network latency and so may not be an issue in practice.

Unfortunately, low- and medium-level approaches to concurrency are very error-prone (in any language). We can avoid such problems by avoiding the use of explicit locks, and by making use of Python's high-level queue and multiprocessing modules' queues, or the concurrent.futures module. We will see how to achieve significant performance improvements using high-level concurrency in Chapter 4.

Sometimes programmers use C, C++, or some other compiled language because of another myth—that Python is slow. While Python is in general slower than compiled languages, on modern hardware Python is often more than fast

---

★This limitation applies to CPython—the reference implementation that most Python programmers use. Some Python implementations don't have this constraint, most notably, Jython (Python implemented in Java).

enough for most applications. And in those cases where Python really isn't fast enough, we can still enjoy the benefits of programming in Python—and at the same time have our code run faster.

To speed up long-running programs we can use the PyPy Python interpreter (pypy.org). PyPy has a just-in-time compiler that can deliver significant speedups. Another way to increase performance is to use code that runs as fast as compiled C; for CPU-bound processing this can comfortably give us $100\times$ speedups. The easiest way to achieve C-like speed is to use Python modules that are already written in C under the hood: for example, use the standard library's array module or the third-party numpy module for incredibly fast and memory-efficient array processing (including multi-dimensional arrays with numpy). Another way is to profile using the standard library's cProfile module to discover where the bottlenecks are, and then write any speed-critical code in Cython—this essentially provides an enhanced Python syntax that compiles into pure C for maximum runtime speed.

Of course, sometimes the functionality we need is already available in a C or C++ library, or a library in another language that uses the C calling convention. In most such cases there will be a third-party Python module that provides access to the library we require—these can be found on the Python Package Index (PyPI; pypi.python.org). But in the uncommon case that such a module isn't available, the standard library's ctypes module can be used to access C library functionality—as can the third-party Cython package. Using preexisting C libraries can significantly reduce development times, as well as usually providing very fast processing. Both ctypes and Cython are covered in Chapter 5.

The Python standard library provides a variety of modules for networking, from the low-level socket module, to the mid-level socketserver module, up to the high-level xmlrpclib module. Although low- and mid-level networking makes sense when porting code from another language, if we are starting out in Python we can often avoid the low-level detail and just focus on what we want our networking applications to do by using high-level modules. In Chapter 6 we will see how to do this using the standard library's xmlrpclib module and the powerful and easy-to-use third-party RPyC module.

Almost every program must provide some kind of user interface so that the program can determine what work it must do. Python programs can be written to support command-line user interfaces, using the argparse module, and full-terminal user interfaces (e.g., on Unix using the third-party urwid package; excess.org/urwid). There are also a great many web frameworks—from the lightweight bottle (bottlepy.org) to heavyweights like Django (www.django-project.com) and Pyramid (www.pylonsproject.org)—all of which can be used to provide applications with a web interface. And, of course, Python can be used to create GUI (graphical user interface) applications.

The death of GUI applications in favor of web applications is often reported—and still hasn't happened. In fact, people seem to prefer GUI applications to web applications. For example, when smartphones became very popular early in the twenty-first century, users invariably preferred to use a purpose-built "app" rather than a web browser and web page for things they did regularly. There are many ways to do GUI programming with Python using third-party packages. However, in Chapter 7 we will see how to create modern-looking GUI applications using Tkinter, which is supplied as part of Python's standard library.

Most modern computers—including laptops and even smartphones—come equipped with powerful graphics facilities, often in the form of a separate GPU (Graphics Processing Unit) that's capable of impressive 2D and 3D graphics. Most GPUs support the OpenGL API, and Python programmers can get access to this API through third-party packages. In Chapter 8, we will see how to make use of OpenGL to do 3D graphics.

The purpose of this book is to illustrate how to write better Python applications that have good performance and maintainable code, and are easy to use. This book assumes prior knowledge of Python programming and is intended to be the kind of book people turn to once they've learned Python, whether from Python's documentation or from other books—such as *Programming in Python 3, Second Edition* (see the Selected Bibliography for details; ➤ 287). The book is designed to provide ideas, inspiration, and practical techniques to help readers take their Python programming to the next level.

All the book's examples have been tested with Python 3.3 (and where possible Python 3.2 and Python 3.1) on Linux, OS X (in most cases), and Windows (in most cases). The examples are available from the book's web site, www.qtrac.eu/pipbook.html, and should work with all future Python 3.x versions.

Acknowledgments

As with all my other technical books, this book has greatly benefited from the advice, help, and encouragement of others: I am very grateful to them all.

Nick Coghlan, a Python core developer since 2005, provided plenty of constructive criticism, and backed this up with lots of ideas and code snippets to show alternative and better ways to do things. Nick's help was invaluable throughout the book, and particularly improved the early chapters.

Doug Hellmann, an experienced Python developer and author, sent me lots of useful comments, both on the initial proposal, and on every chapter of the book itself. Doug gave me many ideas and was kind enough to write the foreword.

Two friends—Jasmin Blanchette and Trenton Schulz—are both experienced programmers, and with their widely differing Python knowledge, they are ideal representatives of many of the book's intended readership. Jasmin and

Trenton's feedback has lead to many improvements and clarifications in the text and in the examples.

I am glad to thank my commissioning editor, Debra Williams Cauley, who once more provided support and practical help as the work progressed.

Thanks also to Elizabeth Ryan who managed the production process so well, and to the proofreader, Anna V. Popick, who did such excellent work.

As always, I thank my wife, Andrea, for her love and support.

1 Creational Design Patterns

Creational design patterns are concerned with how objects are created. Normally we create objects by calling their constructor (i.e., calling their class object with arguments), but sometimes we need more flexibility in how objects are created—which is why the creational design patterns are useful.

For Python programmers, some of these patterns are fairly similar to each other—and some of them, as we will note, aren't really needed at all. This is because the original design patterns were primarily created for the C++ language and needed to work around some of that language's limitations. Python doesn't have those limitations.

1.1. Abstract Factory Pattern

The Abstract Factory Pattern is designed for situations where we want to create complex objects that are composed of other objects and where the composed objects are all of one particular "family".

For example, in a GUI system we might have an abstract widget factory that has three concrete subclass factories: MacWidgetFactory, XfceWidgetFactory, and WindowsWidgetFactory, all of which provide methods for creating the same objects (make_button(), make_spinbox(), etc.), but that do so using the platform-appropriate styling. This allows us to create a generic create_dialog() function that takes a factory instance as argument and produces a dialog with the OS X, Xfce, or Windows look and feel, depending on which factory we pass it.

1.1.1. A Classic Abstract Factory

To illustrate the Abstract Factory Pattern we will review a program that produces a simple diagram. Two factories will be used: one to produce plain text output, and the other to produce SVG (Scalable Vector Graphics) output. Both outputs are shown in Figure 1.1. The first version of the program we will look at, diagram1.py, shows the pattern in its pure form. The second version, diagram2.py, takes advantage of some Python-specific features to make the code slightly shorter and cleaner. Both versions produce identical output.*

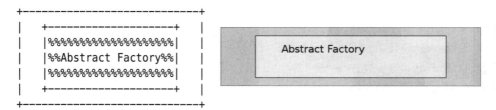

Figure 1.1 *The plain text and SVG diagrams*

We will begin by looking at the code common to both versions, starting with the main() function.

```
def main():
    ...
    txtDiagram = create_diagram(DiagramFactory())    ❶
    txtDiagram.save(textFilename)

    svgDiagram = create_diagram(SvgDiagramFactory())    ❷
    svgDiagram.save(svgFilename)
```

First we create a couple of filenames (not shown). Next, we create a diagram using the plain text (default) factory (❶), which we then save. Then, we create and save the same diagram, only this time using an SVG factory (❷).

```
def create_diagram(factory):
    diagram = factory.make_diagram(30, 7)
    rectangle = factory.make_rectangle(4, 1, 22, 5, "yellow")
    text = factory.make_text(7, 3, "Abstract Factory")
    diagram.add(rectangle)
    diagram.add(text)
    return diagram
```

---

* All the book's examples are available for download from www.qtrac.eu/pipbook.html.

This function takes a diagram factory as its sole argument and uses it to create the required diagram. The function doesn't know or care what kind of factory it receives so long as it supports our diagram factory interface. We will look at the make_...() methods shortly.

Now that we have seen how the factories are used, we can turn to the factories themselves. Here is the plain text diagram factory (which is also the factory base class):

```python
class DiagramFactory:

    def make_diagram(self, width, height):
        return Diagram(width, height)

    def make_rectangle(self, x, y, width, height, fill="white",
            stroke="black"):
        return Rectangle(x, y, width, height, fill, stroke)

    def make_text(self, x, y, text, fontsize=12):
        return Text(x, y, text, fontsize)
```

Despite the word "abstract" in the pattern's name, it is usual for one class to serve both as a base class that provides the interface (i.e., the abstraction), and also as a concrete class in its own right. We have followed that approach here with the DiagramFactory class.

Here are the first few lines of the SVG diagram factory:

```python
class SvgDiagramFactory(DiagramFactory):

    def make_diagram(self, width, height):
        return SvgDiagram(width, height)
    ...
```

The only difference between the two make_diagram() methods is that the Diagram-Factory.make_diagram() method returns a Diagram object and the SvgDiagramFactory.make_diagram() method returns an SvgDiagram object. This pattern applies to the two other methods in the SvgDiagramFactory (which are not shown).

We will see in a moment that the implementations of the plain text Diagram, Rectangle, and Text classes are radically different from those of the SvgDiagram, SvgRectangle, and SvgText classes—although every class provides the same interface (i.e., both Diagram and SvgDiagram have the same methods). This means that we can't mix classes from different families (e.g., Rectangle and SvgText)—and this is a constraint automatically applied by the factory classes.

Plain text Diagram objects hold their data as a list of lists of single character strings where the character is a space or +, |, -, and so on. The plain text Rect-

angle and Text and a list of lists of single character strings that are to replace
those in the overall diagram at their position (and working right and down as
necessary).

```python
class Text:

    def __init__(self, x, y, text, fontsize):
        self.x = x
        self.y = y
        self.rows = [list(text)]
```

This is the complete Text class. For plain text we simply discard the fontsize.

```python
class Diagram:

    ...

    def add(self, component):
        for y, row in enumerate(component.rows):
            for x, char in enumerate(row):
                self.diagram[y + component.y][x + component.x] = char
```

Here is the Diagram.add() method. When we call it with a Rectangle or Text object
(the component), this method iterates over all the characters in the component's
list of lists of single character strings (component.rows) and replaces corresponding characters in the diagram. The Diagram.__init__() method (not shown) has
already ensured that its self.diagram is a list of lists of space characters (of the
given width and height) when Diagram(width, height) is called.

```python
SVG_TEXT = """<text x="{x}" y="{y}" text-anchor="left" \
font-family="sans-serif" font-size="{fontsize}">{text}</text>"""

SVG_SCALE = 20

class SvgText:

    def __init__(self, x, y, text, fontsize):
        x *= SVG_SCALE
        y *= SVG_SCALE
        fontsize *= SVG_SCALE // 10
        self.svg = SVG_TEXT.format(**locals())
```

This is the complete SvgText class and the two constants it depends on.* Incidentally, using **locals() saves us from having to write SVG_TEXT.format(x=x, y=y,
text=text, fontsize=fontsize). From Python 3.2 we could write SVG_TEXT.for-

---

* Our SVG output is rather crudely done—but it is sufficient to show this design pattern. Third-
party SVG modules are available from the Python Package Index (PyPI) at pypi.python.org.

mat_map(locals()) instead, since the str.format_map() method does the mapping unpacking for us. (See the "Sequence and Mapping Unpacking" sidebar, ➤ 13.)

```
class SvgDiagram:
    ...

    def add(self, component):
        self.diagram.append(component.svg)
```

For the SvgDiagram class, each instance holds a list of strings in self.diagram, each one of which is a piece of SVG text. This makes adding new components (e.g., of type SvgRectangle or SvgText) really easy.

1.1.2. A More Pythonic Abstract Factory

The DiagramFactory and its SvgDiagramFactory subclass, and the classes they make use of (Diagram, SvgDiagram, etc.), work perfectly well and exemplify the design pattern.

Nonetheless, our implementation has some deficiencies. First, neither of the factories needs any state of its own, so we don't really need to create factory instances. Second, the code for SvgDiagramFactory is almost identical to that of DiagramFactory—the only difference being that it returns SvgText rather than Text instances, and so on—which seems like needless duplication. Third, our top-level namespace contains all of the classes: DiagramFactory, Diagram, Rectangle, Text, and all the SVG equivalents. Yet we only really need to access the two factories. Furthermore, we have been forced to prefix the SVG class names (e.g., using SvgRectangle rather than Rectangle) to avoid name clashes, which is untidy. (One solution for avoiding name conflicts would be to put each class in its own module. However, this approach would not solve the problem of code duplication.)

In this subsection we will address all these deficiencies. (The code is in diagram2.py.)

The first change we will make is to nest the Diagram, Rectangle, and Text classes inside the DiagramFactory class. This means that these classes must now be accessed as DiagramFactory.Diagram and so on. We can also nest the equivalent classes inside the SvgDiagramFactory class, only now we can give them the same names as the plain text classes since a name conflict is no longer possible—for example, SvgDiagramFactory.Diagram. We have also nested the constants the classes depend on, so our only top-level names are now main(), create_diagram(), DiagramFactory, and SvgDiagramFactory.

```
class DiagramFactory:

    @classmethod
    def make_diagram(Class, width, height):
```

```
        return Class.Diagram(width, height)

    @classmethod
    def make_rectangle(Class, x, y, width, height, fill="white",
            stroke="black"):
        return Class.Rectangle(x, y, width, height, fill, stroke)

    @classmethod
    def make_text(Class, x, y, text, fontsize=12):
        return Class.Text(x, y, text, fontsize)

    ...
```

Here is the start of our new DiagramFactory class. The make_...() methods are now all class methods. This means that when they are called the class is passed as their first argument (rather like self is passed for normal methods). So, in this case a call to DiagramFactory.make_text() will mean that DiagramFactory is passed as the Class, and a DiagramFactory.Text object will be created and returned.

This change also means that the SvgDiagramFactory subclass that inherits from DiagramFactory does not need any of the make_...() methods at all. If we call, say, SvgDiagramFactory.make_rectangle(), since SvgDiagramFactory doesn't have that method the base class DiagramFactory.make_rectangle() method will be called instead—but the Class passed will be SvgDiagramFactory. This will result in an SvgDiagramFactory.Rectangle object being created and returned.

```
def main():
    ...
    txtDiagram = create_diagram(DiagramFactory)
    txtDiagram.save(textFilename)

    svgDiagram = create_diagram(SvgDiagramFactory)
    svgDiagram.save(svgFilename)
```

These changes also mean that we can simplify our main() function since we no longer need to create factory instances.

The rest of the code is almost identical to before, the key difference being that since the constants and non-factory classes are now nested inside the factories, we must access them using the factory name.

```
class SvgDiagramFactory(DiagramFactory):
    ...
    class Text:

        def __init__(self, x, y, text, fontsize):
            x *= SvgDiagramFactory.SVG_SCALE
            y *= SvgDiagramFactory.SVG_SCALE
```

```
            fontsize *= SvgDiagramFactory.SVG_SCALE // 10
            self.svg = SvgDiagramFactory.SVG_TEXT.format(**locals())
```

Here is the `SvgDiagramFactory`'s nested `Text` class (equivalent to `diagram1.py`'s `SvgText` class), which shows how the nested constants must be accessed.

1.2. Builder Pattern

The Builder Pattern is similar to the Abstract Factory Pattern in that both patterns are designed for creating complex objects that are composed of other objects. What makes the Builder Pattern distinct is that the builder not only provides the methods for building a complex object, it also holds the representation of the entire complex object itself.

This pattern allows the same kind of compositionality as the Abstract Factory Pattern (i.e., complex objects are built out of one or more simpler objects), but is particularly suited to cases where the representation of the complex object needs to be kept separate from the composition algorithms.

We will show an example of the Builder Pattern in a program that can produce forms—either web forms using HTML, or GUI forms using Python and Tkinter. Both forms work visually and support text entry; however, their buttons are non-functional.* The forms are shown in Figure 1.2; the source code is in `formbuilder.py`.

Figure 1.2 *The HTML and Tkinter forms on Windows*

Let's begin by looking at the code needed to build each form, starting with the top-level calls.

```
htmlForm = create_login_form(HtmlFormBuilder())
with open(htmlFilename, "w", encoding="utf-8") as file:
    file.write(htmlForm)

tkForm = create_login_form(TkFormBuilder())
```

---

*All the examples must strike a balance between realism and suitability for learning, and as a result a few—as in this case—have only basic functionality.

```
with open(tkFilename, "w", encoding="utf-8") as file:
    file.write(tkForm)
```

Here, we have created each form and written it out to an appropriate file. In both cases we use the same form creation function (create_login_form()), parameterized by an appropriate builder object.

```
def create_login_form(builder):
    builder.add_title("Login")
    builder.add_label("Username", 0, 0, target="username")
    builder.add_entry("username", 0, 1)
    builder.add_label("Password", 1, 0, target="password")
    builder.add_entry("password", 1, 1, kind="password")
    builder.add_button("Login", 2, 0)
    builder.add_button("Cancel", 2, 1)
    return builder.form()
```

This function can create any arbitrary HTML or Tkinter form—or any other kind of form for which we have a suitable builder. The builder.add_title() method is used to give the form a title. All the other methods are used to add a widget to the form at a given row and column position.

Both HtmlFormBuilder and TkFormBuilder inherit from an abstract base class, AbstractFormBuilder.

```
class AbstractFormBuilder(metaclass=abc.ABCMeta):

    @abc.abstractmethod
    def add_title(self, title):
        self.title = title

    @abc.abstractmethod
    def form(self):
        pass

    @abc.abstractmethod
    def add_label(self, text, row, column, **kwargs):
        pass
    ...
```

Any class that inherits this class must implement all the abstract methods. We have elided the add_entry() and add_button() abstract methods because, apart from their names, they are identical to the add_label() method. Incidentally, we are required to make the AbstractFormBuilder have a metaclass of abc.ABCMeta to allow it to use the abc module's @abstractmethod decorator. (See §2.4, ➤ 48 for more on decorators.)

Sequence and Mapping Unpacking

Unpacking means extracting all the items in a sequence or map individually. One simple use case for sequence unpacking is to extract the first or first few items, and then the rest. For example:

```
first, second, *rest = sequence
```

Here we are assuming that `sequence` has at least three items: `first == sequence[0]`, `second == sequence[1]`, and `rest == sequence[2:]`.

Perhaps the most common uses of unpacking are related to function calls. If we have a function that expects a certain number of positional arguments, or particular keyword arguments, we can use unpacking to provide them. For example:

```
args = (600, 900)
kwargs = dict(copies=2, collate=False)
print_setup(*args, **kwargs)
```

The `print_setup()` function requires two positional arguments (`width` and `height`) and accepts up to two optional keyword arguments (`copies` and `collate`). Rather than passing the values directly, we have created an `args` tuple and a `kwargs` dict, and used sequence unpacking (`*args`) and mapping unpacking (`**kwargs`) to pass in the arguments. The effect is exactly the same as if we had written, `print_setup(600, 900, copies=2, collate=False)`.

The other use related to function calls is to create functions that can accept any number of positional arguments, or any number of keyword arguments, or any number of either. For example:

```
def print_args(*args, **kwargs):
    print(args.__class__.__name__, args,
          kwargs.__class__.__name__, kwargs)
print_args() # prints: tuple () dict {}
print_args(1, 2, 3, a="A") # prints: tuple (1, 2, 3) dict {'a': 'A'}
```

The `print_args()` function accepts any number of positional or keyword arguments. Inside the function, `args` is of type `tuple`, and `kwargs` is of type `dict`. If we wanted to pass these on to a function called inside the `print_args()` function, we could, of course, use unpacking in the call (e.g., `function(*args, **kwargs)`). Another common use of mapping unpacking is when calling the `str.format()` method—for example, `s.format(**locals())`—rather than typing all the *key=value* arguments manually (e.g., see SvgText.__init__(); 8 ◄).

Giving a class a metaclass of `abc.ABCMeta` means that the class cannot be instantiated, and so must be used as an abstract base class. This makes particular sense for code being ported from, say, C++ or Java, but does incur a tiny runtime overhead. However, many Python programmers use a more laid back approach: they don't use a metaclass at all, and simply document that the class should be used as an abstract base class.

```
class HtmlFormBuilder(AbstractFormBuilder):

    def __init__(self):
        self.title = "HtmlFormBuilder"
        self.items = {}

    def add_title(self, title):
        super().add_title(escape(title))

    def add_label(self, text, row, column, **kwargs):
        self.items[(row, column)] = ('<td><label for="{}">{}:</label></td>'
                .format(kwargs["target"], escape(text)))

    def add_entry(self, variable, row, column, **kwargs):
        html = """<td><input name="{}" type="{}" /></td>""".format(
                variable, kwargs.get("kind", "text"))
        self.items[(row, column)] = html
    ...
```

Here is the start of the `HtmlFormBuilder` class. We provide a default title in case the form is built without one. All the form's widgets are stored in an `items` dictionary that uses *row, column* 2-tuple keys, and the widgets' HTML as values.

We must reimplement the `add_title()` method since it is abstract, but since the abstract version has an implementation we can simply call that implementation. In this case we must preprocess the title using the `html.escape()` function (or the `xml.sax.saxutil.escape()` function in Python 3.2 or earlier).

The `add_button()` method (not shown) is structurally similar to the other `add_...()` methods.

```
    def form(self):
        html = ["<!doctype html>\n<html><head><title>{}</title></head>"
                "<body>".format(self.title), '<form><table border="0">']
        thisRow = None
        for key, value in sorted(self.items.items()):
            row, column = key
            if thisRow is None:
                html.append("  <tr>")
            elif thisRow != row:
```

```
            html.append("  </tr>\n  <tr>")
        thisRow = row
        html.append("    " + value)
    html.append("  </tr>\n</table></form></body></html>")
    return "\n".join(html)
```

The `HtmlFormBuilder.form()` method creates an HTML page consisting of a `<form>`, inside of which is a `<table>`, inside of which are rows and columns of widgets. Once all the pieces have been added to the `html` list, the list is returned as a single string (with newline separators to make it more human-readable).

```
class TkFormBuilder(AbstractFormBuilder):

    def __init__(self):
        self.title = "TkFormBuilder"
        self.statements = []

    def add_title(self, title):
        super().add_title(title)

    def add_label(self, text, row, column, **kwargs):
        name = self._canonicalize(text)
        create = """self.{}Label = ttk.Label(self, text="{}:")""".format(
            name, text)
        layout = """self.{}Label.grid(row={}, column={}, sticky=tk.W, \
padx="0.75m", pady="0.75m")""".format(name, row, column)
        self.statements.extend((create, layout))

    ...
    def form(self):
        return TkFormBuilder.TEMPLATE.format(title=self.title,
            name=self._canonicalize(self.title, False),
            statements="\n        ".join(self.statements))
```

This is an extract from the `TkFormBuilder` class. We store the form's widgets as a list of statements (i.e., as strings of Python code), two statements per widget.

The `add_label()` method's structure is also used by the `add_entry()` and `add_button()` methods (neither of which is shown). These methods begin by getting a canonicalized name for the widget and then make two strings: `create`, which has the code to create the widget and `layout`, which has the code to lay out the widget in the form. Finally, the methods add the two strings to the list of statements.

The `form()` method is very simple: it just returns a `TEMPLATE` string parameterized by the title and the statements.

```
    TEMPLATE = """#!/usr/bin/env python3
import tkinter as tk
import tkinter.ttk as ttk

class {name}Form(tk.Toplevel):   ❶

    def __init__(self, master):
        super().__init__(master)
        self.withdraw()        # hide until ready to show
        self.title("{title}")  ❷
        {statements}  ❸
        self.bind("<Escape>", lambda *args: self.destroy())
        self.deiconify()    # show when widgets are created and laid out
        if self.winfo_viewable():
            self.transient(master)
        self.wait_visibility()
        self.grab_set()
        self.wait_window(self)

if __name__ == "__main__":
    application = tk.Tk()
    window = {name}Form(application)   ❹
    application.protocol("WM_DELETE_WINDOW", application.quit)
    application.mainloop()
"""
```

The form is given a unique class name based on the title (e.g., `LoginForm`, ❶; ❹). The window title is set early on (e.g., "Login", ❷), and this is followed by all the statements to create and lay out the form's widgets (❸).

The Python code produced by using the template can be run stand-alone thanks to the `if __name__` ... block at the end.

```
    def _canonicalize(self, text, startLower=True):
        text = re.sub(r"\W+", "", text)
        if text[0].isdigit():
            return "_" + text
        return text if not startLower else text[0].lower() + text[1:]
```

The code for the `_canonicalize()` method is included for completeness. Incidentally, although it looks as if we create a fresh regex every time the function is called, in practice Python maintains a fairly large internal cache of compiled regexes, so for the second and subsequent calls, Python just looks up the regex rather than recompiling it.★

1.3. Factory Method Pattern

The Factory Method Pattern is intended to be used when we want subclasses to choose which classes they should instantiate when an object is requested. This is useful in its own right, but can be taken further and used in cases where we cannot know the class in advance (e.g., the class to use is based on what we read from a file or depends on user input).

In this section we will review a program that can be used to create game boards (e.g., a checkers or chess board). The program's output is shown in Figure 1.3, and the four variants of the source code are in the files `gameboard1.py`...`gameboard4.py`.*

We want to have an abstract board class that can be subclassed to create game-specific boards. Each board subclass will populate itself with its initial layout of pieces. And we want every unique kind of piece to belong to its own class (e.g., `BlackDraught`, `WhiteDraught`, `BlackChessBishop`, `WhiteChessKnight`, etc.). Incidentally, for individual pieces, we have used class names like `WhiteDraught` rather than, say, `WhiteChecker`, to match the names used in Unicode for the corresponding characters.

Figure 1.3 *The checkers and chess game boards on a Linux console*

---

* This book assumes a basic knowledge of regexes and Python's re module. Readers needing to learn this can download a free PDF of "Chapter 13. Regular Expressions" from this author's book *Programming in Python 3, Second Edition*; see `www.qtrac.eu/py3book.html`.

° Unfortunately, Windows consoles' UTF-8 support is rather poor, with many characters unavailable, even if code page 65001 is used. So, for Windows, the programs write their output to a temporary file and print the filename they used. None of the standard Windows monospaced fonts seems to have the checkers or chess piece characters, although most of the variable-width fonts have the chess pieces. The free and open-source DejaVu Sans font has them all (`dejavu-fonts.org`).

We will begin by reviewing the top-level code that instantiates and prints the boards. Next, we will look at the board classes and some of the piece classes—starting with hard-coded classes. Then we will review some variations that allow us to avoid hard-coding classes and at the same time use fewer lines of code.

```
def main():
    checkers = CheckersBoard()
    print(checkers)

    chess = ChessBoard()
    print(chess)
```

This function is common to all versions of the program. It simply creates each type of board and prints it to the console, relying on the AbstractBoard's __str__() method to convert the board's internal representation into a string.

```
BLACK, WHITE = ("BLACK", "WHITE")

class AbstractBoard:

    def __init__(self, rows, columns):
        self.board = [[None for _ in range(columns)] for _ in range(rows)]
        self.populate_board()

    def populate_board(self):
        raise NotImplementedError()

    def __str__(self):
        squares = []
        for y, row in enumerate(self.board):
            for x, piece in enumerate(row):
                square = console(piece, BLACK if (y + x) % 2 else WHITE)
                squares.append(square)
            squares.append("\n")
        return "".join(squares)
```

The BLACK and WHITE constants are used here to indicate each square's background color. In later variants they are also used to indicate each piece's color. This class is quoted from gameboard1.py, but it is the same in all versions.

It would have been more conventional to specify the constants by writing: BLACK, WHITE = range(2). However, using strings is much more helpful when it comes to debugging error messages, and should be just as fast as using integers thanks to Python's smart interning and identity checks.

The board is represented by a list of rows of single-character strings—or None for unoccupied squares. The console() function (not shown, but in the source code), returns a string representing the given piece on the given background color. (On Unix-like systems this string includes escape codes to color the background.)

We could have made the AbstractBoard a formally abstract class by giving it a metaclass of abc.ABCMeta (as we did for the AbstractFormBuilder class; 12 ◄). However, here we have chosen to use a different approach, and simply raise a NotImplementedError exception for any methods we want subclasses to reimplement.

```python
class CheckersBoard(AbstractBoard):

    def __init__(self):
        super().__init__(10, 10)

    def populate_board(self):
        for x in range(0, 9, 2):
            for row in range(4):
                column = x + ((row + 1) % 2)
                self.board[row][column] = BlackDraught()
                self.board[row + 6][column] = WhiteDraught()
```

This subclass is used to create a representation of a 10 × 10 international checkers board. This class's populate_board() method is *not* a factory method, since it uses hard-coded classes; it is shown in this form as a step on the way to making it into a factory method.

```python
class ChessBoard(AbstractBoard):

    def __init__(self):
        super().__init__(8, 8)

    def populate_board(self):
        self.board[0][0] = BlackChessRook()
        self.board[0][1] = BlackChessKnight()
        ...
        self.board[7][7] = WhiteChessRook()
        for column in range(8):
            self.board[1][column] = BlackChessPawn()
            self.board[6][column] = WhiteChessPawn()
```

This version of the ChessBoard's populate_board() method—just like the Checkers-Board's one—is *not* a factory method, but it does illustrate how the chess board is populated.

```python
class Piece(str):
    __slots__ = ()
```

This class serves as a base class for pieces. We could have simply used str, but that would not have allowed us to determine if an object is a piece (e.g., using isinstance(x, Piece)). Using __slots__ = () ensures that instances have no data, a topic we'll discuss later on (§2.6, ➤ 65).

```
class BlackDraught(Piece):

    __slots__ = ()

    def __new__(Class):
        return super().__new__(Class, "\N{black draughts man}")

class WhiteChessKing(Piece):

    __slots__ = ()

    def __new__(Class):
        return super().__new__(Class, "\N{white chess king}")
```

These two classes are models for the pattern used for all the piece classes. Every one is an immutable Piece subclass (itself a str subclass) that is initialized with a one-character string holding the Unicode character that represents the relevant piece. There are fourteen of these tiny subclasses in all, each one differing only by its class name and the string it holds: clearly, it would be nice to eliminate all this near-duplication.

```
def populate_board(self):
    for x in range(0, 9, 2):
        for y in range(4):
            column = x + ((y + 1) % 2)
            for row, color in ((y, "black"), (y + 6, "white")):
                self.board[row][column] = create_piece("draught",
                        color)
```

This new version of the CheckersBoard.populate_board() method (quoted from gameboard2.py) is a factory method, since it depends on a new create_piece() factory function rather than on hard-coded classes. The create_piece() function returns an object of the appropriate type (e.g., a BlackDraught or a WhiteDraught), depending on its arguments. This version of the program has a similar Chess-Board.populate_board() method (not shown), which also uses string color and piece names and the same create_piece() function.

```
def create_piece(kind, color):
    if kind == "draught":
        return eval("{}{}()".format(color.title(), kind.title()))
    return eval("{}Chess{}()".format(color.title(), kind.title()))
```

This factory function uses the built-in eval() function to create class instances. For example, if the arguments are "knight" and "black", the string to be eval()'d will be "BlackChessKnight()". Although this works perfectly well, it is potentially risky since pretty well anything could be eval()'d into existence—we will see a solution, using the built-in type() function, shortly.

```
for code in itertools.chain((0x26C0, 0x26C2), range(0x2654, 0x2660)):
    char = chr(code)
    name = unicodedata.name(char).title().replace(" ", "")
    if name.endswith("sMan"):
        name = name[:-4]
    exec("""\
class {}(Piece):

    __slots__ = ()

    def __new__(Class):
        return super().__new__(Class, "{}")""".format(name, char))
```

Instead of writing the code for fourteen very similar classes, here we create all the classes we need with a single block of code.

The itertools.chain() function takes one or more iterables and returns a single iterable that iterates over the first iterable it was passed, then the second, and so on. Here, we have given it two iterables, the first a 2-tuple of the Unicode code points for black and white checkers pieces, and the second a range-object (in effect, a generator) for the black and white chess pieces.

For each code point we create a single character string (e.g., "♞") and then create a class name based on the character's Unicode name (e.g., "black chess knight" becomes BlackChessKnight). Once we have the character and the name we use exec() to create the class we need. This code block is a mere dozen lines—compared with around a hundred lines for creating all the classes individually.

Unfortunately, though, using exec() is potentially even more risky than using eval(), so we must find a better way.

```
DRAUGHT, PAWN, ROOK, KNIGHT, BISHOP, KING, QUEEN = ("DRAUGHT", "PAWN",
        "ROOK", "KNIGHT", "BISHOP", "KING", "QUEEN")

class CheckersBoard(AbstractBoard):
    ...

    def populate_board(self):
        for x in range(0, 9, 2):
            for y in range(4):
                column = x + ((y + 1) % 2)
```

```
        for row, color in ((y, BLACK), (y + 6, WHITE)):
            self.board[row][column] = self.create_piece(DRAUGHT,
                color)
```

This CheckersBoard.populate_board() method is from gameboard3.py. It differs from the previous version in that the piece and color are both specified using constants rather than easy to mistype string literals. Also, it uses a new create_piece() factory to create each piece.

An alternative CheckersBoard.populate_board() implementation is provided in gameboard4.py (not shown)—this version uses a subtle combination of a list comprehension and a couple of itertools functions.

```
class AbstractBoard:

    __classForPiece = {(DRAUGHT, BLACK): BlackDraught,
            (PAWN, BLACK): BlackChessPawn,
            ...
            (QUEEN, WHITE): WhiteChessQueen}
    ...
    def create_piece(self, kind, color):
        return AbstractBoard.__classForPiece[kind, color]()
```

This version of the create_piece() factory (also from gameboard3.py, of course) is a method of the AbstractBoard that the CheckersBoard and ChessBoard classes inherit. It takes two constants and looks them up in a static (i.e., class-level) dictionary whose keys are (*piece kind, color*) 2-tuples, and whose values are class objects. The looked-up value—a class—is immediately called (using the () call operator), and the resulting piece instance is returned.

The classes in the dictionary could have been individually coded (as they were in gameboard1.py) or created dynamically but riskily (as they were in gameboard2.py). But for gameboard3.py, we have created them dynamically and safely, without using eval() or exec().

```
for code in itertools.chain((0x26C0, 0x26C2), range(0x2654, 0x2660)):
    char = chr(code)
    name = unicodedata.name(char).title().replace(" ", "")
    if name.endswith("sMan"):
        name = name[:-4]
    new = make_new_method(char)
    Class = type(name, (Piece,), dict(__slots__=(), __new__=new))
    setattr(sys.modules[__name__], name, Class) # Can be done better!
```

This code has the same overall structure as the code shown earlier for creating the fourteen piece subclasses that the program needs (21 ◄). Only this time instead of using eval() and exec() we take a somewhat safer approach.

Once we have the character and name we create a new function (called new()) by calling a custom make_new_method() function. We then create a new class using the built-in type() function. To create a class this way we must pass in the type's name, a tuple of its base classes (in this case, there's just one, Piece), and a dictionary of the class's attributes. Here, we have set the __slots__ attribute to an empty tuple (to stop the class's instances having a private __dict__ that isn't needed), and set the __new__ method attribute to the new() function we have just created.

Finally, we use the built-in setattr() function to add to the current module (sys.modules[__name__]) the newly created class (Class) as an attribute called name (e.g., "WhiteChessPawn"). In gameboard4.py, we have written the last line of this code snippet in a nicer way:

```
globals()[name] = Class
```

Here, we have retrieved a reference to the dict of globals and added a new item whose key is the name held in name, and whose value is our newly created Class. This does exactly the same thing as the setattr() line used in gameboard3.py.

```
def make_new_method(char): # Needed to create a fresh method each time
    def new(Class): # Can't use super() or super(Piece, Class)
        return Piece.__new__(Class, char)
    return new
```

This function is used to create a new() function (that will become a class's __new__() method). We cannot use a super() call since at the time the new() function is created there is no class context for the super() function to access. Note that the Piece class (19 ◄) doesn't have a __new__() method—but its base class (str) does, so that is the method that will actually be called.

Incidentally, the earlier code block's new = make_new_method(char) line and the make_new_method() function just shown could both be deleted, so long as the line that called the make_new_method() function was replaced with these:

```
new = (lambda char: lambda Class: Piece.__new__(Class, char))(char)
new.__name__ = "__new__"
```

Here, we create a function that creates a function and immediately calls the outer function parameterized by char to return a new() function. (This code is used in gameboard4.py.)

All lambda functions are called "lambda", which isn't very helpful for debugging. So, here, we explicitly give the function the name it should have, once it is created.

```
def populate_board(self):
    for row, color in ((0, BLACK), (7, WHITE)):
        for columns, kind in (((0, 7), ROOK), ((1, 6), KNIGHT),
                ((2, 5), BISHOP), ((3,), QUEEN), ((4,), KING)):
            for column in columns:
                self.board[row][column] = self.create_piece(kind,
                    color)
    for column in range(8):
        for row, color in ((1, BLACK), (6, WHITE)):
            self.board[row][column] = self.create_piece(PAWN, color)
```

For completeness, here is the ChessBoard.populate_board() method from game-board3.py (and gameboard4.py). It depends on color and piece constants (which could be provided by a file or come from menu options, rather than being hard-coded). In the gameboard3.py version, this uses the create_piece() factory function shown earlier (22 ◀). But for gameboard4.py, we have used our final create_piece() variant.

```
def create_piece(kind, color):
    color = "White" if color == WHITE else "Black"
    name = {DRAUGHT: "Draught", PAWN: "ChessPawn", ROOK: "ChessRook",
            KNIGHT: "ChessKnight", BISHOP: "ChessBishop",
            KING: "ChessKing", QUEEN: "ChessQueen"}[kind]
    return globals()[color + name]()
```

This is the gameboard4.py version's create_piece() factory function. It uses the same constants as gameboard3.py, but rather than keeping a dictionary of class objects it dynamically finds the relevant class in the dictionary returned by the built-in globals() function. The looked-up class object is immediately called and the resulting piece instance is returned.

1.4. Prototype Pattern

The Prototype Pattern is used to create new objects by cloning an original object, and then modifying the clone.

As we have already seen, especially in the previous section, Python supports a wide variety of ways of creating new objects, even when their types are only known at runtime—and even if we have only their types' names.

```
class Point:

    __slots__ = ("x", "y")
    def __init__(self, x, y):
        self.x = x
        self.y = y
```

Given this classic Point class, here are seven ways to create new points:

```
def make_object(Class, *args, **kwargs):
    return Class(*args, **kwargs)
point1 = Point(1, 2)
point2 = eval("{}({}, {})".format("Point", 2, 4)) # Risky
point3 = getattr(sys.modules[__name__], "Point")(3, 6)
point4 = globals()["Point"](4, 8)
point5 = make_object(Point, 5, 10)
point6 = copy.deepcopy(point5)
point6.x = 6
point6.y = 12
point7 = point1.__class__(7, 14) # Could have used any of point1 to point6
```

Point point1 is created conventionally (and statically) using the Point class object as a constructor.* All the other points are created dynamically, with point2, point3, and point4 parameterized by the class name. As the creation of point3 (and point4) makes clear, there is no need to use a risky eval() to create instances (as we did for point2). The creation of point4 works exactly the same way as for point3, but using nicer syntax by relying on Python's built-in globals() function. Point point5 is created using a generic make_object() function that accepts a class object and the relevant arguments. Point point6 is created using the classic prototype approach: first, we clone an existing object, then we initialize or configure it. Point point7 is created by using point point1's class object, plus new arguments.

Point point6 shows that Python has built-in support for prototyping using the copy.deepcopy() function. However, point7 shows that Python can do better than prototyping: instead of needing to clone an existing object and modify the clone, Python gives us access to any object's class object, so that we can create a new object directly and much more efficiently than by cloning.

---

* Strictly speaking, an __init__() method is an initializer, and a __new__() method is a constructor. However, since we almost always use __init__() and rarely use __new__(), we will refer to them both as "constructors" throughout the book.

1.5. Singleton Pattern

The Singleton Pattern is used when we need a class that has only a single instance that is the one and only instance accessed throughout the program.

For some object-oriented languages, creating a singleton can be surprisingly tricky, but this isn't the case for Python. The Python Cookbook (code.active-state.com/recipes/langs/python/) provides an easy-to-use Singleton class that any class can inherit to become a singleton—and a Borg class that achieves the same end in a rather different way.

However, the easiest way to achieve singleton functionality in Python is to create a module with the global state that's needed kept in private variables and access provided by public functions. For example, in Chapter 7's currency example (➤ 237), we need a function that will return a dictionary of currency rates (name keys, conversion rate values). We may want to call the function several times, but in most cases we want the rates fetched only once. We can achieve this by using the Singleton Pattern.

```python
_URL = "http://www.bankofcanada.ca/stats/assets/csv/fx-seven-day.csv"

def get(refresh=False):
    if refresh:
        get.rates = {}
    if get.rates:
        return get.rates
    with urllib.request.urlopen(_URL) as file:
        for line in file:
            line = line.rstrip().decode("utf-8")
            if not line or line.startswith(("#", "Date")):
                continue
            name, currency, *rest = re.split(r"\s*,\s*", line)
            key = "{} ({})".format(name, currency)
            try:
                get.rates[key] = float(rest[-1])
            except ValueError as err:
                print("error {}: {}".format(err, line))
    return get.rates
get.rates = {}
```

This is the code for the `currency/Rates.py` module (as usual, excluding the imports). Here, we create a `rates` dictionary as an attribute of the `Rates.get()` function—this is our private value. When the public `get()` function is called for the first time (or if it is called with `refresh=True`), we download the rates afresh; otherwise, we simply return the rates we most recently downloaded. There is no need for a class, yet we have still got a singleton data value—the rates—and we could easily add more singleton values.

All of the creational design patterns are straightforward to implement in Python. The Singleton Pattern can be implemented directly by using a module, and the Prototype Pattern is redundant (although still doable using the copy module), since Python provides dynamic access to class objects. The most useful creational design patterns for Python are the Factory and Builder Patterns; these can be implemented in a number of ways. Once we have created basic objects, we often need to create more complex objects by composing or adapting other objects. We'll look at how this is done in the next chapter.

2

Structural Design Patterns

The primary concern of structural design patterns is how objects are composed together to form new, larger objects. Three themes stand out in structural design patterns: adapting interfaces, adding functionality, and handling collections of objects.

2.1. Adapter Pattern

The Adapter Pattern is a technique for adapting an interface so that one class can make use of another class—that has an incompatible interface—without changing either of the classes being used. This is useful, for example, when we want to use a class that cannot be changed, in a context it wasn't originally designed for.

Let's imagine that we have a simple Page class that can be used to render a page given its title, paragraphs of body text, and an instance of a renderer class. (This section's code is all taken from the render1.py example.)

```
class Page:
    def __init__(self, title, renderer):
```

```
        if not isinstance(renderer, Renderer):
            raise TypeError("Expected object of type Renderer, got {}".
                    format(type(renderer).__name__))
        self.title = title
        self.renderer = renderer
        self.paragraphs = []


    def add_paragraph(self, paragraph):
        self.paragraphs.append(paragraph)


    def render(self):
        self.renderer.header(self.title)
        for paragraph in self.paragraphs:
            self.renderer.paragraph(paragraph)
        self.renderer.footer()
```

The Page class does not know or care what the renderer's class is, only that it provides the page renderer interface; that is, the three methods header(*str*), paragraph(*str*), and footer().

We want to ensure that the renderer passed in is a Renderer instance. A simple but poor solution is: assert isinstance(renderer, Renderer). This has two weaknesses. First, it raises an AssertionError rather than the expected and more specific TypeError. Second, if the user runs the program with the –O ("optimize") option, the assert will be ignored and the user will end up getting an Attribute-Error raised later on, in the render() method. The if not isinstance(...) statement used in the code correctly raises a TypeError and works regardless of the –O option.

One apparent problem with this approach is that it would seem that we must make all our renderers subclasses of a Renderer base class. Certainly, if we were programming in C++, this would be the case; and we could indeed create such a base class in Python. However, Python's abc (abstract base class) module provides us with an alternative and more flexible option that combines the interface checkability benefit of an abstract base class with the flexibility of duck typing. This means that we can create objects that are guaranteed to meet a particular interface (i.e., to have a specified API) but need not be subclasses of any particular base class.

```
class Renderer(metaclass=abc.ABCMeta):

    @classmethod
    def __subclasshook__(Class, Subclass):
        if Class is Renderer:
            attributes = collections.ChainMap(*(Superclass.__dict__
                    for Superclass in Subclass.__mro__))
```

```
            methods = ("header", "paragraph", "footer")
            if all(method in attributes for method in methods):
                return True
        return NotImplemented
```

The Renderer class reimplements the __subclasshook__() special method. This method is used by the built-in isinstance() function to determine if the object it is given as its first argument is a subclass of the class (or any of the tuple of classes) it is passed as its second argument.

The code is rather subtle—and Python 3.3-specific—because it uses the collections.ChainMap() class.* The code is explained next, but understanding it isn't important since all the hard work can be done by the @Qtrac.has_methods class decorator supplied with the book's examples (and covered later; ➤ 36).

The __subclasshook__() special method begins by checking to see if the class instance it is being called on (Class) is Renderer; otherwise, we return NotImplemented. This means that the __subclasshook__ behavior is *not* inherited by subclasses. We do this because we assume that a subclass is adding new criteria to the abstract base class, rather than adding behavior. Naturally, we can still inherit behavior if we wish, simply by calling Renderer.__subclasshook__() explicitly in our __subclasshook__() reimplementation.

If we returned True or False, the abstract base class machinery would be stopped in its tracks and the bool returned. But by returning NotImplemented, we allow the normal inheritance functionality to operate (subclasses, subclasses of explicitly registered classes, subclasses of subclasses).

If the if statement's condition is met, we iterate over every class inherited by the Subclass (including itself), as returned by its __mro__() special method, and access its private dictionary (__dict__). This provides a tuple of __dict__s that we immediately unpack using sequence unpacking (*), so that all the dictionaries get passed to the collections.ChainMap() function. This function takes any number of mappings (such as dicts) as arguments, and returns a single map view as if they were all in the same mapping. Now, we create a tuple of the methods we want to check for. Finally, we iterate over all the methods and check that each one is in the attributes mapping whose keys are the names of all the methods and properties of the Subclass and all its Superclasses, and return True if all the methods are present.

Note that we check only that the subclass (or any of its base classes) has attributes whose names match the required methods—so even a property will match. If we want to be certain of matching only methods, we could add to the

---

* The render1.py example and the Qtrac.py module used by render2.py includes both Python 3.3-specific code and code that works with earlier Python 3 versions.

method in attributes test an additional and callable(method) clause; but in practice this is so rarely a problem that it isn't worth doing.

Creating a class with a __subclasshook__() to provide interface checking is very useful, but writing ten lines of complex code for every such class when they vary only in the base class and the supported methods is just the kind of code duplication we want to avoid. In the next section (§2.2, ➤ 34), we will create a class decorator that means that we can create interface checking classes with just a couple of unique lines of code each time. (The examples also include the render2.py program that makes use of this decorator.)

```python
class TextRenderer:

    def __init__(self, width=80, file=sys.stdout):
        self.width = width
        self.file = file
        self.previous = False

    def header(self, title):
        self.file.write("{0:^{2}}\n{1:^{2}}\n".format(title,
            "=" * len(title), self.width))
```

Here is the start of a simple class that supports the page renderer interface.

The header() method writes the given title centered in the given width, and on the next line writes an = character below every character in the title.

```python
    def paragraph(self, text):
        if self.previous:
            self.file.write("\n")
        self.file.write(textwrap.fill(text, self.width))
        self.file.write("\n")
        self.previous = True

    def footer(self):
        pass
```

The paragraph() method uses the Python standard library's textwrap module to write the given paragraph, wrapped to the given width. We use the self.previous Boolean to ensure that each paragraph is separated by a blank line from the one before. The footer() method does nothing, but must be present since it is part of the page renderer interface.

```python
class HtmlWriter:

    def __init__(self, file=sys.stdout):
        self.file = file
```

```
    def header(self):
        self.file.write("<!doctype html>\n<html>\n")

    def title(self, title):
        self.file.write("<head><title>{}</title></head>\n".format(
                escape(title)))

    def start_body(self):
        self.file.write("<body>\n")

    def body(self, text):
        self.file.write("<p>{}</p>\n".format(escape(text)))

    def end_body(self):
        self.file.write("</body>\n")

    def footer(self):
        self.file.write("</html>\n")
```

The HtmlWriter class can be used to write a simple HTML page, and it takes care of escaping using the html.escape() function (or the xml.sax.saxutil.escape() function in Python 3.2 or earlier).

Although this class has header() and footer() methods, they have different behaviors than those promised by the page renderer interface. So, unlike the Text-Renderer, we cannot pass an HtmlWriter as a page renderer to a Page instance.

One solution would be to subclass HtmlWriter and provide the subclass with the page renderer interface's methods. Unfortunately, this is rather fragile, since the resultant class will have a mixture of the HtmlWriter's methods plus the page renderer interface's methods. A much nicer solution is to create an adapter: a class that aggregates the class we need to use, that provides the required interface, and that handles all the mediation for us. How such an adapter class fits in is illustrated in Figure 2.1 (➤ 34).

```
class HtmlRenderer:

    def __init__(self, htmlWriter):
        self.htmlWriter = htmlWriter

    def header(self, title):
        self.htmlWriter.header()
        self.htmlWriter.title(title)
        self.htmlWriter.start_body()

    def paragraph(self, text):
        self.htmlWriter.body(text)
```

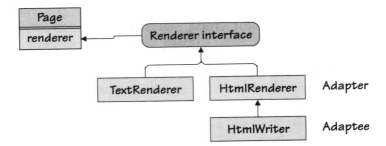

Figure 2.1 *A page renderer adapter class in context*

```
def footer(self):
    self.htmlWriter.end_body()
    self.htmlWriter.footer()
```

This is our adapter class. It takes an htmlWriter of type HtmlWriter at construction time, and it provides the page renderer interface's methods. All the actual work is delegated to the aggregated HtmlWriter, so the HtmlRenderer class is just a wrapper providing a new interface for the existing HtmlWriter class.

```
textPage = Page(title, TextRenderer(22))
textPage.add_paragraph(paragraph1)
textPage.add_paragraph(paragraph2)
textPage.render()

htmlPage = Page(title, HtmlRenderer(HtmlWriter(file)))
htmlPage.add_paragraph(paragraph1)
htmlPage.add_paragraph(paragraph2)
htmlPage.render()
```

Here are a couple of examples showing how instances of the Page class are created with their custom renderer. In this case we've given the TextRenderer a default width of 22 characters. And we have given the HtmlWriter that's used by the HtmlRenderer adapter an open file to write to (whose creation isn't shown) that overrides the default of sys.stdout.

2.2. Bridge Pattern

The Bridge Pattern is used in situations where we want to separate an abstraction (e.g., an interface or an algorithm) from how it is implemented.

The conventional approach without using the Bridge Pattern would be to create one or more abstract base classes and then provide two or more concrete implementations of each of the base classes. But with the Bridge Pattern the approach is to create two independent class hierarchies: the "abstract" one defining the operations (e.g., the interface and high-level algorithms) and the concrete one providing the implementations that the abstract operations will ultimately call. The "abstract" class aggregates an instance of one of the concrete implementation classes—and this instance serves as a *bridge* between the abstract interface and the concrete operations.

In the previous section's Adapter Pattern, the HtmlRenderer class could be said to have used the Bridge Pattern, since it aggregated an HtmlWriter to provide its rendering.

For this section's example, let's suppose that we want to create a class for drawing bar charts using a particular algorithm, but we want to leave the actual rendering of the charts to other classes. We will look at a program that provides this functionality and that uses the Bridge Pattern: barchart1.py.

```
class BarCharter:

    def __init__(self, renderer):
        if not isinstance(renderer, BarRenderer):
            raise TypeError("Expected object of type BarRenderer, got {}".
                    format(type(renderer).__name__))
        self.__renderer = renderer


    def render(self, caption, pairs):
        maximum = max(value for _, value in pairs)
        self.__renderer.initialize(len(pairs), maximum)
        self.__renderer.draw_caption(caption)
        for name, value in pairs:
            self.__renderer.draw_bar(name, value)
        self.__renderer.finalize()
```

The BarCharter class implements a bar chart drawing algorithm (in its render() method) that depends on the renderer implementation it is given meeting a particular bar charting interface. The interface requires the initialize(*int*, *int*), draw_caption(*str*), draw_bar(*str, int*), and finalize() methods.

Just as we did in the previous section, we use an isinstance() test to ensure that the passed-in renderer object supports the interface we require—and without forcing bar renderers to have any particular base class. However, rather than creating a ten-line class as we did before, we have created our interface-checking class with just two lines of code.

```
@Qtrac.has_methods("initialize", "draw_caption", "draw_bar", "finalize")
class BarRenderer(metaclass=abc.ABCMeta): pass
```

This code creates a BarRenderer class that has the necessary metaclass for working with the abc module. This class is then passed to the Qtrac.has_methods()

function, which returns a class decorator. This decorator then adds a custom
__subclasshook__() class method to the class. And this new method checks for
the given methods whenever a BarRenderer is passed as a type to an isinstance()
call. (Readers not familiar with class decorators may find it helpful to skip ahead
and read §2.4, ➤ 48, and especially §2.4.2, ➤ 54, and then return here.)

```python
def has_methods(*methods):
    def decorator(Base):
        def __subclasshook__(Class, Subclass):
            if Class is Base:
                attributes = collections.ChainMap(*(Superclass.__dict__
                    for Superclass in Subclass.__mro__))
                if all(method in attributes for method in methods):
                    return True
            return NotImplemented
        Base.__subclasshook__ = classmethod(__subclasshook__)
        return Base
    return decorator
```

The Qtrac.py module's has_methods() function captures the required methods
and creates a class decorator function, which it then returns. The decorator itself creates a __subclasshook__() function, and then adds it to the base class
as a class method using the built-in classmethod() function. The custom __sub-
classhook__() function's code is essentially the same as we discussed before
(31 ◀), only this time, instead of using a hard-coded base class, we use the decorated class (Base), and instead of a hard-coded set of method names, we use those
passed in to the class decorator (methods).

It is also possible to achieve the same kind of method checking functionality by
inheriting from a generic abstract base class. For example:

```python
class BarRenderer(Qtrac.Requirer):
    required_methods = {"initialize", "draw_caption", "draw_bar",
        "finalize"}
```

This code snippet is from barchart3.py. The Qtrac.Requirer class (not shown,
but in Qtrac.py) is an abstract base class that performs the same checks as the
@has_methods class decorator.

```python
def main():
    pairs = (("Mon", 16), ("Tue", 17), ("Wed", 19), ("Thu", 22),
        ("Fri", 24), ("Sat", 21), ("Sun", 19))
    textBarCharter = BarCharter(TextBarRenderer())
    textBarCharter.render("Forecast 6/8", pairs)
```

```
imageBarCharter = BarCharter(ImageBarRenderer())
imageBarCharter.render("Forecast 6/8", pairs)
```

This `main()` function sets up some data, creates two bar charters—each with
a different renderer implementation—and renders the data. The outputs are
shown in Figure 2.2, and the interface and classes are illustrated in Figure 2.3.

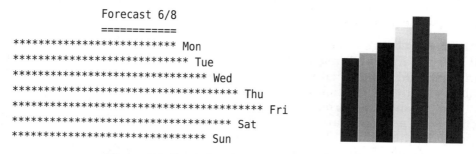

Figure 2.2 *Examples of text and image bar charts*

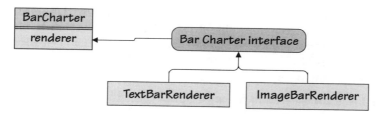

Figure 2.3 *The bar charter interface and classes*

```python
class TextBarRenderer:

    def __init__(self, scaleFactor=40):
        self.scaleFactor = scaleFactor

    def initialize(self, bars, maximum):
        assert bars > 0 and maximum > 0
        self.scale = self.scaleFactor / maximum

    def draw_caption(self, caption):
        print("{0:^{2}}\n{1:^{2}}".format(caption, "=" * len(caption),
                self.scaleFactor))

    def draw_bar(self, name, value):
        print("{} {}".format("*" * int(value * self.scale), name))

    def finalize(self):
```

```
        pass
```

This class implements the bar charter interface and renders its text to `sys.stdout`. Naturally, it would be easy to make the output file user-definable, and for Unix-like systems, to use Unicode box drawing characters and colors for more attractive output.

Notice that although the `TextBarRenderer`'s `finalize()` method does nothing, it must still be present to satisfy the bar charter interface.

Although Python's standard library is very wide ranging ("batteries included"), it has one surprisingly major omission: there is no package for reading and writing standard bitmap and vector images. One solution is to use a third-party library—either a multi-format library like Pillow (github.com/python-imaging/ Pillow), or an image-format–specific library, or even a GUI toolkit library. Another solution is to create our own image handling library—something we will look at later (§3.12, ➤ 124). If we are willing to confine ourselves to GIF images (plus PNG once Python ships with Tk/Tcl 8.6), we can use Tkinter.*

In `barchart1.py`, the `ImageBarRenderer` class uses the `cyImage` module (or failing that, the `Image` module). We will refer to them as the `Image` module when the difference doesn't matter. These modules are supplied with the book's examples and are covered later (Image in §3.12, ➤ 124; cyImage in §5.2.2, ➤ 193). For completeness, the examples also include `barchart2.py`, which is a version of `bar-chart1.py` that uses Tkinter instead of `cyImage` or `Image`; we don't show any of that version's code in the book, though.

Since the `ImageBarRenderer` is more complex than the `TextBarRenderer`, we will separately review its static data and then each of its methods in turn.

```
class ImageBarRenderer:

    COLORS = [Image.color_for_name(name) for name in ("red", "green",
              "blue", "yellow", "magenta", "cyan")]
```

The `Image` module represents pixels using 32-bit unsigned integers into which are encoded four color components: alpha (transparency), red, green, and blue. The module provides the `Image.color_for_name()` function that accepts a color name—either an X11 `rgb.txt` name (e.g., `"sienna"`) or an HTML-style name (e.g., `"#A0522D"`)—and returns the corresponding unsigned integer.

Here, we create a list of colors to be used for the bar chart's bars.

---

* Note that image handling in Tkinter must be done in the main (i.e., GUI) thread. For concurrent image handling we must use another approach, as we will see later (§4.1, ➤ 144).

```
def __init__(self, stepHeight=10, barWidth=30, barGap=2):
    self.stepHeight = stepHeight
    self.barWidth = barWidth
    self.barGap = barGap
```

This method allows the user to set up some preferences that influence how the bar chart's bars will be painted.

```
def initialize(self, bars, maximum):
    assert bars > 0 and maximum > 0
    self.index = 0
    color = Image.color_for_name("white")
    self.image = Image.Image(bars * (self.barWidth + self.barGap),
            maximum * self.stepHeight, background=color)
```

This method (and the ones that follow), must be present since it is part of the bar charter interface. Here, we create a new image whose size is proportional to the number of bars and their width and maximum height, and which is initially colored white.

The self.index variable is used to keep track of which bar we are up to (counting from 0).

```
def draw_caption(self, caption):
    self.filename = os.path.join(tempfile.gettempdir(),
            re.sub(r"\W+", "_", caption) + ".xpm")
```

The Image module has no support for drawing text, so we use the given caption as the basis for the image's filename.

The Image module supports two image formats out of the box: XBM (.xbm) for monochrome images and XPM (.xpm) for color images. (If the PyPNG module is installed—see pypi.python.org/pypi/pypng—the Image module will also support PNG (.png) format.) Here, we have chosen the color XPM format, since our bar chart is in color and this format is always supported.

```
def draw_bar(self, name, value):
    color = ImageBarRenderer.COLORS[self.index %
            len(ImageBarRenderer.COLORS)]
    width, height = self.image.size
    x0 = self.index * (self.barWidth + self.barGap)
    x1 = x0 + self.barWidth
    y0 = height - (value * self.stepHeight)
    y1 = height - 1
    self.image.rectangle(x0, y0, x1, y1, fill=color)
    self.index += 1
```

This method chooses a color from the COLORS sequence (rotating through the same colors if there are more bars than colors). It then calculates the current (self.index) bar's coordinates (top-left and bottom-right corners) and tells the self.image instance (of type Image.Image) to draw a rectangle on itself using the given coordinates and fill color. Then, the index is incremented ready for the next bar.

```
def finalize(self):
    self.image.save(self.filename)
    print("wrote", self.filename)
```

Here, we simply save the image and report this fact to the user.

Clearly, the TextBarRenderer and the ImageBarRenderer have radically different implementations. Yet, either can be used as a bridge to provide a concrete bar-charting implementation for the BarCharter class.

2.3. Composite Pattern

The Composite Pattern is designed to support the uniform treatment of objects in a hierarchy, whether they contain other objects (as part of the hierarchy) or not. Such objects are called *composite*. In the classic approach, composite objects have the same base class for both individual objects and for collections of objects. Both composite and noncomposite objects normally have the same core methods, with composite objects also having additional methods to support adding, removing, and iterating their child objects.

This pattern is often used in drawing programs, such as Inkscape, to support grouping and ungrouping. The pattern is useful in such cases because when the user selects components to group or ungroup, some of the components might be single items (e.g., a rectangle), while others might be composite (e.g., a face made up of many different shapes).

To see an example in practice, let's look at a main() function that creates some individual items and some composite items, and then prints them all out. The code is quoted from stationery1.py, with the output shown after it.

```
def main():
    pencil = SimpleItem("Pencil", 0.40)
    ruler = SimpleItem("Ruler", 1.60)
    eraser = SimpleItem("Eraser", 0.20)
    pencilSet = CompositeItem("Pencil Set", pencil, ruler, eraser)
    box = SimpleItem("Box", 1.00)
    boxedPencilSet = CompositeItem("Boxed Pencil Set", box, pencilSet)
    boxedPencilSet.add(pencil)
    for item in (pencil, ruler, eraser, pencilSet, boxedPencilSet):
```

```
          item.print()
$0.40 Pencil
$1.60 Ruler
$0.20 Eraser
$2.20 Pencil Set
      $0.40 Pencil
      $1.60 Ruler
      $0.20 Eraser
$3.60 Boxed Pencil Set
      $1.00 Box
      $2.20 Pencil Set
            $0.40 Pencil
            $1.60 Ruler
            $0.20 Eraser
      $0.40 Pencil
```

Every SimpleItem has a name and a price, while every CompositeItem has a name and any number of contained SimpleItems—or CompositeItems—so composite items can be nested without limit. The price of a composite item is the sum of its contained items' prices.

In this example, a pencil set consists of a pencil, ruler, and eraser. For the boxed pencil set we begin by creating it with a box and a nested pencil set, and then add an extra pencil. The boxed pencil set's hierarchy is illustrated in Figure 2.4 (➤ 42).

We will review two different implementations of the Composite Pattern, the first using the classic approach, and the second using a single class for representing both composites and noncomposites.

2.3.1. A Classic Composite/Noncomposite Hierarchy

The classic approach is based on having an abstract base class for all kinds of items (i.e., whether composite or not) and an additional abstract base class for composites. The class hierarchy is shown in Figure 2.5 (➤ 43). We will begin by looking at the AbstractItem base class.

```python
class AbstractItem(metaclass=abc.ABCMeta):

    @abc.abstractproperty
    def composite(self):
        pass


    def __iter__(self):
        return iter([])
```

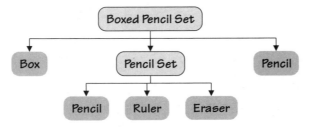

Figure 2.4 *A hierarchy of composite and noncomposite items*

We want all subclasses to say whether or not they are composite. Also, we want all subclasses to be iterable, with a default behavior of returning an iterator to an empty sequence.

Since the AbstractItem class has at least one abstract method or property, we cannot create AbstractItem objects. (Incidentally, from Python 3.3 it is possible to write @property @abstractmethod def *method*(...): ... instead of @abstractproperty def *method*(...): ....)

```
class SimpleItem(AbstractItem):

    def __init__(self, name, price=0.00):
        self.name = name
        self.price = price

    @property
    def composite(self):
        return False
```

The SimpleItem class is used for noncomposite items. In this example, SimpleItems have name and price properties.

Since SimpleItem inherits AbstractItem, it must reimplement all the abstract properties and methods—in this case, just the composite property. Since the AbstractItem's __iter__() method is not abstract and we don't reimplement it here, we get the base class version that safely returns an iterator to an empty sequence. This makes sense because SimpleItems are noncomposite, and yet this still allows us to treat both SimpleItems and CompositeItems uniformly (at least for iteration); for example, by passing a mixture of such items to a function like itertools.chain().

```
    def print(self, indent="", file=sys.stdout):
        print("{}${:.2f} {}".format(indent, self.price, self.name),
                file=file)
```

We have provided a print() method to facilitate the printing of composite and noncomposite items, with nested items using successive levels of indentation.

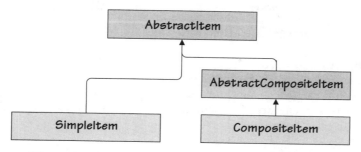

Figure 2.5 *A composite and noncomposite class hierarchy*

```
class AbstractCompositeItem(AbstractItem):
    def __init__(self, *items):
        self.children = []
        if items:
            self.add(*items)
```

This class serves as the base class for CompositeItems and provides the machinery for adding, removing, and iterating composites. It isn't possible to instantiate AbstractCompositeItems, because the class inherits the abstract composite property but doesn't provide an implementation for it.

```
    def add(self, first, *items):
        self.children.append(first)
        if items:
            self.children.extend(items)
```

This method accepts one or more items (both plain SimpleItems and CompositeItems) and adds them to this composite item's list of children. We could not have dropped the first parameter and just used *items, because that would have allowed zero items to be added, which, although harmless here, would probably be masking a logical error in the user's code. (For more about unpacking—e.g., *items—see the "Sequence and Mapping Unpacking" sidebar, 13 ◀). Incidentally, no checks are made to disallow circular references; for example, to prevent adding a composite item to itself.

Later on, we'll implement this method using a single line of code (➤ 46).

```
    def remove(self, item):
        self.children.remove(item)
```

For removing items, we have used a simple approach that allows us to remove only one item at a time. Of course, a removed item might be composite, in which case removing it will remove all its child items, their child items, and so on.

```
    def __iter__(self):
        return iter(self.children)
```

By implementing the __iter__() special method we allow composite items' child items to be iterated over in for loops, comprehensions, and generators. In many cases we would write the method's body as for item in self.children: yield item, but since self.children is a sequence (a list) we can use the built-in iter() function to do the job for us.

```
class CompositeItem(AbstractCompositeItem):

    def __init__(self, name, *items):
        super().__init__(*items)
        self.name = name

    @property
    def composite(self):
        return True
```

This class is used for concrete composite items. It has its own name property but leaves all the composite-handling work (adding, removing, and iterating child items) to the base class. Instances of CompositeItem can be created because the class provides an implementation of the abstract composite property, and there are no other abstract properties or methods.

```
    @property
    def price(self):
        return sum(item.price for item in self)
```

This read-only property is slightly subtle. It calculates this composite item's price by accumulating the sum of its child items' prices—and their child items' prices, in the case of composite child items—recursively, using a generator expression as argument to the built-in sum() function.

The for item in self expression causes Python to in effect call iter(self) to get an iterator for self. This results in the __iter__() special method being called, and this method returns an iterator to self.children.

```
    def print(self, indent="", file=sys.stdout):
        print("{}${:.2f} {}".format(indent, self.price, self.name),
                file=file)
        for child in self:
            child.print(indent + "        ")
```

Again we have provided a convenient print() method, although, unfortunately, the first statement is just a copy of the SimpleItem.print() method's body.

In this example, the `SimpleItem` and `CompositeItem` are designed to serve most use cases. However, it is possible to subclass them—or their abstract base classes—if a finer-grained hierarchy is desired.

The `AbstractItem`, `SimpleItem`, `AbstractCompositeItem`, and `CompositeItem` classes shown here all work perfectly well. However, the code seems to be longer than necessary and doesn't have a uniform interface, since composites have methods (`add()` and `remove()`) that noncomposites don't have. We will address these issues in the next subsection.

2.3.2. A Single Class for (Non)composites

The previous subsection's four classes (two abstract, two concrete), seemed like quite a lot of work. And they don't provide a completely uniform interface because only composites support the `add()` and `remove()` methods. If we are willing to accept a small overhead—one empty list attribute per noncomposite item, and one `float` per composite item—we can use a single class to represent both composite and noncomposite items. This brings with it the benefit of a completely uniform interface, since now we can call `add()` and `remove()` on any item, not just on composites, and get sensible behavior.

In this subsection we will create a new `Item` class that can be either composite or noncomposite, without needing any other class. The code quoted in this subsubsection is from `stationery2.py`.

```
class Item:

    def __init__(self, name, *items, price=0.00):
        self.name = name
        self.price = price
        self.children = []
        if items:
            self.add(*items)
```

The `__init__()` method's arguments aren't very pretty, but this is fine since, as we will see in a moment, we do not expect callers to call `Item()` to create items.

Each item must be given a name. Every item also has a price, for which we provide a default. In addition, an item may have zero or more child items (`*items`), which are stored in `self.children`—this is an empty list for noncomposites.

```
    @classmethod
    def create(Class, name, price):
        return Item(name, price=price)

    @classmethod
```

```
    def compose(Class, name, *items):
        return Item(name, *items)
```

Instead of creating items by calling class objects, we have provided two convenience factory class methods that take nicer arguments and return an Item. So,
now, instead of writing things like SimpleItem("Ruler", 1.60) and CompositeIt-
em("Pencil Set", pencil, ruler, eraser), we write Item.create("Ruler", 1.60) and
Item.compose("Pencil Set", pencil, ruler, eraser). And now, of course, all our
items are of the same type: Item. Naturally, users can still use Item() directly if
they prefer; for example, Item("Ruler", price=1.60) and Item("Pencil Set", pencil, ruler, eraser).

```
def make_item(name, price):
    return Item(name, price=price)

def make_composite(name, *items):
    return Item(name, *items)
```

We have also provided two factory functions that do the same thing as the
class methods. Such functions are convenient when we are using modules.
For example, if our Item class was in the Item.py module we could replace, say,
Item.Item.create("Ruler", 1.60) with Item.make_item("Ruler", 1.60).

```
    @property
    def composite(self):
        return bool(self.children)
```

This property is different from before, since any item may or may not be
composite. For the Item class, a composite item is one whose self.children list
is nonempty.

```
    def add(self, first, *items):
        self.children.extend(itertools.chain((first,), items))
```

We have done the add() method slightly differently from before (43 ◄), using an
approach that should be more efficient. The itertools.chain() function accepts
any number of iterables and returns a single iterable that is effectively the
concatenation of all the iterables passed to it.

This method can be called on any item, whether or not it is composite. And in the
case of noncomposite items, the call causes the item to become composite.

One subtle side effect of changing a noncomposite item into a composite is that
the item's own price is effectively hidden, since its price now becomes the sum of
its child items' prices. Other design decisions—such as keeping the price—are
possible, of course.

```
def remove(self, item):
    self.children.remove(item)
```

If a composite item's last child is removed, the item simply becomes noncomposite. One subtle aspect of such a change is that the item's price then becomes the value of its private self.__price attribute, rather than the sum of its (now nonexistent) childrens' prices. We set an initial price for all items in the __init__() method to ensure that this always works (45 ◄).

```
def __iter__(self):
    return iter(self.children)
```

This method returns an iterator to a composite's list of children, or in the case of a noncomposite, to an empty sequence.

```
@property
def price(self):
    return (sum(item.price for item in self) if self.children else
            self.__price)


@price.setter
def price(self, price):
    self.__price = price
```

The price property must work for both composites (where it is the sum of the child items' prices) and for noncomposites (where it is the item's price).

```
def print(self, indent="", file=sys.stdout):
    print("{}${:.2f} {}".format(indent, self.price, self.name),
            file=file)
    for child in self:
        child.print(indent + "    ")
```

Again, this method must work for both composites and noncomposites, although the code is identical to the previous section's CompositeItem.print() method. When we iterate over a noncomposite, it returns an iterator to an empty sequence, so there is no risk of infinite recursion when we iterate over an item's children.

Python's flexibility makes it straightforward to create composite and noncomposite classes—either as separate classes to minimize storage overhead, or as a single class to provide a completely uniform interface.

We will see a further variation of the Composite Pattern when we review the Command Pattern (§3.2, ➤ 79).

2.4. Decorator Pattern

In general, a *decorator* is a function that takes a function as its sole argument and returns a new function with the same name as the original function but with enhanced functionality. Decorators are often used by frameworks (e.g., web frameworks) to make it easy to integrate our own functions within the framework.

The Decorator Pattern is so useful that Python has built-in support for it. In Python, decorators can be applied to both functions and methods. Furthermore, Python also supports class decorators: functions that take a class as their sole argument and that return a new class with the same name as the original class but with additional functionality. Class decorators can sometimes be used as an alternative to subclassing.

Python's built-in property() function can be used as a decorator, as we have seen already (e.g., the composite and price properties from the previous section; 46 ◀ and 47 ◀). And Python's standard library includes some built-in decorators. For example, the @functools.total_ordering class decorator can be applied to a class that implements the __eq__() and __lt__() special methods (which provide the == and < comparison operators). This will result in the class being replaced with a new version of itself that includes all the other comparison special methods, so that the decorated class supports the full range of comparison operators (i.e., <, <=, ==, !=, =>, and >).

A decorator may accept only a single function, method, or class as its sole argument, so in theory it isn't possible to parameterize decorators. Nonetheless, this isn't any limitation in practice, since, as we will see, we can create parameterized decorator factories that can return a decorator function—which can in turn be used to decorate a function, method, or class.

2.4.1. Function and Method Decorators

All function (and method) decorators have the same overall structure. First, they create a wrapper function (which in this book we always call wrapper()). Inside the wrapper we should call the original function. However, we are free to do any preprocessing we like before the call; we are free to acquire the result and do any postprocessing we like after the call; and we are free to return whatever we like—the original result, a modified result, or anything else we choose. Finally, we return the wrapper function as the decorator's result—and this function replaces the original function using the original function's name.

A decorator is applied to a function, method, or class by writing an @ ("at" symbol) at the same level of indentation as the def or class statement, immediately followed by the decorator's name. It is perfectly possible to stack decorators—that is, to apply a decorator to a decorated function, and so on—as illustrated in Figure 2.6; we will see an example shortly.

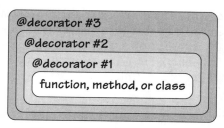

Figure 2.6 *Stacked decorators*

```
@float_args_and_return
def mean(first, second, *rest):
    numbers = (first, second) + rest
    return sum(numbers) / len(numbers)
```

Here, we have used the `@float_args_and_return` decorator (shown in a moment) to decorate the `mean()` function. The undecorated `mean()` function takes two or more numeric arguments and returns their mean as a `float`. But the *decorated* `mean()` function—which we call as `mean()` since it has replaced the original—can accept two or more arguments of any kind that will convert to a `float`. Without the decorator the call `mean(5, "6", "7.5")` would have raised a `TypeError`, because we cannot add `int`s and `str`s, but this works fine with the decorated version, since `float("6")` and `float("7.5")` produce valid numbers.

Incidentally, the decorator syntax is really just syntactic sugar. We could have written the above as:

```
def mean(first, second, *rest):
    numbers = (first, second) + rest
    return sum(numbers) / len(numbers)
mean = float_args_and_return(mean)
```

Here, we have created the function without a decorator and then replaced it with a decorated version by calling the decorator ourselves. Although using decorators is very convenient, sometimes it is necessary to call them directly. We will see an example toward the end of this section when we call the built-in `@property` decorator in the `ensure()` function (➤ 56). We also did this earlier when we called the built-in `@classmethod` decorator in the `has_methods()` function (36 ◄).

```
def float_args_and_return(function):
    def wrapper(*args, **kwargs):
        args = [float(arg) for arg in args]
        return float(function(*args, **kwargs))
    return wrapper
```

The float_args_and_return() function is a function decorator, and so takes a single function as its sole argument. It is conventional for wrapper functions to take *args and **kwargs; that is, any arguments at all. (See the "Sequence and Mapping Unpacking" sidebar, 13 ◄.) Any constraints on the arguments will be handled by the original (wrapped) function, so we must just ensure that all the arguments are passed.

In this example, inside the wrapper function we replace the passed-in positional arguments with a list of floating-point numbers. Then we call the original function with the possibly modified *args and convert its result to a float, which we then return.

Once the wrapper has been created, we return it as the decorator's result.

Unfortunately, as written, the returned decorated function's __name__ attribute is now set to "wrapper" instead of the original function's name, and has no docstring—even if the original function has a docstring. So the replacement isn't perfect. To address this deficiency, Python's standard library includes the @functools.wraps decorator, which can be used to decorate a wrapper function inside a decorator and ensures that the wrapped function's __name__ and __doc__ attributes hold the original function's name and docstring.

```python
def float_args_and_return(function):
    @functools.wraps(function)
    def wrapper(*args, **kwargs):
        args = [float(arg) for arg in args]
        return float(function(*args, **kwargs))
    return wrapper
```

Here is another version of the decorator. This version uses the @functools.wraps decorator to ensure that the wrapper() function created inside the decorator has its __name__ attribute correctly set to the passed-in function's name (e.g., "mean") and has the original function's docstring (which is empty in this example). It is best to always use @functools.wraps, since this will ensure that in tracebacks decorated functions' names will appear correctly (rather than all being called "wrapper") and that we have access to the original functions' docstrings.

```python
@statically_typed(str, str, return_type=str)
def make_tagged(text, tag):
    return "<{0}>{1}</{0}>".format(tag, escape(text))

@statically_typed(str, int, str) # Will accept any return type
def repeat(what, count, separator):
    return ((what + separator) * count)[:-len(separator)]
```

The statically_typed() function used to decorate the make_tagged() and repeat() functions is a *decorator factory*; that is, a decorator-making function. It isn't a decorator because it doesn't take a function, method, or class as its sole parameter. But here we need to parameterize the decorator, since we want to specify the number and types of positional arguments that a decorated function may accept (and optionally specify the type of its return value), and this will vary from function to function. So we have created a statically_typed() function that takes the parameters we need—one type per positional argument and an optional keyword argument for specifying the return type—and *returns* a decorator.

So, when Python encounters @statically_typed(...) in the code, it calls the function with the given arguments and then uses the function that is returned as a decorator for the following function (in this example, make_tagged() or repeat()).

Creating decorator factories follows a pattern. First, we create a decorator function, and inside that function we create a wrapper function; the wrapper follows the same pattern as before. As usual, at the end of the wrapper, the (possibly modified or replaced) result of the original function is returned. And at the end of the decorator function the wrapper is returned. Finally, at the end of the decorator factory function, the decorator is returned.

```python
def statically_typed(*types, return_type=None):
    def decorator(function):
        @functools.wraps(function)
        def wrapper(*args, **kwargs):
            if len(args) > len(types):
                raise ValueError("too many arguments")
            elif len(args) < len(types):
                raise ValueError("too few arguments")
            for i, (arg, type_) in enumerate(zip(args, types)):
                if not isinstance(arg, type_):
                    raise ValueError("argument {} must be of type {}"
                            .format(i, type_.__name__))
            result = function(*args, **kwargs)
            if (return_type is not None and
                not isinstance(result, return_type)):
                raise ValueError("return value must be of type {}".format(
                        return_type.__name__))
            return result
        return wrapper
    return decorator
```

Here we begin by creating a decorator function. We have called it decorator(), but the name doesn't matter. Inside the decorator function we create the wrapper—just as we did before. In this particular case the wrapper is rather involved, because it checks the number and types of all the positional arguments before calling the original function, and then it checks the type of the result if a specific return type was specified. And at the end it returns the result.

Once the wrapper has been created, the decorator returns it. And then, at the very end, the decorator itself is returned. So, when Python reaches, say, `@stat-ically_typed(str, int, str)` in the source code, it will call the `statically_typed()` function. This will return the `decorator()` function it has created—having captured the arguments passed to the `statically_typed()` function. Now, back at the `@`, Python executes the returned `decorator()` function, passing it the function that follows—either a function created with a `def` statement or the function returned by another decorator. In this case, the function is `repeat()`, so that function is passed as the sole argument to the `decorator()` function. The `decorator()` function now creates a new `wrapper()` function parameterized by the captured state (i.e., by the arguments that were given to the `statically_typed()` function) and returns the wrapper, which Python then uses to replace the original `repeat()` function.

Notice that the `wrapper()` function created when the `decorator()` function created by the `statically_typed()` function is called has captured some of its surrounding state—in particular, the `types` tuple and the `return_type` keyword argument. When a function or method captures state like this, it is said to be a *closure*. Python's support for closures is what makes it possible to create parameterized factory functions, decorators, and decorator factories.

Using a decorator to enforce the static type checking of arguments, and optionally of a function's return value, may be appealing to those coming to Python from a statically typed language (e.g., C, C++, or Java), but they add a *runtime* performance penalty that isn't paid by compiled languages. Furthermore, checking types when we have a dynamically typed language isn't very Pythonic, but it does show how flexible Python is. (And if we really want compile-time static typing, we can use Cython, as we will see in a later chapter; §5.2, ➤ 187.) What is probably more useful is parameter validation, something we will look at in the following subsection.

Although it can take a bit of getting used to, the patterns for writing decorators are straightforward. For an unparameterized function or method decorator, simply create a decorator function that creates and returns a wrapper. This pattern is shown by the `@float_args_and_return` decorator we saw earlier (50 ◀) and by the `@Web.ensure_logged_in` decorator that we will look at next. For a parameterized decorator, create a decorator factory that creates a decorator (that in turn creates a wrapper), following the pattern used for the `statically_typed()` function (51 ◀).

```
@application.post("/mailinglists/add")
@Web.ensure_logged_in
def person_add_submit(username):
    name = bottle.request.forms.get("name")
```

```
try:
    id = Data.MailingLists.add(name)
    bottle.redirect("/mailinglists/view")
except Data.Sql.Error as err:
    return bottle.mako_template("error", url="/mailinglists/add",
            text="Add Mailinglist", message=str(err))
```

This code snippet is taken from a web application for managing mailing lists that uses the lightweight `bottle` web framework (`bottlepy.org`). The `@application.post` decorator is provided by the framework and is used to associate a function with a URL. For this particular example, we only want users to access the `mailinglists/add` page if they are logged in—and to be redirected to the login page otherwise. Rather than putting in every function that produces a web page the same code to check whether the user is logged in, we have created the `@Web.ensure_logged_in` decorator, which handles this matter and means that none of our functions needs to be cluttered up with login-related code.

```
def ensure_logged_in(function):
    @functools.wraps(function)
    def wrapper(*args, **kwargs):
        username = bottle.request.get_cookie(COOKIE,
                secret=secret(bottle.request))
        if username is not None:
            kwargs["username"] = username
            return function(*args, **kwargs)
        bottle.redirect("/login")
    return wrapper
```

When the user logs in to the web site, the code behind the `login` page verifies their username and password, and if these are valid, sets a cookie in the user's browser that has a lifetime of a single session.

When the user requests a page whose associated function is protected by the `@ensure_logged_in` decorator, such as the `mailinglists/add` page's `person_add_submit()` function, the `wrapper()` function defined here gets called. The wrapper begins by trying to retrieve the username from the cookie. If this fails, the user isn't logged in, so we redirect them to the web application's `login` page. But if the user is logged in, we add the username to the keyword arguments, and return the result of calling the original function. This means that when the original function is called, it can safely assume that the user is validly logged in, and it has access to their username.

2.4.2. Class Decorators

It is quite common to create classes that have lots of read-write properties. Such classes often have a lot of duplicate or near-duplicate code for the getters and setters. For example, imagine we had a Book class that held a book's title, ISBN, price, and quantity. We would need four @property decorators, all with basically the same code (e.g., @property def title(self): return title). We would also need four setter methods, each with its own validation—although the code for validating the price and quantity properties would be identical apart from the actual minimum and maximum amounts allowed. If we had a lot of classes like this we could end up with a great deal of near-duplicate code.

Fortunately, Python's support of class decorators makes it possible to eliminate such duplication. For example, earlier in this chapter, we used a class decorator to create custom interface-checking classes without the need to duplicate ten lines of code each time (§2.2, 36 ◀). And here is another example, an implementation of a Book class that includes four fully validated properties (plus a read-only computed property):

```
@ensure("title", is_non_empty_str)
@ensure("isbn", is_valid_isbn)
@ensure("price", is_in_range(1, 10000))
@ensure("quantity", is_in_range(0, 1000000))
class Book:

    def __init__(self, title, isbn, price, quantity):
        self.title = title
        self.isbn = isbn
        self.price = price
        self.quantity = quantity

    @property
    def value(self):
        return self.price * self.quantity
```

The self.title, self.isbn, and so on are all properties, so the assignments that take place in the __init__() method are all validated by the relevant property setter. But instead of having to manually write the code for creating these properties with their getters and setters, we have used a class decorator—four times—to provide all of this functionality for us.

The ensure() function accepts two parameters—a property name and a validator function—and returns a class decorator. The class decorator is then applied to the following class.

So, here, the bare Book class is created, then the first (quantity) ensure() call is made, after which the returned class decorator is applied. This results in the

Book class being augmented with a quantity property. Next, the (price) ensure() call is made, and after the returned class decorator is applied, the Book class is now augmented with both quantity and price properties. This process is repeated twice more, until we end up with a final version of the Book class that has all four properties.

Although the process sounds like it is happening backwards, here is effectively what is going on:

```
ensure("title", is_non_empty_str)( # Pseudo-code
    ensure("isbn", is_valid_isbn)(
        ensure("price", is_in_range(1, 10000))(
            ensure("quantity", is_in_range(0, 1000000))(class Book: ...))))
```

The class Book statement must be executed first since the resulting class object is needed as the parameter to the (quantity) ensure() call's call, and the class object returned by this is needed by the one before, and so on.

Notice that both price and quantity use the same validator function, only with different parameters. In fact, the is_in_range() function is a factory function that makes and returns a new is_in_range() function that has the given minimum and maximum values hard-coded into it.

As we will see in a moment, the class decorator returned by the ensure() function adds a property to the class. This property's setter calls the validator function for the given property and passes into the validator two arguments: the name of the property and the new value for the property. The validator should do nothing if the value is valid; otherwise it should raise an exception (e.g., a ValueError). Before looking at ensure()'s implementation, let's look at a couple of validators.

```
def is_non_empty_str(name, value):
    if not isinstance(value, str):
        raise ValueError("{} must be of type str".format(name))
    if not bool(value):
        raise ValueError("{} may not be empty".format(name))
```

This validator is used for a Book's title property to ensure that the title is a nonempty string. As the ValueErrors show, the name of the property is useful for error messages.

```
def is_in_range(minimum=None, maximum=None):
    assert minimum is not None or maximum is not None
    def is_in_range(name, value):
        if not isinstance(value, numbers.Number):
            raise ValueError("{} must be a number".format(name))
        if minimum is not None and value < minimum:
```

```
        raise ValueError("{} {} is too small".format(name, value))
    if maximum is not None and value > maximum:
        raise ValueError("{} {} is too big".format(name, value))
return is_in_range
```

This function is a factory function that creates a new validator function that checks that the value it is given is a number (using the abstract base class numbers.Number) and that the number is in range. Once the validator has been created, it is returned.

```
def ensure(name, validate, doc=None):
    def decorator(Class):
        privateName = "__" + name
        def getter(self):
            return getattr(self, privateName)
        def setter(self, value):
            validate(name, value)
            setattr(self, privateName, value)
        setattr(Class, name, property(getter, setter, doc=doc))
        return Class
    return decorator
```

The ensure() function creates a class decorator parameterized by a property name, a validator function, and an optional docstring. So, each time a class decorator returned by ensure() is used for a particular class, that class is augmented by the addition of a new property.

The class decorator() function receives a class as its sole argument. The decorator() function begins by creating a private name; the property's value will be stored in an attribute with this name. (Thus, in the Book example, the self.title property's value will be stored in the private self.__title attribute.) Next, it creates a getter function that will return the value stored in the attribute with the private name. The built-in getattr() function takes an object and an attribute name and returns the attribute's value—or raises an AttributeError. The function then creates a setter that calls the captured validate() function, and then (assuming that validate() didn't raise an exception) sets the value stored in the attribute with the private name to the new value. The built-in setattr() function takes an object, an attribute name, and a value and sets the attribute's value to the given value, creating a new attribute if necessary.

Once the getter and setter have been created, they are used to create a new property that is added as an attribute to the passed-in class, under the given (public) property name, using the built-in setattr() function. The built-in property() function takes a getter, and optionally a setter, deleter, and docstring, and returns a property; it can also be used as a method decorator, as we have seen. The modified class is then returned by the `decorator()` function, and the `decorator()` function itself is returned by the `ensure()` class decorator factory function.

2.4.2.1. Using a Class Decorator to Add Properties

In the previous example (54 ◀), we had to use the `@ensure` class decorator for every attribute we wanted to validate. Some Python programmers don't like stacking lots of class decorators like this and prefer combining a single class decorator with attributes in a class's body to produce more readable code.

```
@do_ensure
class Book:

    title = Ensure(is_non_empty_str)
    isbn = Ensure(is_valid_isbn)
    price = Ensure(is_in_range(1, 10000))
    quantity = Ensure(is_in_range(0, 1000000))

    def __init__(self, title, isbn, price, quantity):
        self.title = title
        self.isbn = isbn
        self.price = price
        self.quantity = quantity

    @property
    def value(self):
        return self.price * self.quantity
```

This is a new version of the Book class that uses a `@do_ensure` class decorator in conjunction with `Ensure` instances. Each `Ensure` takes a validation function, and the `@do_ensure` class decorator replaces each `Ensure` instance with a validated property of the same name. Incidentally, the validation functions (`is_non_empty_str()` etc.) are the same as those shown earlier.

```
class Ensure:

    def __init__(self, validate, doc=None):
        self.validate = validate
        self.doc = doc
```

This tiny class is used to store the validation function that will end up being used in the property's setter, and optionally, the property's doc string. For example, the Book class's `title` attribute starts out as an `Ensure` instance, but once the Book class has been created, the `@do_ensure` decorator replaces every `Ensure` with a property. So, the `title` attribute ends up being a `title` property (whose setter uses the original `Ensure` instance's validation function).

```
def do_ensure(Class):
    def make_property(name, attribute):
        privateName = "__" + name
        def getter(self):
            return getattr(self, privateName)
        def setter(self, value):
            attribute.validate(name, value)
            setattr(self, privateName, value)
        return property(getter, setter, doc=attribute.doc)
    for name, attribute in Class.__dict__.items():
        if isinstance(attribute, Ensure):
            setattr(Class, name, make_property(name, attribute))
    return Class
```

This class decorator has three parts. In the first part we define a nested function (make_property()). The function takes a name (e.g., "title") and an attribute of type Ensure, and creates and returns a property that stores its value in a private attribute (e.g., "__title"). Furthermore, when the property's setter is accessed, it calls the validation function. In the second part we iterate over all the class's attributes and replace any Ensures with a new property. In the third part we return the modified class.

Once the decorator has finished, the decorated class has had every one of its Ensure attributes replaced by a validated property of the same name.

In theory, we could have avoided the nested function and simply put that code after the if isinstance() test. However, that doesn't work in practice due to problems with late binding, so having a separate function here is essential. This issue isn't uncommon when creating decorators or decorator factories, but using a separate—possibly nested—function is usually a sufficient solution.

2.4.2.2. Using a Class Decorator Instead of Subclassing

Sometimes we create a base class with some methods or data purely so that we can subclass this base class two or more times. This avoids having to duplicate the methods or data and scales well if we create additional subclasses. However, if the inherited methods or data are never modified in the subclasses, it is possible to use a class decorator to achieve the same end.

For example, later on we will make use of a Mediated base class that provides a self.mediator data attribute and an on_change() method (§3.5, ➤ 100). This class is inherited by two classes, Button and Text, which make use of the data and method but don't modify them.

```
class Mediated:
    def __init__(self):
```

```
            self.mediator = None

    def on_change(self):
        if self.mediator is not None:
            self.mediator.on_change(self)
```

This is the base class quoted from `mediator1.py`. It is inherited using the usual syntax; that is, `class Button(Mediated): ...` and `class Text(Mediated): ....` But since no subclass will ever need to modify the inherited `on_change()` method, we can use a class decorator instead of subclassing.

```
def mediated(Class):
    setattr(Class, "mediator", None)
    def on_change(self):
        if self.mediator is not None:
            self.mediator.on_change(self)
    setattr(Class, "on_change", on_change)
    return Class
```

This code is from `mediator1d.py`. The class decorator is applied like any other; that is, `@mediated class Button: ...` and `@mediated class Text: ....` The decorated classes have exactly the same behavior as the subclass versions.

Function and class decorators are a very powerful yet reasonably easy-to-use Python feature. And as we have seen, class decorators can sometimes be used as an alternative to subclassing. Creating decorators is a simple form of metaprogramming, and class decorators can often be used instead of more complex forms of metaprogramming, such as metaclasses.

2.5. Façade Pattern

The Façade Pattern is used to present a simplified and uniform interface to a subsystem whose interface is too complex or too low-level for convenient use.

Python's standard library provides modules for handling gzip-compressed files, tarballs, and zip files, but they all have different interfaces. Let's imagine that we would like to be able to access the names in an archive file, and extract its files, using a simple uniform interface. One solution is to use the Façade Pattern to provide a very simple high-level interface that defers most of the real work to the standard library.

Figure 2.7 (➤ 60) shows the interface we want to provide to users (a `filename` property and `names()` and `unpack()` methods) and the interfaces that we are providing a façade for. An `Archive` instance will hold one archive file's name, and

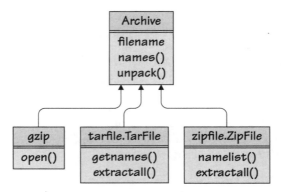

Figure 2.7 *The Archive façade*

only when asked for the archive's names or to unpack the archive will it actually open the archive file. (The code quoted in this section is from Unpack.py.)

```
class Archive:
    def __init__(self, filename):
        self._names = None
        self._unpack = None
        self._file = None
        self.filename = filename
```

The self._names variable is expected to hold a callable that will return a list of the archive's names. Similarly, the self._unpack variable is for holding a callable that will extract all the archive's files into the current directory. The self._file is for holding a file object that has been opened on the archive. And self.filename is a read-write property holding the archive file's filename.

```
    @property
    def filename(self):
        return self.__filename

    @filename.setter
    def filename(self, name):
        self.close()
        self.__filename = name
```

If the user changes the filename (e.g., using *archive*.filename = *newname*), the current archive file is closed (if it is open). We do not immediately open the new archive, though, since the Archive class uses lazy evaluation and so only opens the archive when necessary.

```
    def close(self):
        if self._file is not None:
            self._file.close()
        self._names = self._unpack = self._file = None
```

In theory, users of the Archive class are expected to call the close() method when they have finished with an instance. The method closes the file object (if one is open) and sets the self._names, self._unpack, and self._file variables to None to invalidate them.

We have made the Archive class a context manager (as we will see in a moment) so, in practice, users don't need to call close() themselves, providing they use the class in a with statement. For example:

```
with Archive(zipFilename) as archive:
    print(archive.names())
    archive.unpack()
```

Here we create an Archive for a zip file, print its names to the console, and then extract all its files in the current directory. And because the archive is a context manager, archive.close() is called automatically when the archive goes out of the with statement's scope.

```
    def __enter__(self):
        return self

    def __exit__(self, exc_type, exc_value, traceback):
        self.close()
```

These two methods are sufficient to make an Archive into a context manager. The __enter__() method returns self (an Archive instance), which is assigned to the with ... as statement's variable. The __exit__() method closes the archive's file object (if one is open), and since it (implicitly) returns None, any exceptions that have occurred will be propagated normally.

```
    def names(self):
        if self._file is None:
            self._prepare()
        return self._names()
```

This method returns a list of the archive's filenames, opening the archive and setting self._names and self._unpack to appropriate callables (using self._prepare()) if it isn't open already.

```
def unpack(self):
    if self._file is None:
        self._prepare()
    self._unpack()
```

This method unpacks all the archive's files, but as we will see, only if all of their names are "safe".

```
def _prepare(self):
    if self.filename.endswith((".tar.gz", ".tar.bz2", ".tar.xz",
            ".zip")):
        self._prepare_tarball_or_zip()
    elif self.filename.endswith(".gz"):
        self._prepare_gzip()
    else:
        raise ValueError("unreadable: {}".format(self.filename))
```

This method delegates the preparation to suitable methods. For tarballs and zip files the necessary code is very similar, so they are prepared in the same method. But gzipped files are handled differently and so have their own separate method.

The preparation methods must assign callables to the self._names and self._unpack variables, so that these can be called in the names() and unpack() methods we have just seen.

```
def _prepare_tarball_or_zip(self):
    def safe_extractall():
        unsafe = []
        for name in self.names():
            if not self.is_safe(name):
                unsafe.append(name)
        if unsafe:
            raise ValueError("unsafe to unpack: {}".format(unsafe))
        self._file.extractall()
    if self.filename.endswith(".zip"):
        self._file = zipfile.ZipFile(self.filename)
        self._names = self._file.namelist
        self._unpack = safe_extractall
    else: # Ends with .tar.gz, .tar.bz2, or .tar.xz
        suffix = os.path.splitext(self.filename)[1]
        self._file = tarfile.open(self.filename, "r:" + suffix[1:])
        self._names = self._file.getnames
        self._unpack = safe_extractall
```

This method begins by creating a nested `safe_extractall()` function that checks all the archive's names and raises a `ValueError` if there are any unsafe names, as defined by the `is_safe()` method. If all the names are safe the `tarball.TarFile.extractall()` or `zipfile.ZipFile.extractall()` method is called.

Depending on the archive filename's extension, we open a `tarball.TarFile` or `zipfile.ZipFile` and assign it to `self._file`. We then set `self._names` to the corresponding bound method (`namelist()` or `getnames()`), and `self._unpack` to the `safe_extractall()` function we just created. This function is a closure that has captured `self` and so can access `self._file` and call the appropriate `extractall()` method. (See the "Bound and Unbound Methods" sidebar.)

Bound and Unbound Methods

A *bound method* is a method that is already associated with an instance of its class. Let's imagine we have a `Form` class with an `update_ui()` method. Now, if we write *bound* = `self.update_ui` inside one of the `Form` class's methods, *bound* is assigned an object reference to the `Form.update_ui()` method that is bound to a particular instance of the form (`self`). A bound method can be called directly; for example, *bound*().

An *unbound method* is a method with no associated instance. For example, if we write *unbound* = `Form.update_ui`, *unbound* is assigned an object reference to the `Form.update_ui()` method, but with no binding to any particular instance. This means that if we want to call the unbound method, we must provide a suitable instance as its first argument; for example, *form* = `Form()`; *unbound*(*form*). (Strictly speaking, Python 3 doesn't actually have unbound methods, so *unbound* is really the underlying function object, although this only makes a difference in some metaprogramming corner cases.)

```
def is_safe(self, filename):
    return not (filename.startswith(("/", "\\")) or
        (len(filename) > 1 and filename[1] == ":" and
         filename[0] in string.ascii_letter) or
        re.search(r"[.][.][/\\]", filename))
```

A maliciously created archive file that is unpacked could overwrite important system files with nonfunctional or sinister replacements. In view of this, we should never open archives that contain files with absolute paths or with relative path components, and we should always open archives as an unprivileged user (i.e., never as root or Administrator).

This method returns `False` if the filename it is given starts with a forward slash or a backslash (i.e., an absolute path), or contains `../` or `..\` (a relative path that could lead anywhere), or starts with *D:* where *D* is a Windows drive letter.

In other words, any filename that is absolute or that has relative components is considered to be unsafe. For any other filename the method returns True.

```
    def _prepare_gzip(self):
        self._file = gzip.open(self.filename)
        filename = self.filename[:-3]
        self._names = lambda: [filename]
        def extractall():
            with open(filename, "wb") as file:
                file.write(self._file.read())
        self._unpack = extractall
```

This method provides an open file object for self._file and assigns suitable callables to self._names and self._unpack. For the extractall() function, we have to read and write the data ourselves.

The Façade Pattern can be very useful for creating simplified and convenient interfaces. The upside is that we are insulated from low-level details; the downside is that we may have to give up fine control. However, a façade doesn't hide or do away with the underlying functionality, so we can always use the façade most of the time, and just drop down to lower-level classes if we need more control.

The Façade and Adapter Patterns have a superficial similarity. The difference is that a façade provides a simple interface on top of a complicated interface, whereas an adapter provides a standardized interface on top of another (not necessarily complicated) interface. Both patterns can be used together. For example, we might define an interface for handling archive files (tarballs, zip files, Windows .cab files, and so on), use an adapter for each format, and layer a façade on top so that users would not need to know or care about which particular file format was being used.

2.6. Flyweight Pattern

The Flyweight Pattern is designed for handling large numbers of relatively small objects, where many of the small objects are duplicates of each other. The pattern is implemented by representing each unique object only once, and by sharing this unique instance wherever it is needed.

Python takes a naturally flyweight approach because of its use of object references. For example, if we had a long list of strings—many of which were duplicates—so long as we stored object references (i.e., variables) rather than literal strings, we would make significant memory savings.

```
red, green, blue = "red", "green", "blue"
x = (red, green, blue, red, green, blue, red, green)
y = ("red", "green", "blue", "red", "green", "blue", "red", "green")
```

In the previous code snippet, the x tuple stores 3 strings using 8 object references. The y tuple stores 8 strings using 8 object references, since what we have written is in effect syntactic sugar for _anonymous_item0 = "red", ..., _anonymous_item7 = "green"; y = (_anonymous_item0, ..._anonymous_item7).

Probably the easiest way to take advantage of the Flyweight Pattern in Python is to use a dict, with each unique object held as a value identified by a unique key. For example, if we are creating lots of HTML pages with fonts specified by CSS (Cascading Style Sheets), rather than creating a new font every time one is needed, we could create the ones we need in advance (or as required) and keep them in a dict. Then, whenever we required a font, we could take it from the dict. This would ensure that each unique font would be created only once, no matter how many times it was used.

In some situations we may have a large number of not necessarily small objects, where all or most of them are unique. One easy way to reduce the memory footprint in such cases is to use __slots__.

```
class Point:

    __slots__ = ("x", "y", "z", "color")

    def __init__(self, x=0, y=0, z=0, color=None):
        self.x = x
        self.y = y
        self.z = z
        self.color = color
```

Here is a simple Point class that holds a three-dimensional position and a color. Thanks to the __slots__, no Point has its own private dict (self.__dict__). However, this also means that no arbitrary attributes can be added to individual points. (This class is quoted from pointstore1.py.)

On one test machine it took around 2½ seconds to create a tuple of one million of these points, and the program (which did little else) occupied 183 MiB of RAM. Without the slots, this program ran a fraction of a second faster but occupied 312 MiB of RAM.

By default, Python always sacrifices memory for the sake of speed, but we can often reverse this trade-off if doing so suits us better.

```
class Point:

    __slots__ = ()
    __dbm = shelve.open(os.path.join(tempfile.gettempdir(), "point.db"))
```

Here is the beginning of our second Point class (quoted from pointstore2.py). It uses a DBM (key–value) database that is stored in a file on disk to store its data. An object reference to the DBM is stored in the static (i.e., class-level)

`Point.__dbm` variable. All `Points` share the same underlying DBM file. We begin by opening the DBM file ready for use. The `shelve` module's default behavior is to automatically create the DBM file if it doesn't already exist. (We'll see how we ensure that the DBM file is properly closed later.)

The `shelve` module pickles the values we store and unpickles the values we retrieve. (Python's pickle format is inherently insecure because the unpickling process in effect executes arbitrary Python code. In view of this we should never use pickles from untrusted sources or for data to which untrusted access is possible. Alternatively, if we want to use pickles in such circumstances, we should apply our own security measures, such as checksums and encryption.)

```
def __init__(self, x=0, y=0, z=0, color=None):
    self.x = x
    self.y = y
    self.z = z
    self.color = color
```

This method is exactly the same as the one in `pointstore1.py`, but under the hood the values are assigned into the underlying DBM file.

```
def __key(self, name):
    return "{:X}:{}".format(id(self), name)
```

This method provides the key string for any of the x, y, z, and color `Point` attributes. The key is made up of the instance's ID (a unique number returned by the built-in `id()` function) in hexadecimal and the attribute name. For example, if we had a `Point` with an ID of, say, 3 954 827, its x attribute would be stored using the key `"3C588B:x"`, its y attribute using the key `"3C588B:y"`, and so on.

```
def __getattr__(self, name):
    return Point.__dbm[self.__key(name)]
```

This method is called whenever a `Point` attribute is accessed (e.g., *x = point.x*).

DBM databases' keys and values must be bytes. Fortunately, Python's DBM modules will accept either `str` or `bytes` keys, converting the former to `bytes` using the default encoding (UTF-8) under the hood. And if we use the `shelve` module (as we have done here), we can store any pickleable values we like, relying on the `shelve` module to convert to and from `bytes` as required.

So, here, we get the appropriate key and retrieve the corresponding value. And thanks to the `shelve` module, the retrieved value is converted from (pickled) bytes to the type originally set (e.g., to an `int` or `None` for a point color).

```
def __setattr__(self, name, value):
    Point.__dbm[self.__key(name)] = value
```

Whenever a `Point` attribute is set (e.g., `point.y = y`), this method is called. Here, we get the appropriate key and set its value, relying on the `shelve` module to convert the value to (pickled) bytes.

```
atexit.register(__dbm.close)
```

At the end of `Point` class, we register the DBM's `close()` method to be called when the program terminates, using the `atexit` module's `register()` function.

On the test machine, it took about a minute to create a database of a million points, but the program only occupied 29 MiB of RAM (plus a 361 MiB disk file), compared with 183 MiB of RAM for the first version. Although the time taken to populate the DBM is considerable, once this is done, lookup speed should be fast, since most operating systems will cache a disk file that's frequently used.

2.7. Proxy Pattern

The Proxy Pattern is used when we want one object to stand in for another. Four use cases are presented in the *Design Patterns* book. The first is a remote proxy where a local object proxies a remote object. The RPyC library is a perfect example of this: it allows us to create objects on a server and proxies for those objects on one or more clients. (This library is introduced in Chapter 6; §6.2, ➤ 219.) The second is a virtual proxy that allows us to create lightweight objects instead of heavyweight objects, only creating the heavyweight objects if they are actually needed. We will review an example of this in this section. The third is a protection proxy that provides different levels of access depending on a client's access rights. And the fourth is a smart reference that "performs additional actions when an object is accessed". We can use the same coding approach for all proxies, although the fourth use case's behavior could also be achieved using a descriptor (e.g., replacing an object with a property using the `@property` decorator).★

This pattern can also be used in unit testing. For example, if we need to test some code that accesses a resource that isn't always available, or a class that is being developed but is incomplete, we could create a proxy for the resource or class that provided the full interface, but with stubs for missing functionality. This approach can be so useful that Python 3.3 includes the `unittest.mock` library for creating mock objects and for adding stubs in place of missing methods. (See `docs.python.org/py3k/library/unittest.mock.html`.)

★ Descriptors are covered in *Programming in Python 3, Second Edition* (see the Selected Bibliography for details; ➤ 287), and in the online documentation: `docs.python.org/3/reference/datamodel.html#descriptors`.

For this section's example, we will assume that we need to create multiple images speculatively, with only one of them actually used in the end. We have an Image module and a faster near-equivalent cyImage module (covered in §3.12, ➤ 124 and §5.2.2, ➤ 193), but these modules create their images in memory. Since we will need only one of the speculatively created images, it would be better if we created lightweight image proxies and only when we knew which image we were really going to need go on to create an actual image.

The Image.Image class's interface consists of ten methods in addition to the constructor: load(), save(), pixel(), set_pixel(), line(), rectangle(), ellipse(), size(), subsample(), and scale(). (This doesn't include some additional static convenience methods that are also available as module functions, such as Image.Image.color_for_name() and Image.color_for_name().)

Figure 2.8 *A drawn image*

For our proxy class we will only implement the subset of the Image.Image's methods that is sufficient for our needs. Let's begin by looking at how the proxy is used. The code is quoted from imageproxy1.py; the image produced is shown in Figure 2.8.

```
YELLOW, CYAN, BLUE, RED, BLACK = (Image.color_for_name(color)
    for color in ("yellow", "cyan", "blue", "red", "black"))
```

First, we create some color constants using the Image module's color_for_name() function.

```
image = ImageProxy(Image.Image, 300, 60)
image.rectangle(0, 0, 299, 59, fill=YELLOW)
image.ellipse(0, 0, 299, 59, fill=CYAN)
image.ellipse(60, 20, 120, 40, BLUE, RED)
image.ellipse(180, 20, 240, 40, BLUE, RED)
image.rectangle(180, 32, 240, 41, fill=CYAN)
image.line(181, 32, 239, 32, BLUE)
image.line(140, 50, 160, 50, BLACK)
image.save(filename)
```

Here, we create an image proxy, passing in the image class we want it to use. Then we draw on it, and at the end we save the resultant image. This code would work just as well had we created the image using Image.Image() rather than ImageProxy(). However, by using an image proxy, the actual image is not created until the save() method is called—so the cost of creating the image prior to saving it is extremely low (both in memory and processing), and if we end up discarding the image without saving it, we have lost very little. Compare this with using an Image.Image where we pay a high price up front (i.e., by effectively creating a width × height array of color values) and do expensive processing when drawing (e.g., setting every pixel in a filled rectangle, as well as computing which ones to set), even if we end up discarding the image.

```
class ImageProxy:

    def __init__(self, ImageClass, width=None, height=None, filename=None):
        assert (width is not None and height is not None) or \
                filename is not None
        self.Image = ImageClass
        self.commands = []
        if filename is not None:
            self.load(filename)
        else:
            self.commands = [(self.Image, width, height)]

    def load(self, filename):
        self.commands = [(self.Image, None, None, filename)]
```

The ImageProxy class can stand in for an Image.Image (or any other image class passed to it that supports the Image interface), providing that the incomplete interface that the image proxy provides is sufficient. An ImageProxy does not store an image; instead, it keeps a list of command tuples where the first item in each tuple is a function or an unbound method and the remaining items are the arguments to be passed when the function or method is called.

When an ImageProxy is created, it must be given a width and height (to create a new image of the given size) or a filename. If it is given a filename, it stores the same commands as when an ImageProxy.load() call is made: the Image.Image() constructor, and, as arguments None and None for the width and height and the filename. Notice that if ImageProxy.load() is called at any later time, all previous commands are discarded and the load command becomes the first and only command in self.commands. If a width and height are given, the Image.Image() constructor is stored, along with the width and height as arguments.

If any unsupported method is called (e.g., pixel()), the method won't be found and Python will automatically do what we want: raise an AttributeError. An alternative approach for handling methods that can't be proxied is to create an actual image as soon as one of these methods is called, and from then on, use the actual image. (The examples' imageproxy2.py program—not shown—takes this approach.)

```
    def set_pixel(self, x, y, color):
        self.commands.append((self.Image.set_pixel, x, y, color))

    def line(self, x0, y0, x1, y1, color):
        self.commands.append((self.Image.line, x0, y0, x1, y1, color))

    def rectangle(self, x0, y0, x1, y1, outline=None, fill=None):
        self.commands.append((self.Image.rectangle, x0, y0, x1, y1,
                outline, fill))

    def ellipse(self, x0, y0, x1, y1, outline=None, fill=None):
        self.commands.append((self.Image.ellipse, x0, y0, x1, y1,
                outline, fill))
```

The Image.Image class's drawing interface consists of the four methods: line(), rectangle(), ellipse(), and set_pixel(). Our ImageProxy class fully supports this interface, only instead of executing these commands, it simply adds them—along with their arguments—to the self.commands list.

```
    def save(self, filename=None):
        command = self.commands.pop(0)
        function, *args = command
        image = function(*args)
        for command in self.commands:
            function, *args = command
            function(image, *args)
        image.save(filename)
        return image
```

Only if we choose to save the image, do we have to actually create a real image and pay the price in processing and memory consumption. The design of the ImageProxy means that the first command is always one that creates a new image (either one of a given width and height, or by loading one). So, we treat the first command specially by saving its return value, which we know will be an Image.Image (or a cyImage.Image). Then, we iterate over the remaining commands, calling each one in turn, and passing in the image as the first (self) argument, since they are really unbound method calls. And at the end, we save the image using the Image.Image.save() method.

The Image.Image.save() method has no return value (although it can raise an exception if an error occurs). However, we have modified its interface slightly for the ImageProxy by returning the Image.Image that has been created, in case it was needed for further processing. This should be a harmless change since if the return value is ignored (as it would be if we were calling Image.Image.save()), it will be silently discarded. The imageproxy2.py program doesn't require this modification, since it has an `image` property of type `Image.Image` that forces the image to be created (if it hasn't been already) when it is accessed.

Storing up commands, as we have done here, has the potential for adaptation to support do–undo; for more on that, see the Command Pattern (§3.2, ➤ 79). See, also, the State Pattern (§3.8, ➤ 111).

The structural design patterns can all be implemented in Python. The Adapter and Façade Patterns make it straightforward to reuse classes in new contexts, and the Bridge Pattern makes it possible to embed the sophisticated functionality of one class inside another. The Composite Pattern makes it easy to create hierarchies of objects—although there is less need for this in Python, since using `dicts` is often sufficient for this purpose. The Decorator Pattern is so useful that the Python language has direct support for it and even extends the idea to classes. Python's use of object references means that the language itself uses a variation of the Flyweight Pattern. And the Proxy Pattern is particularly easy to implement in Python. The design patterns go beyond the creation of basic and complex objects and into the realms of behavior: how individual objects or groups of objects can get things done. We will look at behavioral patterns in the next chapter.

3

Behavioral Design Patterns

The behavioral patterns are concerned with how things get done; that is, with algorithms and object interactions. They provide powerful ways of thinking about and organizing computations, and like a few of the patterns seen in the previous two chapters, some of them are supported directly by built-in Python syntax.

The Perl programming language's well-known motto is, "there's more than one way to do it"; whereas in Tim Peters' Zen of Python, "there should be one—and preferably only one—obvious way to do it".* Yet, like any programming language, there are sometimes two or more ways to do things in Python, especially since the introduction of comprehensions (use a comprehension or a for loop) and generators (use a generator expression or a function with a yield statement). And as we will see in this chapter, Python's support for coroutines adds a new way to do certain things.

3.1. Chain of Responsibility Pattern

The Chain of Responsibility Pattern is designed to decouple the sender of a request from the recipient that processes the request. So, instead of one function directly calling another, the first function sends a request to a chain of receivers. The first receiver in the chain either can handle the request and stop the chain (by not passing the request on) or can pass on the request to the next receiver in the chain. The second receiver has the same choices, and so on, until the last one is reached (which could choose to throw the request away or to raise an exception).

Let's imagine that we have a user interface that receives events to be handled. Some of the events come from the user (e.g., mouse and key events), and some come from the system (e.g., timer events). In the following two subsections we will look at a conventional approach to creating an event-handling chain, and then at a pipeline-based approach using coroutines.

3.1.1. A Conventional Chain

In this subsection we will review a conventional event-handling chain where each event has a corresponding event-handling class.

```
handler1 = TimerHandler(KeyHandler(MouseHandler(NullHandler())))
```

Here is how the chain might be set up using four separate handler classes. The chain is illustrated in Figure 3.1. Since we throw away unhandled events, we could have just passed None—or nothing—as the MouseHandler's argument.

---

* To see the Zen of Python, enter import this at an interactive Python prompt.

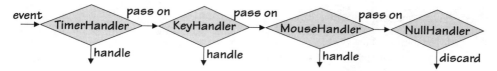

Figure 3.1 *An event-handling chain*

The order in which we create the handlers should not matter since each one handles events only of the type it is designed for.

```
while True:
    event = Event.next()
    if event.kind == Event.TERMINATE:
        break
    handler1.handle(event)
```

Events are normally handled in a loop. Here, we exit the loop and terminate the application if there is a TERMINATE event; otherwise, we pass the event to the event-handling chain.

```
handler2 = DebugHandler(handler1)
```

Here we have created a new handler (although we could just as easily have assigned back to handler1). This handler *must* be first in the chain, since it is used to eavesdrop on the events passing into the chain and to report them, but not to handle them (so it passes on every event it receives).

We can now call handler2.handle(event) in our loop, and in addition to the normal event handlers we will now have some debugging output to see the events that are received.

```
class NullHandler:

    def __init__(self, successor=None):
        self.__successor = successor

    def handle(self, event):
        if self.__successor is not None:
            self.__successor.handle(event)
```

This class serves as the base class for our event handlers and provides the infrastructure for handling events. If an instance is created with a successor handler, then when this instance is given an event, it simply passes the event down the chain to the successor. However, if there is no successor, we have decided to simply discard the event. This is the standard approach in GUI (graphical user interface) programming, although we could easily log or raise an exception for unhandled events (e.g., if our program was a server).

```
class MouseHandler(NullHandler):

    def handle(self, event):
        if event.kind == Event.MOUSE:
            print("Click:    {}".format(event))
        else:
            super().handle(event)
```

Since we haven't reimplemented the __init__() method, the base class one will
be used, so the self.__successor variable will be correctly created.

This handler class handles only those events that it is interested in (i.e., of type
Event.MOUSE) and passes any other kind of event on to its successor in the chain
(if there is one).

The KeyHandler and TimerHandler classes (neither of which is shown) have exactly
the same structure as the MouseHandler. These other classes only differ in which
kind of event they respond to (e.g., Event.KEYPRESS and Event.TIMER) and the
handling they perform (i.e., they print out different messages).

```
class DebugHandler(NullHandler):

    def __init__(self, successor=None, file=sys.stdout):
        super().__init__(successor)
        self.__file = file

    def handle(self, event):
        self.__file.write("*DEBUG*: {}\n".format(event))
        super().handle(event)
```

The DebugHandler class is different from the other handlers in that it never
handles any events, and it must be first in the chain. It takes a file or file-like
object to direct its reports to, and when an event occurs, it reports the event and
then passes it on.

3.1.2. A Coroutine-Based Chain

A generator is a function or method that has one or more yield expressions instead of returns. Whenever a yield is reached, the value yielded is produced, and
the function or method is suspended with all its state intact. At this point the
function has yielded the processor (to the receiver of the value it has produced),
so although suspended, the function does not block. Then, when the function or
method is used again, execution resumes from the statement following the yield.
So, values are *pulled* from a generator by iterating over it (e.g., using for *value*
in *generator*:) or by calling next() on it.

A coroutine uses the same yield expression as a generator but has different behavior. A coroutine executes an infinite loop and starts out suspended at its first (or only) yield expression, waiting for a value to be sent to it. If and when a value is sent, the coroutine receives this as the value of its yield expression. The coroutine can then do any processing it wants and when it has finished, it loops and again becomes suspended waiting for a value to arrive at its next yield expression. So, values are *pushed* into a coroutine by calling the coroutine's send() or throw() methods.

In Python, any function or method that contains a yield is a generator. However, by using a @coroutine decorator, and by using an infinite loop, we can turn a generator into a coroutine. (We discussed decorators and the @functools.wraps decorator in the previous chapter; §2.4, 48 ◄.)

```
def coroutine(function):
    @functools.wraps(function)
    def wrapper(*args, **kwargs):
        generator = function(*args, **kwargs)
        next(generator)
        return generator
    return wrapper
```

The wrapper calls the generator function just once and captures the generator it produces in the generator variable. This generator is really the original function with its arguments and any local variables captured as its state. Next, the wrapper advances the generator—just once, using the built-in next() function—to execute it up to its first yield expression. The generator—with its captured state—is then returned. This returned generator function is a coroutine, ready to receive a value at its first (or only) yield expression.

If we call a generator, it will resume execution where it left off (i.e., continue after the last—or only—yield expression it executed). However, if we send a value into a coroutine (using Python's *generator*.send(*value*) syntax), this value will be received inside the coroutine as the current yield expression's result, and execution will resume from that point.

Since we can both receive values from and send values to coroutines, they can be used to create pipelines, including event-handling chains. Furthermore, we don't need to provide a successor infrastructure, since we can use Python's generator syntax instead.

```
pipeline = key_handler(mouse_handler(timer_handler()))
```

Here, we create our chain (pipeline) using a bunch of nested function calls. Every function called is a coroutine, and each one executes up to its first (or only) yield expression, here suspending execution, ready to be used again or sent a value. So, the pipeline is created immediately, with no blocking.

Instead of having a null handler, we pass nothing to the last handler in the chain. We will see how this works when we look at a typical handler coroutine (key_handler()).

```
while True:
    event = Event.next()
    if event.kind == Event.TERMINATE:
        break
    pipeline.send(event)
```

Just as with the conventional approach, once the chain is ready to handle events, we handle them in a loop. Because each handler function is a coroutine (a generator function), it has a send() method. So, here, each time we have an event to handle, we send it into the pipeline. In this example, the value will first be sent to the key_handler() coroutine, which will either handle the event or pass it on. As before, the order of the handlers often doesn't matter.

```
pipeline = debug_handler(pipeline)
```

This is the one case where it does matter which order we use for a handler. Since the debug_handler() coroutine is intended to spy on the events and simply pass them on, it must be the first handler in the chain. With this new pipeline in place, we can once again loop over events, sending each one to the pipeline in turn using pipeline.send(event).

```
@coroutine
def key_handler(successor=None):
    while True:
        event = (yield)
        if event.kind == Event.KEYPRESS:
            print("Press:    {}".format(event))
        elif successor is not None:
            successor.send(event)
```

This coroutine accepts a successor coroutine to send to (or None) and begins executing an infinite loop. The @coroutine decorator ensures that the key_handler() is executed up to its yield expression, so when the pipeline chain is created, this function has reached its yield expression and is blocked, waiting for the yield to produce a (sent) value. (Of course, it is only the coroutine that is blocked, not the program as a whole.)

Once a value is sent to this coroutine—either directly, or from another coroutine in the pipeline—it is received as the event value. If the event is of a kind that this coroutine handles (i.e., of type Event.KEYPRESS), it is handled—in this example, just printed—and not sent any further. However, if the event is not of the right type for this coroutine, and providing that there is a successor coroutine, it is sent on to its successor to handle. If there is no successor, and the event isn't handled here, it is simply discarded.

After handling, sending, or discarding an event, the coroutine returns to the top of the while loop, and then, once again, waits for the yield to produce a value sent into the pipeline.

The mouse_handler() and timer_handler() coroutines (neither of which is shown), have exactly the same structure as the key_handler(); the only differences being the type of event they handle and the messages they print.

```
@coroutine
def debug_handler(successor, file=sys.stdout):
    while True:
        event = (yield)
        file.write("*DEBUG*: {}\n".format(event))
        successor.send(event)
```

The debug_handler() waits to receive an event, prints the event's details, and then sends it on to the next coroutine to be handled.

Although coroutines use the same machinery as generators, they work in a very different way. With a normal generator, we *pull* values out one at a time (e.g., for x in range(10):). But with coroutines, we *push* values in one at a time using send(). This versatility means that Python can express many different kinds of algorithm in a very clean and natural way. For example, the coroutine-based chain shown in this subsection was implemented using far less code than the conventional chain shown in the previous subsection.

We will see coroutines in action again when we look at the Mediator Pattern (§3.5, ➤ 100).

The Chain of Responsibility Pattern can, of course, be applied in many other contexts than those illustrated in this section. For example, we could use the pattern to handle requests coming into a server.

3.2. Command Pattern

The Command Pattern is used to encapsulate commands as objects. This makes it possible, for example, to build up a sequence of commands for deferred execution or to create undoable commands. We have already seen a basic use of the Command Pattern in the ImageProxy example (§2.7, 67 ◄), and in this section we will go a step further and create classes for undoable individual commands and for undoable macros (i.e., undoable sequences of commands).

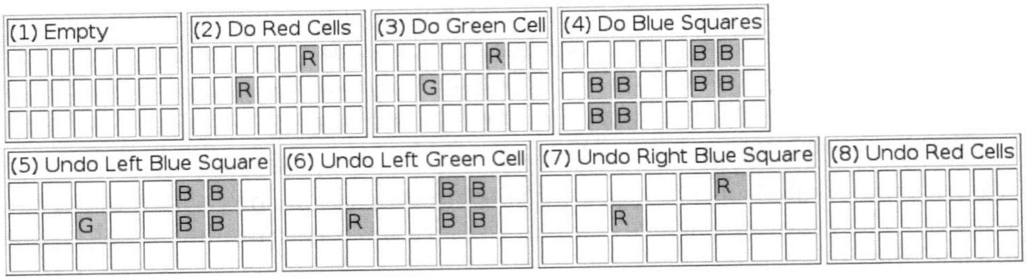

Figure 3.2 *A grid being done and undone*

Let's begin by seeing some code that uses the Command Pattern, and then we will look at the classes it uses (UndoableGrid and Grid) and the Command module that provides the do–undo and macro infrastructure.

```
grid = UndoableGrid(8, 3)    # (1) Empty
redLeft = grid.create_cell_command(2, 1, "red")
redRight = grid.create_cell_command(5, 0, "red")
redLeft()                     # (2) Do Red Cells
redRight.do()                 # OR: redRight()
greenLeft = grid.create_cell_command(2, 1, "lightgreen")
greenLeft()                   # (3) Do Green Cell
rectangleLeft = grid.create_rectangle_macro(1, 1, 2, 2, "lightblue")
rectangleRight = grid.create_rectangle_macro(5, 0, 6, 1, "lightblue")
rectangleLeft()               # (4) Do Blue Squares
rectangleRight.do()           # OR: rectangleRight()
rectangleLeft.undo()          # (5) Undo Left Blue Square
greenLeft.undo()              # (6) Undo Left Green Cell
rectangleRight.undo()         # (7) Undo Right Blue Square
redLeft.undo()                # (8) Undo Red Cells
redRight.undo()
```

Figure 3.2 shows the grid rendered as HTML eight different times. The first one shows the grid after it has been created in the first place (i.e., when it is empty). Then, each subsequent one shows the state of things after each command or macro is created and then called (either directly or using its do() method) and after every undo() call.

```
class Grid:

    def __init__(self, width, height):
        self.__cells = [["white" for _ in range(height)]
                        for _ in range(width)]

    def cell(self, x, y, color=None):
        if color is None:
```

```
        return self.__cells[x][y]
    self.__cells[x][y] = color

@property
def rows(self):
    return len(self.__cells[0])

@property
def columns(self):
    return len(self.__cells)
```

This `Grid` class is a simple image-like class that holds a list of lists of color names.

The `cell()` method serves as both a getter (when the `color` argument is None) and a setter (when a `color` is given). The `rows` and `columns` read-only properties return the grid's dimensions.

```
class UndoableGrid(Grid):

    def create_cell_command(self, x, y, color):
        def undo():
            self.cell(x, y, undo.color)
        def do():
            undo.color = self.cell(x, y) # Subtle!
            self.cell(x, y, color)
        return Command.Command(do, undo, "Cell")
```

To make the `Grid` support undoable commands, we have created a subclass that adds two additional methods, the first of which is shown here.

Every command must be of type `Command.Command` or `Command.Macro`. The former takes do and undo callables and an optional description. The latter has an optional description and can have any number of `Command.Commands` added to it.

In the `create_cell_command()` method, we accept the position and color of the cell to set and then create the two functions required to create a `Command.Command`. Both commands simply set the given cell's color.

Of course, at the time the `do()` and `undo()` functions are created, we cannot know what the color of the cell will be *immediately before* the `do()` command is applied, so we don't know what color to undo it to. We have solved this problem by retrieving the cell's color inside the `do()` function—at the time the function is called—and setting it as an attribute of the `undo()` function. Only then do we set the new color. Note that this works because the `do()` function is a closure that not only captures the x, y, and `color` parameters as part of its state, but also the `undo()` function that has just been created.

Once the do() and undo() functions have been created, we create a new Command.Command that incorporates them, plus a simple description, and return the command to the caller.

```
def create_rectangle_macro(self, x0, y0, x1, y1, color):
    macro = Command.Macro("Rectangle")
    for x in range(x0, x1 + 1):
        for y in range(y0, y1 + 1):
            macro.add(self.create_cell_command(x, y, color))
    return macro
```

This is the second UndoableGrid method for creating doable–undoable commands. This method creates a macro that will create a rectangle spanning the given co-ordinates. For each cell to be colored, a cell command is created using the class's other method (create_cell_command()), and this command is added to the macro. Once all the commands have been added, the macro is returned.

As we will see, both commands and macros support do() and undo() methods. Since commands and macros support the same methods, and macros contain commands, their relationship to each other is a variation of the Composite Pattern (§2.3, 40 ◄).

```
class Command:

    def __init__(self, do, undo, description=""):
        assert callable(do) and callable(undo)
        self.do = do
        self.undo = undo
        self.description = description


    def __call__(self):
        self.do()
```

A Command.Command expects two callables: the first is the "do" command, and the second is the "undo" command. (The callable() function is a Python 3.3 built-in; for earlier versions an equivalent function can be created with: def callable(function): return isinstance(function, collections.Callable).)

A Command.Command can be executed simply by calling it (thanks to our imple-mentation of the __call__() special method) or equivalently by calling its do() method. The command can be undone by calling its undo() method.

```
class Macro:

    def __init__(self, description=""):
        self.description = description
        self.__commands = []
```

```
    def add(self, command):
        if not isinstance(command, Command):
            raise TypeError("Expected object of type Command, got {}".
                format(type(command).__name__))
        self.__commands.append(command)

    def __call__(self):
        for command in self.__commands:
            command()

    do = __call__

    def undo(self):
        for command in reversed(self.__commands):
            command.undo()
```

The Command.Macro class is used to encapsulate a sequence of commands that should all be done—or undone—as a single operation.* The Command.Macro offers the same interface as Command.Commands: do() and undo() methods, and the ability to be called directly. In addition, macros provide an add() method through which Command.Commands can be added.

For macros, commands must be undone in reverse order. For example, suppose we created a macro and added the commands A, B, and C. When we executed the macro (i.e., called it or called its do() method), it would execute A, then B, and then C. So when we call undo(), we must execute the undo() methods for C, then B, and then A.

In Python, functions, bound methods, and other callables are first-class objects that can be passed around and stored in data structures such as lists and dicts. This makes Python an ideal language for implementations of the Command Pattern. And the pattern itself can be used to great effect, as we have seen here, in providing do–undo functionality, as well as being able to support macros and deferred execution.

3.3. Interpreter Pattern

The Interpreter Pattern formalizes two common requirements: providing some means by which users can enter nonstring values into applications, and allowing users to program applications.

At the most basic level, an application will receive strings from the user—or from other programs—that must be interpreted (and perhaps executed) appropriately. Suppose, for example, we receive a string from the user that is supposed

---

* Although we speak of macros executing in a single operation, this operation is not atomic from a concurrency point of view, although it could be made atomic if we used appropriate locks.

to represent an integer. An easy—and unwise—way to get the integer's value is like this: i = eval(*userCount*). This is dangerous, because although we hope the string is something innocent like "1234", it could be "os.system('rmdir /s /q C:\\\\')".

In general, if we are given a string that is supposed to represent the value of a specific data type, we can use Python to obtain the value directly and safely.

```
try:
    count = int(userCount)
    when = datetime.datetime.strptime(userDate, "%Y/%m/%d").date()
except ValueError as err:
    print(err)
```

In this snippet, we get Python to safely try to parse two strings, one into an int and the other into a datetime.date.

Sometimes, of course, we need to go beyond interpreting single strings into values. For example, we might want to provide an application with a calculator facility or allow users to create their own code snippets to be applied to application data. One popular approach to these kinds of requirements is to create a DSL (Domain Specific Language). Such languages can be created with Python out of the box—for example, by writing a recursive descent parser. However, it is much simpler to use a third-party parsing library such as PLY (www.dabeaz.com/ply), PyParsing (pyparsing.wikispaces.com), or one of the many other libraries that are available.[*]

If we are in an environment where we can trust our applications' users, we can give them access to the Python interpreter itself. The IDLE IDE (Integrated Development Environment) that is included with Python does exactly this, although IDLE is smart enough to execute user code in a separate process, so that if it crashes IDLE isn't affected.

3.3.1. Expression Evaluation with eval()

The built-in eval() function evaluates a single string as an expression (with access to any global or local context we give it) and returns the result. This is sufficient to build the simple calculator.py application that we will review in this subsection. Let's begin by looking at some interaction.

```
$ ./calculator.py
Enter an expression (Ctrl+D to quit): 65
A=65
```

---

[*] Parsing, including using PLY and PyParsing, is introduced in this author's book, *Programming in Python 3, Second Edition*; see the Selected Bibliography for details (➤ 287).

```
ANS=65
Enter an expression (Ctrl+D to quit): 72
A=65, B=72
ANS=72
Enter an expression (Ctrl+D to quit): hypotenuse(A, B)
name 'hypotenuse' is not defined
Enter an expression (Ctrl+D to quit): hypot(A, B)
A=65, B=72, C=97.0
ANS=97.0
Enter an expression (Ctrl+D to quit): ^D
```

The user entered two sides of a right-angled triangle and then used the
math.hypot() function (after making a mistake) to calculate the hypotenuse. After each expression is entered, the calculator.py program prints the variables
it has created so far (and that are accessible to the user) and the answer to the
current expression. (We have indicated user-entered text using bold—with Enter
or Return at the end of each line implied—and Ctrl+D with ^D.)

To make the calculator as convenient as possible, the result of each expression
entered is stored in a variable, starting with A, then B, and so on, and restart-
ing at A if Z is reached. Furthermore, we have imported all the math module's
functions and constants (e.g., hypot(), e, pi, sin(), etc.) into the calculator's
namespace so that the user can access them without qualifying them (e.g., cos()
rather than math.cos()).

If the user enters a string that cannot be evaluated, the calculator prints an
error message and then repeats the prompt, and all the existing context is kept
intact.

```python
def main():
    quit = "Ctrl+Z,Enter" if sys.platform.startswith("win") else "Ctrl+D"
    prompt = "Enter an expression ({} to quit): ".format(quit)
    current = types.SimpleNamespace(letter="A")
    globalContext = global_context()
    localContext = collections.OrderedDict()
    while True:
        try:
            expression = input(prompt)
            if expression:
                calculate(expression, globalContext, localContext, current)
        except EOFError:
            print()
            break
```

We have used EOF (End Of File) to signify that the user has finished. This means that the calculator can be used in a shell pipeline, accepting input redirected from a file, as well as for interactive user input.

We need to keep track of the name of the current variable (A or B or ...) so that we can update it each time a calculation is done. However, we can't simply pass it as a string, since strings are copied and cannot be changed. A poor solution is to use a global variable. A better and much more common solution is to create a one-item list; for example, current = ["A"]. This list can be passed as current and its string can be read or changed by accessing it as current[0].

For this example, we have taken a more modern approach and created a tiny namespace with a single attribute (letter) whose value is "A". We can freely pass the current simple namespace instance around, and since it has a letter attribute, we can read or change the attribute's value using the nice current.letter syntax.

The types.SimpleNamespace class was introduced in Python 3.3. For earlier versions an equivalent effect can be achieved by writing current = type("_", (), dict(letter="A"))(). This creates a new class called _ with a single attribute called letter with an initial value of "A". The built-in type() function returns the type of an object if called with one argument, or creates a new class if given a class name, a tuple of base classes, and a dictionary of attributes. If we pass an empty tuple, the base class will be object. Since we don't need the class but only an instance, having called type(), we immediately call the class itself—hence the extra parentheses—to return the instance of it that we assign to current.

Python can supply the current global context using the built-in globals() function; this returns a dict that we can modify (e.g., add to, as we saw earlier; 23 ◄). Python can also supply the local context using the built-in locals() function, although the dict returned by this function must *not* be modified.

We want to provide a global context supplemented with the math module's constants and functions and an initially empty local context. Although the global context *must* be a dict, the local context can be supplied as a dict—or as any other mapping object. Here, we have chosen to use a collections.OrderedDict—an insertion-ordered dictionary—as the locals context.

Since the calculator can be used interactively, we have created an event loop that is terminated when EOF is encountered. Inside the loop we prompt the user for input (also telling them how to quit), and if they enter any text, we call our calculate() function to perform the calculation and to print the results.

```
import math

def global_context():
    globalContext = globals().copy()
    for name in dir(math):
```

```
        if not name.startswith("_"):
            globalContext[name] = getattr(math, name)
    return globalContext
```

This helper function starts by creating a local (shallow-copied) dict of the program's global modules, functions, and variables. Then it iterates over all the public constants and functions in the math module and, for each one, adds its unqualified name to the globalContext dict and sets its value to be the actual math module constant or function it refers to. So, for example, when the name is "factorial", this name is added as a key in the globalContext, and its value is set to be the (i.e., a reference to the) math.factorial() function. This is what allows the calculator's users to use unqualified names.

A simpler approach would have been to do from math import * and then use globals() directly, with no need for the globalContext dict. Such an approach is probably okay for the math module, but the way we have done it here provides finer control that might be more appropriate for other modules.

```
def calculate(expression, globalContext, localContext, current):
    try:
        result = eval(expression, globalContext, localContext)
        update(localContext, result, current)
        print(", ".join(["{}={}".format(variable, value)
                for variable, value in localContext.items()]))
        print("ANS={}".format(result))
    except Exception as err:
        print(err)
```

This is the function where we ask Python to evaluate the string expression using the global and local context dictionaries that we have created. If the eval() succeeds, we update the local context with the result and print the variables and the result. And if an exception occurs, we safely print it. Since we used a collections.OrderedDict for the local context, the items() method returns the items in insertion order without the need for an explicit sort. (Had we used a plain dict we would have needed to write sorted(localContext.items()).)

Although it is usually poor practice to use the Exception catch-all exception, it seems reasonable in this case, because the user's expression could raise any kind of exception at all.

```
def update(localContext, result, current):
    localContext[current.letter] = result
    current.letter = chr(ord(current.letter) + 1)
    if current.letter > "Z": # We only support 26 variables
        current.letter = "A"
```

This function assigns the result to the next variable in the cyclic sequence A …
Z A … Z …. This means that after the user has entered 26 expressions, the result
of the last one is set as Z's value, and the result of the next one will overwrite A's
value, and so on.

The eval() function will evaluate *any* Python expression. This is potentially dan‐
gerous if the expression is received from an untrusted source. An alternative
is to use the standard library's more restrictive—and safe—ast.literal_eval()
function.

3.3.2. Code Evaluation with exec()

The built-in exec() function can be used to execute arbitrary pieces of Python
code. Unlike eval(), exec() is not restricted to a single expression and always
returns None. Context can be passed to exec() in the same way as for eval(), via
globals and locals dictionaries. Results can be retrieved from exec() through the
local context it is passed.

In this subsection, we will review the genome1.py program. This program creates
a genome variable (a string of random *A*, *C*, *G*, and *T* letters) and executes eight
pieces of user code with the genome in the code's context.

```
context = dict(genome=genome, target="G[AC]{2}TT", replace="TCGA")
execute(code, context)
```

This code snippet shows the creation of the context dictionary with some data
for the user's code to work on and the execution of a user's Code object (code) with
the given context.

```
TRANSFORM, SUMMARIZE = ("TRANSFORM", "SUMMARIZE")
Code = collections.namedtuple("Code", "name code kind")
```

We expect user code to be provided in the form of Code named tuples, with a
descriptive name, the code itself (as a string), and a kind—either TRANSFORM or
SUMMARIZE. When executed, the user code should create either a result object
or an error object. If their code's kind is TRANSFORM, the result is expected to be
a new genome string, and if the kind is SUMMARIZE, result is expected to be a
number. Naturally, we will try to make our code robust enough to cope with user
code that doesn't meet these requirements.

```
def execute(code, context):
    try:
        exec(code.code, globals(), context)
        result = context.get("result")
        error = context.get("error")
```

```
        handle_result(code, result, error)
    except Exception as err:
        print("'{}' raised an exception: {}\n".format(code.name, err))
```

This function performs the exec() call on the user's code, using the program's own global context and the provided local context. It then tries to retrieve the result and error objects, one of which the user code should have created, and passes them on to the custom handle_result() function.

Just as with the previous subsection's eval() example, we have used the (normally to be avoided) Exception exception, since the user code could raise any kind of exception.

```
def handle_result(code, result, error):
    if error is not None:
        print("'{}' error: {}".format(code.name, error))
    elif result is None:
        print("'{}' produced no result".format(code.name))
    elif code.kind == TRANSFORM:
        genome = result
        try:
            print("'{}' produced a genome of length {}".format(code.name,
                    len(genome)))
        except TypeError as err:
            print("'{}' error: expected a sequence result: {}".format(
                    code.name, err))
    elif code.kind == SUMMARIZE:
        print("'{}' produced a result of {}".format(code.name, result))
    print()
```

If the error object is not None, it is printed. Otherwise, if the result is None, we print a "produced no result" message. If we have a result and the user code's kind is TRANSFORM, we assign result to genome, and in this case we simply print the genome's new length. The try ... except block is designed to protect our program from a user code error (e.g., returning a single value rather than a string or other sequence for a TRANSFORM). If the result's kind is SUMMARIZE, we just print a summary line containing the result.

The genome1.py program has eight Code items: the first two (which we will see shortly) produce legitimate results, the third has a syntax error, the fourth reports an error, the fifth does nothing, the sixth has the wrong kind set, the seventh calls sys.exit(), and the eighth is never reached because the seventh terminates the program. Here is the program's output.

```
$ ./genome1.py
'Count' produced a result of 12

'Replace' produced a genome of length 2394

'Exception Test' raised an exception: invalid syntax (<string>, line 4)

'Error Test' error: 'G[AC]{2}TT' not found

'No Result Test' produced no result

'Wrong Kind Test' error: expected a sequence result: object of type 'int' has
no len()
```

As the output makes clear, because the user code is executing in the same interpreter as the program itself, the user code can terminate or crash the program. (Note that the last line has been wrapped to fit on the page.)

```
    Code("Count",
"""
import re
matches = re.findall(target, genome)
if matches:
    result = len(matches)
else:
    error = "'{}' not found".format(target)
""", SUMMARIZE)
```

This is the "Count" Code item. The item's code does much more than is possible in a single expression of the kind that eval() could handle. The target and genome strings are taken from the context object that is passed as the exec()'s local context—and it is this same context object that any new variables (such as result and error) are implicitly stored in.

```
    Code("Replace",
"""
import re
result, count = re.subn(target, replace, genome)
if not count:
    error = "no '{}' replacements made".format(target)
""", TRANSFORM)
```

The "Replace" Code item's code performs a simple transformation on the genome string, replacing nonoverlapping substrings that match the target regex with the replace string.

The re.subn() function (and *regex*.subn() method) performs substitutions exactly the same as re.sub() (and *regex*.sub()). However, whereas the sub()

function (and method) returns a string where all the replacements have been made, the subn() function (and method) returns both the string and a count of how many replacements were made.

Although the genome1.py program's execute() and handle_result() functions are easy to use and understand, in one respect the program is fragile: if the user code crashes—or simply calls sys.exit()—our program will terminate. In the next subsection we will explore a solution to this problem.

3.3.3. Code Evaluation Using a Subprocess

One possible answer to executing user code without compromising our application is to execute it in a separate process. This subsection's genome2.py and genome3.py programs show how we can execute a Python interpreter in a subprocess, feed the interpreter with a program to execute through its standard input, and retrieve its results by reading its standard output.

We have given the genome2.py and genome3.py programs exactly the same eight Code items as the genome1.py program. Here is genome2.py's output (genome3.py's is identical):

```
$ ./genome2.py
'Count' produced a result of 12

'Replace' produced a genome of length 2394

'Exception Test' has an error on line 3
    if genome[i] = "A":
                  ^
SyntaxError: invalid syntax

'Error Test' error: 'G[AC]{2}TT' not found

'No Result Test' produced no result

'Wrong Kind Test' error: expected a sequence result: object of type 'int' has
no len()

'Termination Test' produced no result

'Length' produced a result of 2406
```

Notice that even though the seventh Code item calls sys.exit(), the genome2.py program continues afterward, merely reporting "produced no result" for that piece of code, and then going on to execute the "Length" code. (The genome1.py program was terminated by the sys.exit() call, so its last line of output was "...error: expected a sequence...".) Another point to note is that genome2.py produces much better error reporting (e.g., the "Exception Test" code's syntax error).

```
context = dict(genome=genome, target="G[AC]{2}TT", replace="TCGA")
execute(code, context)
```

The creation of the context and the execution of the user's code with the context is exactly the same as for the genome1.py program.

```
def execute(code, context):
    module, offset = create_module(code.code, context)
    with subprocess.Popen([sys.executable, "-"], stdin=subprocess.PIPE,
            stdout=subprocess.PIPE, stderr=subprocess.PIPE) as process:
        communicate(process, code, module, offset)
```

This function begins by creating a string of code (module) containing the user's code plus some supporting code that we will see in a moment. The offset is the number of lines we have added before the user's code—this will help us to provide accurate line numbers in error messages. The function then starts a subprocess in which it executes a new instance of the Python interpreter, whose name is in sys.executable, and whose – (hyphen) argument means that the interpreter will expect to execute Python code sent to its sys.stdin.* The interaction with the process—including sending it the module code—is handled by our custom communicate() function.

```
def create_module(code, context):
    lines = ["import json", "result = error = None"]
    for key, value in context.items():
        lines.append("{} = {!r}".format(key, value))
    offset = len(lines) + 1
    outputLine = "\nprint(json.dumps((result, error)))"
    return "\n".join(lines) + "\n" + code + outputLine, offset
```

This function creates a list of lines that will form a new Python module to be executed by a Python interpreter in a subprocess. The first line imports the json module that we will use to return results to the initiating process (i.e., to the genome2.py program). The second line initializes the result and error variables to ensure that they exist. Then, we add a line for each of the context variables. Finally, we store the result and error (which the user's code might have changed) inside a string using JSON (JavaScript Object Notation) that will be printed to sys.stdout after the user's code has been executed.

```
UTF8 = "utf-8"

def communicate(process, code, module, offset):
```

---

* The subprocess.Popen() function added support for context managers (i.e., the with statement) in Python 3.2.

```
    stdout, stderr = process.communicate(module.encode(UTF8))
    if stderr:
        stderr = stderr.decode(UTF8).lstrip().replace(", in <module>", ":")
        stderr = re.sub(", line (\d+)",
                lambda match: str(int(match.group(1)) - offset), stderr)
        print(re.sub(r'File."[^"]+?"', "'{}' has an error on line "
                .format(code.name), stderr))
        return
    if stdout:
        result, error = json.loads(stdout.decode(UTF8))
        handle_result(code, result, error)
        return
    print("'{}' produced no result\n".format(code.name))
```

The `communicate()` function begins by sending the module code we created earlier to the subprocess's Python interpreter to execute, and then blocks waiting for results to be produced. Once the interpreter finishes execution, its standard output and standard error output are collected in our local `stdout` and `stderr` variables. Note that all communication takes place using raw bytes—hence our need to encode the `module` string into UTF-8-encoded bytes.

If there is any error output (i.e., if an exception was raised, or if anything is written to `sys.stderr`), we replace the reported line number (which includes the lines we added before the user's code) with the actual line number in the user's code, and we replace the "File "<stdin>"" text with the `Code` object's name. Then, we print the error text as a string.

The `re.sub()` call matches—and captures—the line number's digits with `(\d+)` and replaces them with the result of the call to the `lambda` function given as its second argument. (More commonly, we give a string as second argument, but here we need to do some computation.) The `lambda` function converts the digits into an integer and subtracts the offset, then returns the new line number as a string to replace the original. This ensures that the error message's line number is correct for the user's code, regardless of how many lines we put in front of it when creating the module we sent to be interpreted.

If there was no error output, but there was standard output, we decode the output's bytes into a string (which we expect to be in JSON format) and parse this into Python objects—in this case a 2-tuple of a `result` and an `error`. Then we call our custom `handle_result()` function. (This function is identical in `genome1.py`, `genome2.py`, and `genome3.py`, and was shown earlier; 89 ◄.)

The `genome2.py` program's user code is identical to `genome1.py`'s, although for `genome2.py` we provide some additional supporting code before and after the user code. Using JSON format to return results is safe and convenient but limits the data types we can return (e.g., `result`'s type) to `dict`, `list`, `str`, `int`, `float`, `bool`, or `None`, and where a `dict` or `list` may only contain objects of these types.

The genome3.py program is almost the same as genome2.py but returns its results in a pickle. This means that most Python types can be used.

```
def create_module(code, context):
    lines = ["import pickle", "import sys", "result = error = None"]
    for key, value in context.items():
        lines.append("{} = {!r}".format(key, value))
    offset = len(lines) + 1
    outputLine = "\nsys.stdout.buffer.write(pickle.dumps((result, error)))"
    return "\n".join(lines) + "\n" + code + outputLine, offset
```

This function is very similar to the genome2.py version. A minor difference is that we must import sys. The major difference is that whereas the json module's loads() and dumps() methods work on strs, the pickle module's equivalent functions work on bytes. So, here, we must write the raw bytes directly to sys.stdout's underlying buffer to avoid the bytes being erroneously encoded.

```
def communicate(process, code, module, offset):
    stdout, stderr = process.communicate(module.encode(UTF8))
    ...
    if stdout:
        result, error = pickle.loads(stdout)
        handle_result(code, result, error)
        return
```

The genome3.py program's communicate() method is the same as for genome2.py (93 ◄) except for the line that has the loads() method call. For the JSON data we had to decode the bytes into a UTF-8-encoded str, but here we work directly on the raw bytes.

Using exec() to execute arbitrary pieces of Python code received from the user or from other programs gives that code access to the full power of the Python interpreter—and to its entire standard library. And by executing the user code in a separate Python interpreter in a subprocess, we can protect our program from being crashed or terminated by it. However, we cannot really stop the user code from doing anything malicious. To execute untrusted code we would need to use some kind of sandbox; for example, the one provided by the PyPy Python interpreter (pypy.org).

For some programs, blocking while waiting for user code to finish execution might be acceptable, but it does run the risk of waiting "forever" if the user code has a bug (e.g., an infinite loop). One possible solution would be to create the subprocess in a separate thread and use a timer in the main thread. If the timer times out, we could then forcibly terminate the subprocess and report the problem to the user. Concurrent programming is introduced in the next chapter.

3.4. Iterator Pattern

The Iterator Pattern provides a way of sequentially accessing the items inside a collection or an aggregate object without exposing any of the internals of the collection or aggregate's implementation. This pattern is so useful that Python provides built-in support for it, as well as providing special methods that we can implement in our own classes to make them seamlessly support iteration.

Iteration can be supported by satisfying the sequence protocol, or by using the two-argument form of the built-in `iter()` function, or by satisfying the iterator protocol. We will see examples of all these in the following subsections.

3.4.1. Sequence Protocol Iterators

One way to provide iterator support for our own classes is to make them support the sequence protocol. This means that we must implement a __getitem__() special method that can accept an integer index argument that starts from 0 and that raises an `IndexError` exception if no further iteration is possible.

```
for letter in AtoZ():
    print(letter, end="")
print()

for letter in iter(AtoZ()):
    print(letter, end="")
print()
```

```
ABCDEFGHIJKLMNOPQRSTUVWXYZ
ABCDEFGHIJKLMNOPQRSTUVWXYZ
```

These two code snippets create an `AtoZ()` object and then iterate over it. The object first returns the single character string "A", then "B", and so on, up to "Z". The object could have been made iterable in a number of ways, although in this case we've provided a __getitem__() method, as we will see in a moment.

In the second loop we have used the built-in `iter()` function to obtain an iterator to an instance of the AtoZ class. Clearly, this isn't necessary in this case, but as we will see in a moment (and elsewhere in the book), `iter()` does have its uses.

```
class AtoZ:

    def __getitem__(self, index):
        if 0 <= index < 26:
            return chr(index + ord("A"))
        raise IndexError()
```

This is the complete AtoZ class. We have provided it with a __getitem__() method that satisfies the sequence protocol. When an object of this class is iterated, on the twenty-seventh iteration it will raise an IndexError. If this occurs inside a for loop, the exception is discarded, the loop is cleanly terminated, and execution resumes from the first statement after the loop.

3.4.2. Two-Argument iter() Function Iterators

Another way to provide iteration support is to use the built-in iter() function, but passing it two arguments instead of one. When this form is used, the first argument must be a callable (a function, a bound method, or any other callable object), and the second argument must be a sentinel value. When this form is used the callable is called at each iteration—with no arguments—and iteration will stop only if the callable raises a StopIteration exception or if it returns the sentinel value.

```
for president in iter(Presidents("George Bush"), None):
    print(president, end=" * ")
print()

for president in iter(Presidents("George Bush"), "George W. Bush"):
    print(president, end=" * ")
print()

George Bush * Bill Clinton * George W. Bush * Barack Obama *
George Bush * Bill Clinton *
```

The Presidents() call creates an instance of the Presidents class, and—thanks to the implementation of the __call__() special method—such instances are callable. So, here, we create a Presidents object that is a callable (as required by the two-argument form of the built-in iter() function), and we provide a sentinel of None. A sentinel must be provided, even if it is None, so that Python knows to use the two-argument iter() function rather than the one-argument version.

The Presidents constructor creates a callable that will return each president in turn, starting with George Washington or, optionally, from the president we give it. In this case we told it to start from George Bush. Here, the first time we iterate, we have used a sentinel of None to signify "go to the end", which, at the time of this writing, is Barack Obama. The second time we iterate we have provided the name of a president as the sentinel; this means that the callable will output each president from the first up to the one before the sentinel.

```
class Presidents:

    __names = ("George Washington", "John Adams", "Thomas Jefferson",
        ...
```

```
                "Bill Clinton", "George W. Bush", "Barack Obama")
    def __init__(self, first=None):
        self.index = (-1 if first is None else
                        Presidents.__names.index(first) - 1)

    def __call__(self):
        self.index += 1
        if self.index < len(Presidents.__names):
            return Presidents.__names[self.index]
        raise StopIteration()
```

The Presidents class keeps a static (that is, class-wide) __names list with the names of all the U.S. presidents. The __init__() method sets the initial index to one less than either the first president in the list or the president the user has specified.

The instances of any class that implements the __call__() special method are callable. And when such an instance is called, it is this __call__() method that is actually executed.*

In this class's __call__() special method, we either return the name of the next president in the list, or we raise a StopIteration exception. In the first iteration where the sentinel was None, the sentinel was never reached (since __call__() never returns None), but iteration still stopped cleanly because once we ran out of presidents, we raised the StopIteration exception. But in the second iteration, as soon as the sentinel president was returned to the built-in iter() function, the function itself raised StopIteration to terminate the loop.

3.4.3. Iterator Protocol Iterators

Probably the easiest way to provide iterator support in our own classes is to make them support the iterator protocol. This protocol requires that a class implements the __iter__() special method and that this method returns an iterator object. The iterator object must have its own __iter__() method that returns the iterator itself and a __next__() method that returns the next item—or that raises a StopIteration exception if there are no more items. Python's for loop and in statement make use of this protocol under the hood. One simple way to implement an __iter__() method is to make it a generator—or to make it return a generator, since generators satisfy the iterator protocol. (See §3.1.2, 76 ◀ for more about generators.)

In this subsection we will create a simple bag class (also called a multiset). A bag is a collection class that is like a set but which allows duplicate items. An

---

* In languages that don't support functions as first-class objects, callable instances are called *functors*.

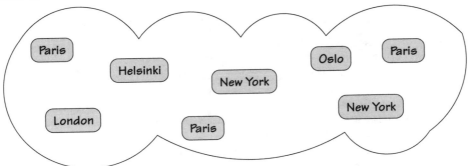

Figure 3.3 *A bag is an unsorted collection of values with duplicates allowed*

example bag is illustrated in Figure 3.3. Naturally, we will make the bag iterable and show three ways to do so. All the code is quoted from Bag1.py except where stated otherwise.

```
class Bag:

    def __init__(self, items=None):
        self.__bag = {}
        if items is not None:
            for item in items:
                self.add(item)
```

The bag's data is stored in the private self.__bag dictionary. The dictionary's keys are anything hashable (i.e., they are the bag's items), and the values are counts (i.e., how many of the item are in the bag). Users can add some initial items to a newly created bag if they wish.

```
    def add(self, item):
        self.__bag[item] = self.__bag.get(item, 0) + 1
```

Since self.__bag is not a collections.defaultdict, we must be careful to only increment an item that already exists; otherwise, we would get a KeyError exception. We use the dict.get() method to retrieve an existing item's count, or 0 if there isn't such an item, and set the dictionary to have an item with this number plus 1, creating the item if necessary.

```
    def __delitem__(self, item):
        if self.__bag.get(item) is not None:
            self.__bag[item] -= 1
            if self.__bag[item] <= 0:
                del self.__bag[item]
        else:
            raise KeyError(str(item))
```

If an attempt is made to delete an item that isn't in the bag, we raise a KeyError exception containing the item in string form. On the other hand, if the item is in the bag, we begin by reducing its count. If this drops to zero or less, we delete it from the bag.

We have not implemented the __getitem__() or __setitem__() special methods, because neither of them make sense for bags (since bags are unordered). Instead, we use *bag*.add() to add items, del *bag*[*item*] to delete items, and *bag*.count(*item*) to check how many of a particular item are in the bag.

```
def count(self, item):
    return self.__bag.get(item, 0)
```

This method simply returns how many occurrences of the given item are in the bag—or zero if the item isn't in the bag. A perfectly reasonable alternative would be to raise a KeyError for attempts to count an item that isn't in the bag. This could be done simply by changing the method's body to return self.__bag[item].

```
def __len__(self):
    return sum(count for count in self.__bag.values())
```

This method is subtle since we must count all the duplicate items in the bag separately. To do this, we iterate over all the bag's values (i.e., its item counts) and sum them using the built-in sum() function.

```
def __contains__(self, item):
    return item in self.__bag
```

This method returns True if the bag contains at least one of the given item (since if an item is in the bag at all, its count is at least 1); otherwise, it returns False.

We have now seen all of the bag's methods except for its iteration support. First, we'll look at the Bag1.py module's Bag.__iter__() method.

```
def __iter__(self): # This needlessly creates a list of items!
    items = []
    for item, count in self.__bag.items():
        for _ in range(count):
            items.append(item)
    return iter(items)
```

This method is a first attempt. It builds up a list of items—as many of each as its count indicates—and then returns an iterator for the list. For a large bag, this could result in the creation of a very large list, which is rather inefficient, so we will look at two better approaches.

```
    def __iter__(self):
        for item, count in self.__bag.items():
            for _ in range(count):
                yield item
```

This code is from the Bag2.py module and is the only method that is different from Bag1.py's Bag class.

Here, we iterate over the bag's items, retrieving each item and its count, and yielding each item count times. There is a tiny fixed overhead for making the method a generator, but this is independent of the number of items, and of course, no separate list needs to be created, so this method is much more efficient than the Bag1.py version.

```
    def __iter__(self):
        return (item for item, count in self.__bag.items()
                for _ in range(count))
```

Here is the Bag3.py module's version of the Bag.__iter__() method. It is effectively the same as the Bag2.py module's version, only instead of making the method into a generator, it returns a generator expression.

Although the book's bag implementations work perfectly well, keep in mind that the standard library has its own bag implementation: collections.Counter.

3.5. Mediator Pattern

The Mediator Pattern provides a means of creating an object—the mediator —that can encapsulate the interactions between other objects. This makes it possible to achieve interactions between objects that have no direct knowledge of each other. For example, if a button object is clicked, it need only tell the mediator; then, it is up to the mediator to notify any objects that are interested in the button click. A mediator for a form with some text and button widgets, and a couple of associated methods, is illustrated in Figure 3.4.

This pattern is clearly of great utility in GUI programming. In fact, all of the GUI toolkits available for Python (e.g., Tkinter, PyQt/PySide, PyGObject, wxPython) provide some equivalent facility. We will see Tkinter examples of this in Chapter 7 (➤ 231).

In this section's two subsections, we will look at two approaches to implementing a mediator. The first is quite conventional; the second uses coroutines. Both make use of Form, Button, and Text classes (whose implementations we will see) for a fictitious user interface toolkit.

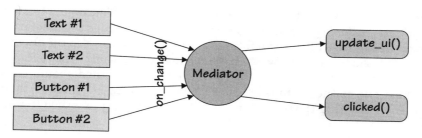

Figure 3.4 *A form's widget mediator*

3.5.1. A Conventional Mediator

In this subsection we will create a conventional mediator—a class that will orchestrate interactions—in this case, for a form. All the code shown here is from the mediator1.py program.

```
class Form:

    def __init__(self):
        self.create_widgets()
        self.create_mediator()
```

Like most functions and methods shown in this book, this method has been ruthlessly refactored, in this case to the point where it passes on all its work.

```
    def create_widgets(self):
        self.nameText = Text()
        self.emailText = Text()
        self.okButton = Button("OK")
        self.cancelButton = Button("Cancel")
```

This form has two text entry widgets for a user's name and email address, and two buttons, OK and Cancel. Naturally, in a real user interface we would have to include label widgets, and then lay out the widgets, but here our example is purely to show the Mediator Pattern, so we don't do any of that. We will see the Text and Button classes shortly.

```
    def create_mediator(self):
        self.mediator = Mediator(((self.nameText, self.update_ui),
                (self.emailText, self.update_ui),
                (self.okButton, self.clicked),
                (self.cancelButton, self.clicked)))
        self.update_ui()
```

We create a single mediator object for the entire form. This object takes one or more *widget–callable* pairs, which describe the relationships the mediator must support. In this case all the callables are bound methods. (See the "Bound and Unbound Methods" sidebar, 63 ◀.) Here, we are saying that if the text of one of the text entry widgets changes, the Form.update_ui() method should be called; and that if one of the buttons is clicked, the Form.clicked() method should be called. After creating the mediator, we call the update_ui() method to initialize the form.

```python
def update_ui(self, widget=None):
    self.okButton.enabled = (bool(self.nameText.text) and
                             bool(self.emailText.text))
```

This method enables the OK button if both the text entry widgets have some text in them; otherwise it disables the button. Clearly, this method should be called whenever the text of one of the text entry widgets is changed.

```python
def clicked(self, widget):
    if widget == self.okButton:
        print("OK")
    elif widget == self.cancelButton:
        print("Cancel")
```

This method is designed to be called whenever a button is clicked. In a real application it would do something more interesting than printing the button's text.

```python
class Mediator:

    def __init__(self, widgetCallablePairs):
        self.callablesForWidget = collections.defaultdict(list)
        for widget, caller in widgetCallablePairs:
            self.callablesForWidget[widget].append(caller)
            widget.mediator = self
```

This is the first of the Mediator class's two methods. We want to create a dictionary whose keys are widgets and whose values are lists of one or more callables. This is achieved by using a default dictionary. When we access an item in a default dictionary, if the item is not present, it is created and added with the value being created by the callable given to the dictionary in the first place. In this case, we gave the dictionary a list object, which when called returns a new empty list. So, the first time a particular widget is looked up in the dictionary, a new item is inserted with the widget as the key and an empty list as the value, and we immediately append the caller to the list. And whenever a widget is looked up subsequently, the caller is appended to the item's existing list. We also set the widget's mediator attribute (creating it if necessary) to this mediator (self).

The method adds the bound methods in the order they appear in the pairs; if we didn't care about the order we could pass set instead of list when creating the default dictionary, and use set.add() instead of list.append() to add the bound methods.

```
def on_change(self, widget):
    callables = self.callablesForWidget.get(widget)
    if callables is not None:
        for caller in callables:
            caller(widget)
    else:
        raise AttributeError("No on_change() method registered for {}"
            .format(widget))
```

Whenever a mediated object—that is, any widget passed to a Mediator—has a change of state, it is expected to call its mediator's on_change() method. This method then retrieves and calls every bound method associated with the widget.

```
class Mediated:

    def __init__(self):
        self.mediator = None

    def on_change(self):
        if self.mediator is not None:
            self.mediator.on_change(self)
```

This is a convenience class designed to be inherited by mediated classes. It keeps a reference to the mediator object, and if its on_change() method is called, it calls the mediator's on_change() method, parameterized by this widget (i.e., self, the widget that has had a change of state).

Since this base class's method is never modified in any of its subclasses, we could replace the base class with a class decorator, as we saw earlier (§2.4.2.2, 58 ◄).

```
class Button(Mediated):

    def __init__(self, text=""):
        super().__init__()
        self.enabled = True
        self.text = text

    def click(self):
        if self.enabled:
            self.on_change()
```

This `Button` class inherits `Mediated`. This gives the button a `self.mediator` attribute and an `on_change()` method that it is expected to call when it experiences a change of state; for example, when it is clicked.

So, in this example, a call to `Button.click()` will result in a call to `Button.on_change()` (inherited from `Mediated`), which will result in a call to the mediator's `on_change()` method, which will then call whatever method or methods are associated with this button—in this case, the `Form.clicked()` method, with the button as the `widget` argument.

```
class Text(Mediated):

    def __init__(self, text=""):
        super().__init__()
        self.__text = text

    @property
    def text(self):
        return self.__text

    @text.setter
    def text(self, text):
        if self.text != text:
            self.__text = text
            self.on_change()
```

Structurally, the `Text` class is the same as the `Button` class and also inherits `Mediated`.

For any widget (button, text entry, and so on), so long as we make them a `Mediated` subclass and call `on_change()` whenever they have a change of state, we can leave it to the `Mediator` to take care of the interactions. Of course, when we create the `Mediator`, we must also register the widgets and the associated methods we want called. This means that all of a form's widgets are loosely coupled, thereby avoiding direct—and potentially fragile—relationships.

3.5.2. A Coroutine-Based Mediator

A mediator can be viewed as a pipeline that receives messages (`on_change()` calls) and passes these on to interested objects. As we have already seen (§3.1.2, 76 ◄), coroutines can be used to provide such facilities. All the code shown here is from the `mediator2.py` program, and all the code not shown is identical to that shown in the previous subsection from the `mediator1.py` program.

The approach used in this subsection is different from that taken in the previous subsection. There, we associated pairs of widgets and methods, and whenever the widget notified it had changed, the mediator called the associated methods.

Here, every widget is given a mediator that is actually a pipeline of coroutines. Whenever a widget has a change of state, it sends itself into the pipeline, and it is up to the pipeline components (i.e., the coroutines) to decide whether they want to perform any action in response to a change in the widget they are sent.

```python
def create_mediator(self):
    self.mediator = self._update_ui_mediator(self._clicked_mediator())
    for widget in (self.nameText, self.emailText, self.okButton,
            self.cancelButton):
        widget.mediator = self.mediator
    self.mediator.send(None)
```

For the coroutine version we don't need a separate mediator class. Instead, we create a pipeline of coroutines; in this case, one with two components, self._update_ui_mediator() and self._clicked_mediator(). (These are all Form methods.)

Once the pipeline is in place, we set each widget's mediator attribute to the pipeline. And at the end, we send None down the pipeline. Since no widget is None, no widget-specific actions will be triggered, but any form-level actions (such as enabling or disabling the OK button in _update_ui_mediator()) will be performed.

```python
@coroutine
def _update_ui_mediator(self, successor=None):
    while True:
        widget = (yield)
        self.okButton.enabled = (bool(self.nameText.text) and
                                 bool(self.emailText.text))
        if successor is not None:
            successor.send(widget)
```

This coroutine is part of the pipeline. (The @coroutine decorator was shown and discussed earlier; 77 ◄.)

Whenever a widget reports a change, the widget is passed into the pipeline and is returned by the yield expression into the widget variable. When it comes to enabling or disabling the OK button, we do this regardless of which widget has changed. (After all, it may be that no widget has changed, that widget is None, and so the form is simply being initialized.) After dealing with the button the coroutine passes on the changed widget to the next coroutine in the chain (if there is one).

```python
@coroutine
def _clicked_mediator(self, successor=None):
    while True:
```

```
            widget = (yield)
            if widget == self.okButton:
                print("OK")
            elif widget == self.cancelButton:
                print("Cancel")
            elif successor is not None:
                successor.send(widget)
```

This pipeline coroutine is only concerned with OK and Cancel button clicks. If either of these buttons is the changed widget, this coroutine handles it; otherwise, it passes on the widget to the next coroutine, if any.

```
class Mediated:

    def __init__(self):
        self.mediator = None

    def on_change(self):
        if self.mediator is not None:
            self.mediator.send(self)
```

The Button and Text classes are the same as for mediator1.py, but the Mediated class has one tiny change: if its on_change() method is called, it sends the changed widget (self) into the mediator pipeline.

As we mentioned in the previous subsection, the Mediated class could be replaced with a class decorator. The book's examples include a mediator2d.py version of this example where this is done. (See §2.4.2.2, 58 ◀.)

The Mediator Pattern can also be varied to provide multiplexing; that is, many-to-many communications between objects. See, also, the Observer Pattern (§3.7, ▶ 107) and the State Pattern (§3.8, ▶ 111).

3.6. Memento Pattern

The Memento Pattern is a means of saving and restoring an object's state without violating encapsulation.

Python has support for this pattern out of the box: we can use the pickle module to pickle and unpickle arbitrary Python objects (with a few constraints; e.g., we cannot pickle a file object). In fact, Python can pickle None, bools, bytearrays, bytes, complexes, floats, ints, and strs, as well as dicts, lists, and tuples that contain only pickleable objects (including collections), top-level functions, top-level classes, and instances of custom top-level classes whose __dict__ is pickleable; that is, objects of most custom classes. It is also possible to achieve the same effect using the json module, although this only supports Python's basic types along with dictionaries and lists. (We saw examples of `json` and `pickle` use in §3.3.3, 91 ◄).

Even in the quite rare cases where we hit a limitation in what can be pickled, we can always add our own custom pickling support; for example, by implementing the `__getstate__()` and `__setstate__()` special methods, and possibly the `__get-newargs__()` method. Similarly, if we want to use JSON format with our own custom classes, we can extend the `json` module's encoder and decoder.

We could also create our own format and protocols, but there is little point in doing so, given Python's rich support for this pattern.

Unpickling essentially involves executing arbitrary Python code, so it is poor practice to unpickle pickles that are received from untrusted sources such as physical media or over a network connection. In such cases JSON is safer, or we can use checksums and encryption with pickling to ensure that the pickle hasn't been meddled with.

3.7. Observer Pattern

The Observer Pattern supports many-to-many dependency relationships between objects, such that when one object changes state, all its related objects are notified. Nowadays, probably the most common expression of this pattern and its variants is the model/view/controller (MVC) paradigm. In this paradigm, a model represents data, one or more views visualize that data, and one or more controllers mediate between input (e.g., user interaction) and the model. And any changes to the model are automatically reflected in the associated views.

One popular simplification of the MVC approach is to use a model/view where the views both visualize the data and mediate input to the model; that is, the views and controllers are combined. In terms of the Observer Pattern, this means that the views are observers of the model, and the model is the subject being observed.

In this section we will create a model that represents a value with a minimum and a maximum (such as a scrollbar or slider widget or a temperature monitor). And we will create two separate observers (views) for the model: one to output the model's value whenever it changes (as a kind of progress bar using HTML), and another to keep a history of the changes (their values and timestamps). Here is a sample run of the `observer.py` program.

```
$ ./observer.py > /tmp/observer.html
 0 2013-04-09 14:12:01.043437
 7 2013-04-09 14:12:01.043527
23 2013-04-09 14:12:01.043587
37 2013-04-09 14:12:01.043647
```

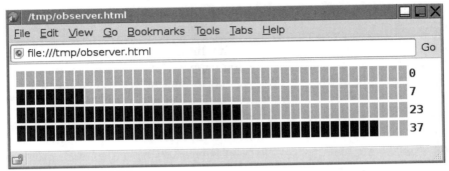

Figure 3.5 *The observer example's HTML output as the model changes*

The history data is sent to sys.stderr and the HTML to sys.stdout, which we have redirected into an HTML file. The HTML page is shown in Figure 3.5. The program outputs four one-row HTML tables, the first when the (empty) model is first observed, and then each time the model is changed. Figure 3.6 illustrates the example's model/view architecture.

This section's example, observer.py, uses an Observed base class to provide the functionality for adding, removing, and notifying observers. The SliderModel class provides a value with a minimum and maximum, and inherits the Observed class so that it can support being observed. And then we have two views that observe the model, HistoryView and LiveView. Naturally, we will review all of these classes, but first we will look at the program's main() function to see how they are used and how the output shown earlier and in Figure 3.5 was obtained.

```
def main():
    historyView = HistoryView()
    liveView = LiveView()
    model = SliderModel(0, 0, 40) # minimum, value, maximum
    model.observers_add(historyView, liveView)  # liveView produces output
    for value in (7, 23, 37):
        model.value = value                      # liveView produces output
    for value, timestamp in historyView.data:
        print("{:3} {}".format(value, datetime.datetime.fromtimestamp(
                timestamp)), file=sys.stderr)
```

We begin by creating the two views. Next we create a model with a minimum of 0, a current value of 0, and a maximum of 40. Then we add the two views as observers of the model. As soon as the LiveView is added as an observer it produces its first output, and as soon as the HistoryView is added it records its first value and timestamp. We then update the model's value three times, and at each update the LiveView outputs a new one-row HTML table and the HistoryView records the value and the timestamp.

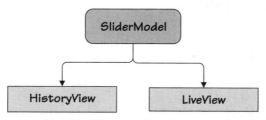

Figure 3.6 *A model and two views*

At the end we print out the entire history to `sys.stderr` (i.e., to the console). The `datetime.datetime.fromtimestamp()` function accepts a timestamp (number of seconds since the epoch as returned by `time.time()`) and returns an equivalent `datetime.datetime` object. The `str.format()` method is smart enough to output `datetime.datetime`s in ISO-8601 format.

```
class Observed:

    def __init__(self):
        self.__observers = set()

    def observers_add(self, observer, *observers):
        for observer in itertools.chain((observer,), observers):
            self.__observers.add(observer)
            observer.update(self)

    def observer_discard(self, observer):
        self.__observers.discard(observer)

    def observers_notify(self):
        for observer in self.__observers:
            observer.update(self)
```

This class is designed to be inherited by models or by any other class that wants to support observation. The `Observed` class maintains a set of observing objects. Whenever an object is added, its `update()` method is called to initialize it with the model's current state. Then, whenever the model changes state it is expected to call its inherited `observers_notify()` method, so that every observer's `update()` method can be called to ensure that every observer (i.e., every view) is representing the model's new state.

The `observers_add()` method is subtle. We want to accept one or more observers to add, but using just `*observers` would allow zero or more. So, we require at least one observer (`observer`) and accept zero or more in addition (`*observers`). We could have done this using tuple concatenation (e.g., `for observer in (observer,) + observers:`), but we have used the more efficient `itertools.chain()` function instead. As noted earlier (46 ◄), this function accepts any number of iterables and returns a single iterable that is effectively the concatenation of all the iterables passed to it.

```python
class SliderModel(Observed):

    def __init__(self, minimum, value, maximum):
        super().__init__()
        # These must exist before using their property setters
        self.__minimum = self.__value = self.__maximum = None
        self.minimum = minimum
        self.value = value
        self.maximum = maximum


    @property
    def value(self):
        return self.__value


    @value.setter
    def value(self, value):
        if self.__value != value:
            self.__value = value
            self.observers_notify()
    ...
```

This is the particular model class for this example, but of course, it could be any kind of model. By inheriting Observed, the class gains a private set of observers (initially empty) and the observers_add(), observer_discard(), and observers_notify() methods. Whenever the model's state changes—for example, when its value is changed—it must call its observers_notify() method so that any observers can respond accordingly.

The class also has minimum and maximum properties whose code has been elided; they are structurally identical to the value property, and, of course, their setters also call observers_notify().

```python
class HistoryView:

    def __init__(self):
        self.data = []


    def update(self, model):
        self.data.append((model.value, time.time()))
```

This view is an observer of the model since it provides an update() method that accepts the observed model as its only argument besides self. Whenever the update() method is called, it adds a *value–timestamp* 2-tuple to its self.data list, thus preserving a history of all the changes that are applied to the model.

```
class LiveView:

    def __init__(self, length=40):
        self.length = length
```

This is another view that observes the model. The length is the number of cells used to represent the model's value in a one-row HTML table.

```
    def update(self, model):
        tippingPoint = round(model.value * self.length /
                (model.maximum - model.minimum))
        td = '<td style="background-color: {}"> </td>'
        html = ['<table style="font-family: monospace" border="0"><tr>']
        html.extend(td.format("darkblue") * tippingPoint)
        html.extend(td.format("cyan") * (self.length - tippingPoint))
        html.append("<td>{}</td></tr></table>".format(model.value))
        print("".join(html))
```

When the model is first observed, and whenever it is subsequently updated, this method is called. It outputs a one-row HTML table with self.length cells to represent the model, using cyan for empty cells and dark blue for filled cells. It determines how many of which kind of cell there are by calculating the tipping point between the filled cells (if there are any) and the empty cells.

The Observer Pattern is widely used in GUI programming and also has uses in the context of other event-processing architectures, such as simulations and servers. Examples include database triggers, Django's signaling system, the Qt GUI application framework's signals and slots mechanism, and many uses of WebSockets.

3.8. State Pattern

The State Pattern is intended to provide objects whose behavior changes when their state changes; that is, objects that have modes.

To illustrate this design pattern we will create a multiplexer class that has two states, and whose methods' behavior changes depending on which state a multiplexer instance is in. When the multiplexer is in its active state, it can accept "connections"—that is, *event name–callback* pairs—where the callback is any Python callable (e.g., a lambda, a function, a bound method, etc.). After the connections have been made, whenever an event is sent to the multiplexer, the associated callbacks are called (providing the multiplexer is in its active state). If the multiplexer is dormant, calling its methods safely does nothing.

To show the multiplexer in use, we will create some callback functions that count the number of events they receive and connect them to an active multiplexer. Then we will send some random events to the multiplexer, and afterwards, print out the counts that the callbacks have accumulated. All the code is in the `multi-plexer1.py` program, and the program's output for a sample run is shown here:

```
$ ./multiplexer1.py
After 100 active events:   cars=150 vans=42 trucks=14 total=206
After 100 dormant events:  cars=150 vans=42 trucks=14 total=206
After 100 active events:   cars=303 vans=83 trucks=30 total=416
```

After sending the active multiplexer one-hundred random events, we change the multiplexer's state to dormant, and then send it another hundred events—all of which should be ignored. Then we set the multiplexer back to its active state and send it more events; these it should respond to by calling the associated callbacks.

We will begin by looking at how the multiplexer is constructed, how the connections are made, and how events are sent. Then we will look at the callback functions and the event class. Finally, we will look at the multiplexer itself.

```
totalCounter = Counter()
carCounter = Counter("cars")
commercialCounter = Counter("vans", "trucks")

multiplexer = Multiplexer()
for eventName, callback in (("cars", carCounter),
        ("vans", commercialCounter), ("trucks", commercialCounter)):
    multiplexer.connect(eventName, callback)
    multiplexer.connect(eventName, totalCounter)
```

Here, we begin by creating some counters. Instances of these classes are callable, so they can be used wherever a function (e.g., a callback) is required. They maintain one independent count per name they are given, or if anonymous (like `totalCounter`) they maintain a single count.

Then we create a new multiplexer (which starts out active by default). Next, we connect callback functions to events. There are three event names we are interested in: "cars", "vans", and "trucks". The `carCounter()` function is connected to the "cars" event; the `commercialCounter()` function is connected to the "vans" and "trucks" events; and the `totalCounter()` function is connected to all three events.

```
for event in generate_random_events(100):
    multiplexer.send(event)
print("After 100 active events:  cars={} vans={} trucks={} total={}"
        .format(carCounter.cars, commercialCounter.vans,
                commercialCounter.trucks, totalCounter.count))
```

In this snippet, we generate one-hundred random events and send each one to the multiplexer. If, for example, an event is a "cars" event, the multiplexer will call the `carCounter()` and `totalCounter()` functions, passing the event as the sole argument for each call. Similarly, if the event is a "vans" or "trucks" event, both the `commercialCounter()` and `totalCounter()` functions are called.

```python
class Counter:

    def __init__(self, *names):
        self.anonymous = not bool(names)
        if self.anonymous:
            self.count = 0
        else:
            for name in names:
                if not name.isidentifier():
                    raise ValueError("names must be valid identifiers")
                setattr(self, name, 0)
```

If no names are given, an instance of an anonymous counter is created whose count is kept in `self.count`. Otherwise, independent counts are created for the name or names passed in using the built-in `setattr()` function. For example, the `carCounter` instance is given a `self.cars` attribute, and the `commercialCounter` is given `self.vans` and `self.trucks` attributes.

```python
    def __call__(self, event):
        if self.anonymous:
            self.count += event.count
        else:
            count = getattr(self, event.name)
            setattr(self, event.name, count + event.count)
```

When a `Counter` instance is called, the call is passed to this special method. If the counter is anonymous (e.g., `totalCounter`), the `self.count` is incremented. Otherwise, we try to retrieve the counter attribute corresponding to the event name. For example, if the event name is `"trucks"`, we set `count` to be the value of `self.trucks`. Then we update the attribute's value with the old count plus the new event count.

Since we haven't provided a default value for the built-in `getattr()` function, if the attribute doesn't exist (e.g., `"truck"`), the method will correctly raise an `AttributeError`. This also ensures that we don't create a misnamed attribute by mistake since in such cases the `setattr()` call is never reached.

```python
class Event:

    def __init__(self, name, count=1):
        if not name.isidentifier():
```

```
        raise ValueError("names must be valid identifiers")
    self.name = name
    self.count = count
```

This is the entire Event class. It is very simple since we just need it as part of the infrastructure for showing the State Pattern that's exemplified by the Multiplexer class. Incidentally, the Multiplexer is also an example of the Observer Pattern (§3.7, 107 ◄).

3.8.1. Using State-Sensitive Methods

There are two main approaches that we can take to handling state within a class. One approach is to use state-sensitive methods, as we will see in this subsection. The other approach is to use state-specific methods, which we will cover in the next subsection (§3.8.2, ➤ 115).

```
class Multiplexer:

    ACTIVE, DORMANT = ("ACTIVE", "DORMANT")

    def __init__(self):
        self.callbacksForEvent = collections.defaultdict(list)
        self.state = Multiplexer.ACTIVE
```

The Multiplexer class has two states (or modes): ACTIVE and DORMANT. When a Multiplexer instance is ACTIVE, its state-sensitive methods do useful work, but when it is DORMANT, its state-sensitive methods do nothing. We ensure that when a new Multiplexer is created, it starts off in the ACTIVE state.

The self.callbacksForEvent dictionary's keys are event names and its values are lists of callables.

```
    def connect(self, eventName, callback):
        if self.state == Multiplexer.ACTIVE:
            self.callbacksForEvent[eventName].append(callback)
```

This method is used to create an association between a named event and a callback. If the given event name isn't already in the dictionary, the fact that self.callbacksForEvent is a default dictionary will ensure that an item with the event name as key is created with an empty list as its value, which it will then return. And if the event name is already in the dictionary, its list will be returned. So, in either case, we get a list that we can then append the new callback to. (We discussed default dictionaries earlier; 102 ◄.)

```
    def disconnect(self, eventName, callback=None):
        if self.state == Multiplexer.ACTIVE:
            if callback is None:
                del self.callbacksForEvent[eventName]
            else:
                self.callbacksForEvent[eventName].remove(callback)
```

If this method is called without specifying a callback, we interpret that to mean that the user wants to disconnect all the callbacks associated with the given event name. Otherwise, we remove only the specified callback from the given event name's list of callbacks.

```
    def send(self, event):
        if self.state == Multiplexer.ACTIVE:
            for callback in self.callbacksForEvent.get(event.name, ()):
                callback(event)
```

If an event is sent to the multiplexer, and if the multiplexer is active, this method iterates over all the given event's associated callbacks (of which there might not be any), and for each one, calls it with the event as argument.

3.8.2. Using State-Specific Methods

The multiplexer2.py program is almost the same as multiplexer1.py, only its Multiplexer class uses state-specific methods rather than the state-sensitive methods shown in the previous subsection. The Multiplexer class has the same two states and the same __init__() method as before. However, the self.state attribute is now a property.

```
    @property
    def state(self):
        return (Multiplexer.ACTIVE if self.send == self.__active_send
                else Multiplexer.DORMANT)
```

This version of the multiplexer doesn't store the state as such. Instead, it computes the state by checking if one of the public methods has been set to an active or passive private method, as we'll see next.

```
    @state.setter
    def state(self, state):
        if state == Multiplexer.ACTIVE:
            self.connect = self.__active_connect
            self.disconnect = self.__active_disconnect
            self.send = self.__active_send
        else:
```

```
        self.connect = lambda *args: None
        self.disconnect = lambda *args: None
        self.send = lambda *args: None
```

Whenever the state is changed, the state property's setter sets the multiplexer to have a set of methods that are appropriate to the state. For example, if the state is set to be DORMANT, the anonymous lambda versions of the methods are assigned to the public methods.

```
    def __active_connect(self, eventName, callback):
        self.callbacksForEvent[eventName].append(callback)
```

Here, we have created a private active method: either this or an anonymous "do nothing" lambda method is assigned to the corresponding public method at any one time. We haven't shown the private active disconnect or send methods, because they follow the same pattern. The key point to notice is that none of these methods checks the instance's state (since they are only ever called in the appropriate state), which slightly simplifies them and makes them minutely faster.

Naturally, it is easy to do a coroutine-based version of the Multiplexer, but since we've already seen some coroutine examples, we won't show another one here. (However, the examples' multiplexer3.py program shows one approach to coroutine-based multiplexing.)

Although we have used the State Pattern for a multiplexer, having stateful (or modal) objects is quite common in a wide range of contexts.

3.9. Strategy Pattern

The Strategy Pattern provides a means of encapsulating a set of algorithms that can be used interchangeably, depending on the user's needs.

For example, in this section we will create two different algorithms for arranging a list containing an arbitrary number of items in a table with a specified number of rows. One algorithm will produce a snippet of HTML output; Figure 3.7 shows the results for tables with two, three, and four rows. The other algorithm will produce plain text output, the results of which (for tables of four and five rows) are shown here:

```
$ ./tabulator3.py
...
+--------------------+--------------------+--------------------+
| Nikolai Andrianov  | Matt Biondi        | Bjørn Dæhlie       |
| Birgit Fischer     | Sawao Kato         | Larisa Latynina    |
| Carl Lewis         | Michael Phelps     | Mark Spitz         |
```

```
| Jenny Thompson     |                    |                    |                    |
+--------------------+--------------------+--------------------+--------------------+

+--------------------+--------------------+
| Nikolai Andrianov  | Matt Biondi        |
| Bjørn Dæhlie       | Birgit Fischer     |
| Sawao Kato         | Larisa Latynina    |
| Carl Lewis         | Michael Phelps     |
| Mark Spitz         | Jenny Thompson     |
+--------------------+--------------------+
```

There are a number of approaches we could take to parameterizing by algorithm. One obvious approach is to create a Layout class that accepts a Tabulator instance, which performs the appropriate tabulated layout. The tabulator1.py program (not shown) takes this approach. A refinement, for tabulators that don't need to maintain state, is to use static methods and to pass the tabulator class rather than an instance to provide the algorithm. The tabulator2.py program (again, not shown) does this.

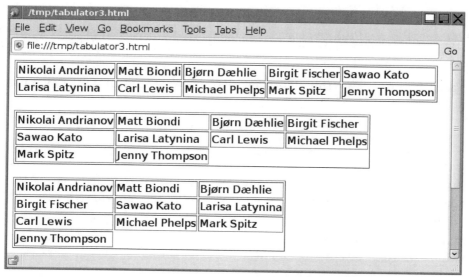

Figure 3.7 *The tabulator program's HTML table output*

In this section, we will show a simpler and even more refined technique: a Layout class that accepts a tabulation function that implements the desired algorithm.

```
WINNERS = ("Nikolai Andrianov", "Matt Biondi", "Bjørn Dæhlie",
        "Birgit Fischer", "Sawao Kato", "Larisa Latynina", "Carl Lewis",
        "Michael Phelps", "Mark Spitz", "Jenny Thompson")
```

```
def main():
    htmlLayout = Layout(html_tabulator)
    for rows in range(2, 6):
        print(htmlLayout.tabulate(rows, WINNERS))
    textLayout = Layout(text_tabulator)
    for rows in range(2, 6):
        print(textLayout.tabulate(rows, WINNERS))
```

In this function we create two Layout objects, each parameterized by a different tabulator function. For each layout we print a table with two rows, with three rows, with four rows, and with five rows.

```
class Layout:

    def __init__(self, tabulator):
        self.tabulator = tabulator

    def tabulate(self, rows, items):
        return self.tabulator(rows, items)
```

This class supports only one algorithm: tabulate. The function that implements the algorithm is expected to accept a row count and a sequence of items and to return the tabulated results.

In fact, we could reduce this class even more: here is the tabulator4.py version.

```
class Layout:

    def __init__(self, tabulator):
        self.tabulate = tabulator
```

Here, we have made the self.tabulate attribute a callable (the passed-in tabulator function). The calls shown in main() work exactly the same for tabulator3.py's and tabulator4.py's Layout classes.

Although the actual tabulation algorithms aren't relevant to the design pattern itself, we will very briefly review one of them for the sake of completeness.

```
def html_tabulator(rows, items):
    columns, remainder = divmod(len(items), rows)
    if remainder:
        columns += 1
    column = 0
    table = ['<table border="1">\n']
    for item in items:
        if column == 0:
            table.append("<tr>")
```

```
        table.append("<td>{}</td>".format(escape(str(item))))
        column += 1
        if column == columns:
            table.append("</tr>\n")
        column %= columns
    if table[-1][-1] != "\n":
        table.append("</tr>\n")
    table.append("</table>\n")
    return "".join(table)
```

For both tabulator functions, we must calculate the number of columns needed to put all the items in a table with the specified number of rows. Once we have this number (columns), we can iterate over all the items while keeping track of the current column in the current row.

The text_tabulator() function (not shown) is slightly longer but uses essentially the same approach.

In more realistic contexts we might use algorithms that are radically different —both in terms of their code and their performance characteristics—so as to allow users to choose the most appropriate trade-offs for their particular uses. Plugging in different algorithms as callables—lambdas, functions, bound methods—is straightforward because Python treats callables as first-class objects; that is, as objects that can be passed and stored in collections like any other kind of object.

3.10. Template Method Pattern

The Template Method Pattern allows us to define the steps of an algorithm but defer the execution of some of those steps to subclasses.

In this section we will create an AbstractWordCounter class that provides two methods. The first, can_count(filename), is expected to return a Boolean indicating whether the class can count the words in the given file (based on the file's extension). The second, count(filename), is expected to return a word count. We will also create two subclasses: one for word-counting plain text files and the other for word-counting HTML files. Let's start by seeing the classes in action (with the code taken from wordcount1.py):

```
def count_words(filename):
    for wordCounter in (PlainTextWordCounter, HtmlWordCounter):
        if wordCounter.can_count(filename):
            return wordCounter.count(filename)
```

We have made all the methods in all the classes static. This means that no per-instance state can be maintained (because there are no instances as such) and that we can work directly on class objects rather than on instances. (It would be easy to make the methods nonstatic and use instances if we did need to maintain any state.)

Here, we iterate over our two word-counting subclasses' class objects, and if one of them is able to count the words in the given file, we perform and return the count. If neither of them can, we (implicitly) return None to signify that we couldn't do a count at all.

```python
class AbstractWordCounter:

    @staticmethod
    def can_count(filename):
        raise NotImplementedError()

    @staticmethod
    def count(filename):
        raise NotImplementedError()
```

```python
class AbstractWordCounter(
        metaclass=abc.ABCMeta):

    @staticmethod
    @abc.abstractmethod
    def can_count(filename):
        pass

    @staticmethod
    @abc.abstractmethod
    def count(filename):
        pass
```

This purely abstract class provides the word-counter interface, whose methods subclasses must reimplement. The left-hand code snippet, from wordcount1.py, takes a more traditional approach. The right-hand code snippet, from wordcount2.py, takes a more modern approach using the abc (abstract base class) module.

```python
class PlainTextWordCounter(AbstractWordCounter):

    @staticmethod
    def can_count(filename):
        return filename.lower().endswith(".txt")

    @staticmethod
    def count(filename):
        if not PlainTextWordCounter.can_count(filename):
            return 0
        regex = re.compile(r"\w+")
        total = 0
        with open(filename, encoding="utf-8") as file:
            for line in file:
                for _ in regex.finditer(line):
                    total += 1
        return total
```

This subclass implements the word-counter interface using a very simplistic notion of what constitutes a word, and assuming that all .txt files are encoded using UTF-8 (or 7-bit ASCII, since that's a subset of UTF-8).

```python
class HtmlWordCounter(AbstractWordCounter):

    @staticmethod
    def can_count(filename):
        return filename.lower().endswith((".htm", ".html"))

    @staticmethod
    def count(filename):
        if not HtmlWordCounter.can_count(filename):
            return 0
        parser = HtmlWordCounter.__HtmlParser()
        with open(filename, encoding="utf-8") as file:
            parser.feed(file.read())
        return parser.count
```

This subclass provides the word-counter interface for HTML files. It uses its own private HTML parser (itself an html.parser.HTMLParser subclass embedded inside the HtmlWordCounter class, which we will see in a moment). With the private HTML parser in place, all we need to do to count the words in an HTML file is create an instance of the parser and give it the HTML to parse. Once parsing is complete, we return the word count that the parser has accumulated for us.

For completeness, we will review the embedded HtmlWordCounter.__HtmlParser that does the actual counting. The Python standard library's HTML parser works rather like a SAX (Simple API for XML) parser, in that it iterates over the text and calls particular methods when corresponding events (i.e., "start tag", "end tag", etc.) occur. So, to make use of the parser we must subclass it and reimplement those methods that correspond to the events we are interested in.

```python
class __HtmlParser(html.parser.HTMLParser):

    def __init__(self):
        super().__init__()
        self.regex = re.compile(r"\w+")
        self.inText = True
        self.text = []
        self.count = 0
```

We have made the embedded html.parser.HTMLParser subclass private and added four items of data to it. The self.regex holds our simple definition of a "word" (a sequence of one or more letters, digits, or underscores). The self.inText bool indicates whether text we encounter is a piece of a value such as user-visible text (as opposed to being inside a <script> or <style> tag). The self.text will hold the piece or pieces of text that make up the current value, and the self.count is the word count.

```
def handle_starttag(self, tag, attrs):
    if tag in {"script", "style"}:
        self.inText = False
```

This method's name and signature (and that of all the handle_...() methods) is determined by the base class. By default, handler methods do nothing, so, naturally, we must reimplement any that we are interested in.

We do not want to count the words inside embedded scripts or style sheets, so if we encounter their start tags, we switch off text accumulation.

```
def handle_endtag(self, tag):
    if tag in {"script", "style"}:
        self.inText = True
    else:
        for _ in self.regex.finditer(" ".join(self.text)):
            self.count += 1
        self.text = []
```

If we reach the end of a script or style sheet tag, we switch text accumulation back on. In all other cases we iterate over the accumulated text and count the words. Then we reset the accumulated text to be an empty list.

```
def handle_data(self, text):
    if self.inText:
        text = text.rstrip()
        if text:
            self.text.append(text)
```

If we receive text and we are not inside a script or style sheet, we accumulate the text.

Thanks to the power and flexibility of Python's support for private nested classes, and its library's html.parser.HTMLParser, we can do fairly sophisticated parsing while hiding all the details from users of the HtmlWordCounter class.

The Template Method Pattern is in some ways similar to the Bridge Pattern we saw earlier (§2.2, 34 ◄).

3.11. Visitor Pattern

The Visitor Pattern is used to apply a function to every item in a collection or aggregate object. This is different from a typical use of the Iterator Pattern (§3.4, 95 ◄)—where we would iterate over a collection or aggregate and call a method on each item—since with a "visitor", we are applying an external function rather than calling a method.

Python has built-in support for this pattern. For example, `newList = map(function, oldSequence)` will call the `function()` on every item in the `oldSequence` to produce the `newList`. The same can be done using a list comprehension: `newList = [function(item) for item in oldSequence]`.

If we need to apply a function to every item in a collection or aggregate object, then we can iterate over it using a for loop: `for item in collection: function(item)`. If the items are of different types, we can use `if` statements and the built-in `isinstance()` function to distinguish between them to choose the type-appropriate code to execute inside the `function()`.

Some of the behavioral patterns have direct support in the Python language; those that don't are simple to implement. The Chain of Responsibility, Mediator, and Observer Patterns can all be implemented conventionally or using coroutines, and they all provide variations on the theme of decoupled inter-object communication. The Command Pattern can be used to provide lazy evaluation and do–undo facilities. Since Python is a (byte-code) interpreted language, we can implement the Interpreter Pattern using Python itself and can even isolate the interpreted code in a separate process. Support for the Iterator Pattern (and, implicitly, the Visitor Pattern) is built in to Python. The Memento Pattern is well supported by Python's standard library (e.g., using the `pickle` or `json` modules). The State, Strategy, and Template Method Patterns have no direct support, but are all easy to implement.

Design patterns provide useful ways of thinking about, organizing, and implementing code. Some of the patterns are only applicable to the object-oriented programming paradigm, while others can be used for both procedural and object-oriented programming. Since the publication of the original design patterns book, there has been—and there continues to be—a great deal of research into the subject. The best starting point for learning more is the educational, not-for-profit Hillside Group's web site (`hillside.net`).

In the next chapter, we will look at a different programming paradigm—concurrency—to try to achieve improved performance by taking advantage of modern multi-core hardware. But before looking into concurrency, we will do our first case study, developing an image-handling package that we will use and refer to in various ways at several points throughout the book.

3.12. Case Study: An Image Package

The Python standard library does not include any image processing modules, as such. However, it is possible to create, load, and save images using Tkinter's `tk.PhotoImage` class. (The `barchart2.py` example shows how this can be done.) Unfortunately, Tkinter can only read and write the unpopular GIF, PPM, and PGM image formats, although once Python comes with Tcl/Tk 8.6, the popular PNG format will be supported. Even so, the `tk.PhotoImage` class can only be used in a single thread (the main GUI thread), so it is of no use if we want to handle multiple images concurrently.

We could, of course, use a third-party image library like Pillow (`github.com/python-imaging/Pillow`) or use another GUI toolkit.* But we have decided to implement our own image package to provide this case study and to serve as the basis for another one later on.

We want our image package to store its image data efficiently and to be able to work with Python out of the box. To this end, we will represent an image as a linear array of colors. Each color (i.e., each pixel) will be represented by an unsigned 32-bit integer whose four bytes represent the alpha (transparency), red, green, and blue color components; this is sometimes called ARGB format. Since we are using a one-dimensional array, the pixel at image coordinate x, y is in array element $(y \times width) + x$. This is illustrated in Figure 3.8, where the highlighted pixel in an 8×8 image is at coordinate (5, 1); that is, index position 13 ($(1 \times 8) + 5$) in the array.

The Python standard library provides the `array` module for one-dimensional, type-specific arrays, and so is ideal for our purpose. However, the third-party `numpy` module offers highly optimized code for handling arrays (of any number of dimensions), so it would be good to take advantage of this module when it is available. Therefore, we will design the Image package to use `numpy` when possible, with `array` as a fallback. This means that Image will work in all cases but won't be able to take as much advantage of `numpy` as possible, because the code must work interchangeably with both `array.array`s and `numpy.ndarray`s.

We want to create and modify arbitrary images; however, we also want to be able to load existing images and to save created or modified images. Since loading and saving depends on the image format, we have designed the image package to have one module for handling images generically and separate modules (one per image format) for handling loading and saving. Furthermore, we will make the package capable of automatically taking advantage of any new image format modules that are added to the package—even after deployment—providing they meet the image package's interface requirements.

---

* If we wanted to plot 2D data, we could use the third-party `matplotlib` package (`matplotlib.org`).

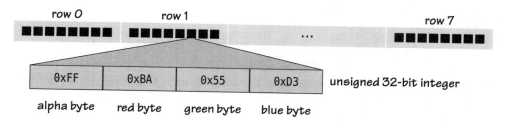

Figure 3.8 *An array of Image color values for an 8 × 8 image*

The Image package consists of four modules. The Image/__init__.py module provides all the generic functionality. The other three modules provide format-specific loading and saving code. These are Image/Xbm.py for XBM (.xbm) format monochrome bitmaps, Image/Xpm.py for XPM (.xpm) format color pixmaps, and Image/Png.py for PNG (.png) format. The PNG format is very complicated, and there is already a Python module that supports it—PyPNG (github.com/drj11/pypng)—so our Png.py module will simply provide a thin wrapper (using the Adapter Pattern; §2.1, 29 ◀) around PyPNG, if it is available.

We will begin by looking at the generic image module (Image/__init__.py). Then we will review the Image/Xpm.py module, skipping the low-level details. Finally, we will look at the complete Image/Png.py wrapper module.

3.12.1. The Generic Image Module

The Image module provides the Image class plus a number of convenience functions and constants to support image processing.

```
try:
    import numpy
except ImportError:
    numpy = None
    import array
```

One key issue is whether the image data is represented using an array.array or a numpy.ndarray, so after the normal imports, we try to import numpy. If the import fails, we fall back to importing the standard library's array module to provide the necessary functionality, and create a numpy variable with value None for those few places where the difference between array and numpy matters.

We want our users to be able to access the image module with a simple import Image statement. And when they do this, we want all the available image-format–specific modules that provide load and save functions to be automatically available. This means that the user should be able to create and save a red 64 × 64 square using code like this:

```
import Image
image = Image.Image.create(64, 64, Image.color_for_name("red"))
image.save("red_64x64.xpm")
```

We want this to work even though the user hasn't explicitly imported the
Image/Xpm.py module. And, of course, we want this to work with any other image
format modules that happen to be in the Image directory, even if they are added
after the image package is initially deployed.

To support this functionality, we have included code in Image/__init__.py that
automatically tries to load image format modules.

```
_Modules = []
for name in os.listdir(os.path.dirname(__file__)):
    if not name.startswith("_") and name.endswith(".py"):
        name = "." + os.path.splitext(name)[0]
        try:
            module = importlib.import_module(name, "Image")
            _Modules.append(module)
        except ImportError as err:
            warnings.warn("failed to load Image module: {}".format(err))
del name, module
```

This code populates the private _Modules list with any modules that are found
and imported from the Image directory, except for __init__.py (or any other
module whose name begins with an underscore).

The code works by iterating over the files in the Image directory (wherever it
happens to be in the file system). For each suitable .py file, we obtain the module
name based on the filename. We must be careful to precede the module's name
with . since we want to import the module relative to the Image package. When
using a relative import like this we must provide the package name as the
importlib.import_module() function's second argument. If the import succeeds,
we add the corresponding Python module object to the list of modules; we'll see
how they are used shortly.

To avoid cluttering up the Image namespace, we have deleted the name and module
variables once they are no longer needed.

The plugin approach used here is easy to use and understand and works well
in most cases. However, it does suffer from a limitation: it won't work if the
Image package is put inside a .zip file. (Recall that Python can import modules
that are inside .zip files: we just have to insert the .zip file into the sys.path
list and then import as if the .zip file were a normal module; see docs.python.
org/dev/library/zipimport.html.) A solution to this problem is to use the standard library's pkgutil.walk_packages() function (instead of os.listdir(), and
adapting the code accordingly), since this function can work both with normal

packages and with those inside .zip files; it can also cope with implementations provided as C extensions and precompiled byte code files (.pyc and .pyo).

```
class Image:

    def __init__(self, width=None, height=None, filename=None,
            background=None, pixels=None):
        assert (width is not None and (height is not None or
                pixels is not None) or (filename is not None))
        if filename is not None: # From file
            self.load(filename)
        elif pixels is not None: # From data
            self.width = width
            self.height = len(pixels) // width
            self.filename = filename
            self.meta = {}
            self.pixels = pixels
        else: # Empty
            self.width = width
            self.height = height
            self.filename = filename
            self.meta = {}
            self.pixels = create_array(width, height, background)
```

The image's __init__() method has a rather complicated signature, but this doesn't matter, because we will encourage our users to use much simpler convenience class methods to create images instead (for example, the Image.Image. create() method we saw earlier; 126 ◀).

```
    @classmethod
    def from_file(Class, filename):
        return Class(filename=filename)

    @classmethod
    def create(Class, width, height, background=None):
        return Class(width=width, height=height, background=background)

    @classmethod
    def from_data(Class, width, pixels):
        return Class(width=width, pixels=pixels)
```

Here are the three image-creating factory class methods. These methods can be called on the class itself (e.g., image = Image.Image.create(200, 400)) and will work correctly for Image subclasses.

The from_file() method creates an image from a filename. The create() method creates an empty image with the given background color (or with a transparent background, if no color is specified). The from_data() method creates an image of the given width and with the pixels (i.e., colors) from the one-dimensional pixels array (of type array.array or numpy.ndarray).

```
def create_array(width, height, background=None):
    if numpy is not None:
        if background is None:
            return numpy.zeros(width * height, dtype=numpy.uint32)
        else:
            iterable = (background for _ in range(width * height))
            return numpy.fromiter(iterable, numpy.uint32)
    else:
        typecode = "I" if array.array("I").itemsize >= 4 else "L"
        background = (background if background is not None else
                      ColorForName["transparent"])
        return array.array(typecode, [background] * width * height)
```

This function creates a one-dimensional array of 32-bit unsigned integers (see Figure 3.8; 125 ◄). If numpy is present and the background is transparent, we can use the numpy.zeros() factory function to create the array with every integer set to zero (i.e., to 0x00000000). Any number with a zero alpha component is fully transparent. If a background color has been given, we create a generator expression that will produce width × height values (all of which are the same: background) and pass this iterator to the numpy.fromiter() factory function.

If numpy is not available, we must create an array.array. Unlike numpy, this module does not allow us to specify the exact size of the integers we want it to hold, so we do the best we can. We use the "I" type specifier (unsigned integer, minimum size two bytes) if it is actually four or more bytes; otherwise, we use the "L" type specifier (unsigned integer, minimum size four bytes). This is to ensure that we use the smallest-sized integer that can hold four bytes, even on 64-bit machines where an unsigned integer would normally occupy eight bytes. We then create an array to hold items of the type specifier's type and populate it with width × height background values. (We discuss the ColorForName default dictionary further on; ➤ 134.)

```
class Error(Exception): pass
```

This class provides us with an Image.Error exception type. We could have simply used one of the built-in exceptions (e.g., ValueError), but this makes it easier for Image users to catch image-specific exceptions without risking masking any other exceptions.

```
    def load(self, filename):
        module = Image._choose_module("can_load", filename)
        if module is not None:
            self.width = self.height = None
            self.meta = {}
            module.load(self, filename)
            self.filename = filename
        else:
            raise Error("no Image module can load files of type {}".format(
                os.path.splitext(filename)[1]))
```

The Image.__init__.py module has no knowledge of image file formats. However, the image-specific modules do have such knowledge, and they were loaded earlier when we populated the _Modules list (126 ◄). The image-specific modules could be considered variations of the Template Method Pattern (§3.10, 119 ◄) or of the Strategy Pattern (§3.9, 116 ◄).

Here, we try to retrieve a module that can load the given filename. If we get a suitable module, we initialize some of the image's instance variables and tell the module to load the file. If the module's load() method succeeds, it will populate self.pixels with an array of color values and set self.width and self.height appropriately; otherwise, it will raise an exception. (We'll see examples of format-specific load() methods in subsections §3.12.2, ➤ 136, and §3.12.3, ➤ 138.)

```
    @staticmethod
    def _choose_module(actionName, filename):
        bestRating = 0
        bestModule = None
        for module in _Modules:
            action = getattr(module, actionName, None)
            if action is not None:
                rating = action(filename)
                if rating > bestRating:
                    bestRating = rating
                    bestModule = module
        return bestModule
```

This static method is used to find a module in the private _Modules list that can perform the action (actionName) on the file (filename). It iterates over all the loaded modules and for each one tries to retrieve the actionName function (e.g., can_load() or can_save()) using the built-in getattr() function. For each action function found, the method calls the function with the given filename.

The action function is expected to return an integer of value 0 if it cannot perform the action at all, 100 if it can perform the action perfectly, or somewhere in between if it can perform the action imperfectly. For example, the Image/Xbm.py module returns 100 for files with the .xbm extension, since the module fully supports the format, but returns 0 for all other extensions. However, the Image/Xpm.py module returns only 80 for .xpm files, because it does not support the full XPM specification (although it works perfectly on all the .xpm files it has been tested on).

At the end, the module with the highest rating is returned, or if there is no suitable module None is returned.

```
def save(self, filename=None):
    filename = filename if filename is not None else self.filename
    if not filename:
        raise Error("can't save without a filename")
    module = Image._choose_module("can_save", filename)
    if module is not None:
        module.save(self, filename)
        self.filename = filename
    else:
        raise Error("no Image module can save files of type {}".format(
                os.path.splitext(filename)[1]))
```

This method is very similar to the load() method in that it tries to get a module that can save a file with the given filename (i.e., one that can save in the format indicated by the file's extension) and performs the save.

```
def pixel(self, x, y):
    return self.pixels[(y * self.width) + x]
```

The pixel() method returns the color at the given position as an ARGB value (i.e., an unsigned 32-bit integer).

```
def set_pixel(self, x, y, color):
    self.pixels[(y * self.width) + x] = color
```

The set_pixel() method sets the given pixel to the given ARGB value if the x and y coordinates are in range; otherwise, it raises an IndexError exception.

The Image module provides some basic drawing methods including line(), ellipse(), and rectangle(). We will just show one representative method here.

```
def line(self, x0, y0, x1, y1, color):
    Δx = abs(x1 - x0)
    Δy = abs(y1 - y0)
    xInc = 1 if x0 < x1 else -1
    yInc = 1 if y0 < y1 else -1
    δ = Δx - Δy
```

```
        while True:
            self.set_pixel(x0, y0, color)
            if x0 == x1 and y0 == y1:
                break
            δ2 = 2 * δ
            if δ2 > -Δy:
                δ -= Δy
                x0 += xInc
            if δ2 < Δx:
                δ += Δx
                y0 += yInc
```

This method uses Bresenham's line algorithm (which requires only integer arithmetic) to draw a line from point (x0, y0) to point (x1, y1).* Thanks to Python 3's Unicode support, we are able to use variable names that are natural for this context; for example, Δx and Δy to represent differences in *x* and *y* coordinate values, and δ and δ2 for the error values.

```
    def scale(self, ratio):
        assert 0 < ratio < 1
        rows = round(self.height * ratio)
        columns = round(self.width * ratio)
        pixels = create_array(columns, rows)
        yStep = self.height / rows
        xStep = self.width / columns
        index = 0
        for row in range(rows):
            y0 = round(row * yStep)
            y1 = round(y0 + yStep)
            for column in range(columns):
                x0 = round(column * xStep)
                x1 = round(x0 + xStep)
                pixels[index] = self._mean(x0, y0, x1, y1)
                index += 1
        return self.from_data(columns, pixels)
```

This method creates and returns a new image that is a scaled-down version of this image. The ratio should be in the interval (0.0, 1.0), with a ratio of 0.75 producing an image with its width and height ¾ their original sizes, and a ratio of 0.5 producing an image ¼ of the original size, that is, with half the width and height. Each pixel (i.e., each color) in the resultant image is the average (mean) of the colors in the rectangle of the source image that the pixel must represent.

---

* This algorithm is explained at en.wikipedia.org/wiki/Bresenham's_line_algorithm.

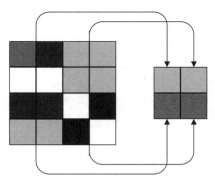

Figure 3.9 *Scaling a 4 × 4 image by 0.5*

The image's x, y coordinates are integers, but to avoid inaccuracies we must use floating-point arithmetic (e.g., using / rather than //) as we step through the pixel data. So, we use the built-in round() function whenever we need integers. And at the end, we use the Image.Image.from_data() convenience factory class method to create a new image based on the computed number of columns and using the pixels array we have created and populated with colors.

```
def _mean(self, x0, y0, x1, y1):
    αTotal, redTotal, greenTotal, blueTotal, count = 0, 0, 0, 0, 0
    for y in range(y0, y1):
        if y >= self.height:
            break
        offset = y * self.width
        for x in range(x0, x1):
            if x >= self.width:
                break
            α, r, g, b = self.argb_for_color(self.pixels[offset + x])
            αTotal += α
            redTotal += r
            greenTotal += g
            blueTotal += b
            count += 1
    α = round(αTotal / count)
    r = round(redTotal / count)
    g = round(greenTotal / count)
    b = round(blueTotal / count)
    return self.color_for_argb(α, r, g, b)
```

This private method accumulates the sums of the alpha, red, green, and blue components of all the pixels in the rectangle specified by the x0, y0, x1, y1 coordinates. Each of these sums is then divided by the number of pixels that were examined to produce a color that is the average of them all. This process is illustrated in Figure 3.9.

```
MAX_ARGB = 0xFFFFFFFF
MAX_COMPONENT = 0xFF
```

The minimum 32-bit ARGB value is `0x0` (i.e., `0x00000000`, transparent—strictly speaking, transparent black). These two `Image` module constants specify the maximum ARGB value (solid white) and the maximum value of any color component (255).

```python
@staticmethod
def argb_for_color(color):
    if numpy is not None:
        if isinstance(color, numpy.uint32):
            color = int(color)
    if isinstance(color, str):
        color = color_for_name(color)
    elif not isinstance(color, int) or not (0 <= color <= MAX_ARGB):
        raise Error("invalid color {}".format(color))
    α = (color >> 24) & MAX_COMPONENT
    r = (color >> 16) & MAX_COMPONENT
    g = (color >> 8) & MAX_COMPONENT
    b = (color & MAX_COMPONENT)
    return α, r, g, b
```

This static method (and module function) returns the four color components (each in the range 0 to 255) for a given color. The color passed in can be an `int`, a `numpy.uint32`, or a `str` color name. The individual color components (bytes) of the `int` that represents the color are then extracted (as `int`s) using bitwise shifts (`>>`) and bitwise and-ing (`&`).

```python
@staticmethod
def color_for_name(name):
    if name is None:
        return ColorForName["transparent"]
    if name.startswith("#"):
        name = name[1:]
        if len(name) == 3: # add solid alpha
            name = "F" + name # now has 4 hex digits
        if len(name) == 6: # add solid alpha
            name = "FF" + name # now has the full 8 hex digits
        if len(name) == 4: # originally #FFF or #FFFF
            components = []
            for h in name:
```

```
            components.extend([h, h])
        name = "".join(components) # now has the full 8 hex digits
    return int(name, 16)
    return ColorForName[name.lower()]
```

This static method (and module function) returns a 32-bit ARGB value for a given str color. If the color passed is None, the method returns transparent. If the string begins with #, it is assumed to be an HTML-style color of one of the forms "#HHH", "#HHHH", "#HHHHHH", or "#HHHHHHHH", where H is a hexadecimal digit. If the number of digits supplied is only sufficient for an RGB value, we prefix it with two "F"s to make the color have an opaque alpha channel. Otherwise, we return the color from the ColorForName dictionary; this always succeeds because ColorForName is a default dictionary.

```
ColorForName = collections.defaultdict(lambda: 0xFF000000, {
    "transparent": 0x00000000, "aliceblue": 0xFFF0F8FF,
    ...
    "yellow4": 0xFF8B8B00, "yellowgreen": 0xFF9ACD32})
```

The ColorForName is a collections.defaultdict that returns a 32-bit unsigned integer that encodes the given named color's alpha, red, green, and blue color components or, if the name isn't in the dictionary, silently returns solid black (0xFF000000). Although Image users are free to use this dictionary, the color_ for_name() function is more convenient and versatile. The color names are taken from the rgb.txt file supplied with X11, with the addition of transparent.

The collections.defaultdict() function accepts a factory function as its first argument, followed by any arguments that a plain dict accepts. The factory function is used to produce the value for any item that is brought into existence when a missing key is accessed. Here, we have used a lambda that always returns the same value (solid black). Although it is possible to pass keyword arguments (e.g., transparent=0x00000000), we have more colors than Python's limit of 255 arguments, so we initialize the default dictionary with a normal dictionary created using the {key: value} syntax, which has no such limit.

```
argb_for_color = Image.argb_for_color
rgb_for_color = Image.rgb_for_color
color_for_argb = Image.color_for_argb
color_for_rgb = Image.color_for_rgb
color_for_name = Image.color_for_name
```

After the Image class we have created some convenience functions based on some of the class's static methods. This means, for example, that after doing import Image, the user can call Image.color_for_name() or, if they have an Image.Image instance, *image*.color_for_name().

We have now completed our review of the core Image module (in Image/__init__.py). We have omitted a couple of less interesting constants, a few Image.Image methods (rectangle(), ellipse(), and subsample()), the size property (which just returns a width and height 2-tuple), and various color manipulating static methods. The module is sufficient for creating, loading, drawing on, and saving image files using the XBM and XPM formats, and if the PyPNG module is installed, the PNG format.

Now we will look at two image-format–specific modules that the Image module relies on. We will omit coverage of the Image/Xbm.py module, though, since apart from the low-level details of the XBM format covering it would not teach us any more than we can learn from the Image/Xpm.py module that we will look at next.

3.12.2. An Overview of the Xpm Module

Every image-format–specific module is expected to provide four functions. Two of these are can_load() and can_save(). Both of these functions should return 0 to indicate they can't, 100 to indicate they can, or some value in between if they can imperfectly. The module is also expected to provide load() and save() functions, and these may assume that they will only ever be called with a filename for which the corresponding can_load() or can_save() function returned a nonzero value.

```
def can_load(filename):
    return 80 if os.path.splitext(filename)[1].lower() == ".xpm" else 0
def can_save(filename):
    return can_load(filename)
```

The Image/Xpm.py module implements most of the XPM specification, leaving out some rarely used features. In view of this, it reports a rating of 80 (i.e., less than perfect), both for loading and saving.★ This means that if a new XPM-handling module was added—say as Image/Xpm2.py—providing it reports a rating greater than 80, the new module will be used instead of this one. (We discussed this when we covered the Image._choose_module() method; 129 ◀.)

```
(_WANT_XPM, _WANT_NAME, _WANT_VALUES, _WANT_COLOR, _WANT_PIXELS,
 _DONE) = ("WANT_XPM", "WANT_NAME", "WANT_VALUES", "WANT_COLOR",
        "WANT_PIXELS", "DONE")
_CODES = "".join((chr(x) for x in range(32, 127) if chr(x) not in '\\"'))
```

★ An alternative to checking a file's type by extension is to read its first few bytes—its "magic" number. For example, XPM files begin with the bytes 0x2F 0x2A 0x20 0x58 0x50 0x4D 0x20 0x2A 0x2F ("/* XPM */") and PNG files with 0x89 0x50 0x4E 0x47 0x0D 0x0A 0x1A 0x0A ("·PNG····").

The XPM format is a plain text (7-bit ASCII) format that must be parsed to extract its data. The format consists of some metadata (width, height, number of colors, and so on), a color table, and pixel data that identifies each pixel by reference to the color table. The details would take us too far from Python to go into further; however, we use a simple, hand-coded parser, and these constants provide the parser's states.

```python
def load(image, filename):
    colors = cpp = count = None
    state = _WANT_XPM
    palette = {}
    index = 0
    with open(filename, "rt", encoding="ascii") as file:
        for lino, line in enumerate(file, start=1):
            line = line.strip()
            ...
```

This is the start of the module's load() function. The image passed in is of type Image.Image, and inside the function (but not shown), the image's pixels, width, and height attributes are all set directly. The pixels array is created using the Image.create_array() function so that the Xpm.py module doesn't have to know or care whether the array is an array.array or a numpy.ndarray, so long as the array is one dimensional and of length width × height. This does mean, though, that we must only access the pixels array using methods that are common to both types.

```python
def save(image, filename):
    name = Image.sanitized_name(filename)
    palette, cpp = _palette_and_cpp(image.pixels)
    with open(filename, "w+t", encoding="ascii") as file:
        _write_header(image, file, name, cpp, len(palette))
        _write_palette(file, palette)
        _write_pixels(image, file, palette)
```

Both XBM and XPM formats include a name in the actual file that is based on their filename but which must be a valid identifier in the C language. We obtain this name using the Image.sanitized_name() function. Almost all of the saving work is passed on to private helper functions, none of which is of intrinsic interest, and so they aren't shown.

```python
def sanitized_name(name):
    name = re.sub(r"\W+", "", os.path.basename(os.path.splitext(name)[0]))
    if not name or name[0].isdigit():
        name = "z" + name
    return name
```

The `Image.sanitized_name()` function takes a filename and produces a name based on it that includes only unaccented Latin letters, digits, and underscores, and that starts with a letter or underscore. In the regex, `\W+` matches one or more non-word characters (i.e., characters that are not valid in C identifiers).

Support for any other image format can be added to the `Image` module by creating a suitable module to go in the `Image` directory, which has the four required functions: `can_load()`, `can_save()`, `load()`, and `save()`, where the first two return appropriate integers for the filenames they are given. One very popular image format is PNG format, but it is pretty complicated. Fortunately, we can adapt the existing PyPNG module to take advantage of it with minimal effort, as we will see in the next subsection.

3.12.3. The PNG Wrapper Module

The PyPNG module (`github.com/drj11/pypng`) provides good support for the PNG image format. However, it doesn't have the interface that the `Image` module requires for an image-specific format module. So, in this subsection we will create the `Image/Png.py` module, which will use the Adapter Pattern (§2.1, 29 ◄) to add support for PNG images to the `Image` module. And unlike the previous subsection, where we only showed a small sample of the code, here we will see all of the `Image/Png.py` module's code.

```
try:
    import png
except ImportError:
    png = None
```

We begin by attempting to import PyPNG's `png` module. If this fails we create a `png` variable of value `None` that we can check later.

```
def can_load(filename):
    return (80 if png is not None and
            os.path.splitext(filename)[1].lower() == ".png" else 0)
def can_save(filename):
    return can_load(filename)
```

If the `png` module was successfully imported, we return a rating of 80 (slightly imperfect) as our indication of this module's PNG support. We use 80 rather than 100 to allow for another module to supercede this one. Just as for the XPM format, we return the same rating for both loading and saving; however, it is perfectly acceptable to return different ratings.

```
def load(image, filename):
    reader = png.Reader(filename=filename)
```

```
image.width, image.height, pixels, _ = reader.asRGBA8()
image.pixels = Image.create_array(image.width, image.height)
index = 0
for row in pixels:
    for r, g, b, α in zip(row[::4], row[1::4], row[2::4], row[3::4]):
        image.pixels[index] = Image.color_for_argb(α, r, g, b)
        index += 1
```

We begin by creating a png.Reader, giving it the filename we have been given:
this will result in the PNG file being loaded into the reader instance. Then we
extract the image's width, height, and pixels and discard the metadata.

The PyPNG module uses RGBA format, whereas our Image module uses ARGB
format, so we must account for this difference. This is done by extracting the
pixels using the png.Reader.asRGBA8() method, which returns a two-dimensional
array of rows of color component values. For example, the pixels for an image
whose first row began with a solid red pixel followed by a solid blue pixel would
have for its first row a list of values that starts like this: 0xFF, 0x00, 0x00, 0xFF,
0x00, 0x00, 0xFF, 0xFF.

Once we have the RGBA pixels, we create a new array of the right size and
with all the pixels set as transparent. We then iterate over each row of color
components and use slicing to extract each kind of component. For example,
the red components are at row positions 0, 4, 8, 12, ..., the green at positions 1,
5, 9, 13, ..., the blue at 2, 6, 10, 14, ..., and the alpha at 3, 7, 11, 15, ... We then
use the built-in zip() function to produce color component 4-tuples. So, the first
4-tuple is from the first row at index positions (0, 1, 2, 3), the second 4-tuple is
from index positions (4, 5, 6, 7), and so on. For each tuple, we create an ARGB
color value and insert it into our image's one-dimensional array of pixels.

```
def save(image, filename):
    with open(filename, "wb") as file:
        writer = png.Writer(width=image.width, height=image.height,
                alpha=True)
        writer.write_array(file, list(_rgba_for_pixels(image.pixels)))
```

The save() function delegates most of its work to the png module. It begins by
creating a png.Writer with some appropriate metadata, and then it writes all the
pixels to it. Since Image uses ARGB values and png uses RGBA values, we have
used a private helper function to convert from one to the other.

```
def _rgba_for_pixels(pixels):
    for color in pixels:
        α, r, g, b = Image.argb_for_color(color)
        for component in (r, g, b, α):
            yield component
```

This function iterates over the array it is given (i.e., `image.pixels`) and separates out each color's color components. It then yields each of these components (in RGBA order) to its caller.

The code shown in this subsection is complete, because all the hard work is done by PyPNG's `png` module.

The `Image` module provides a useful interface for drawing (`set_pixel()`, `line()`, `rectangle()`, `ellipse()`), and support for loading and saving in XBM, XPM, and (if PyPNG is installed) PNG formats. It also provides a `subsample()` method (for fast rough scaling) and a `scale()` method (for smooth scaling), as well as some convenience color manipulation functions and static methods.

The `Image` module can be used in concurrent contexts—for example, to create, load, draw on, and save images in multiple threads or processes—making it more convenient than, say, Tkinter, which can only handle images in the main (GUI) thread. Unfortunately, though, the scaling is rather slow. One way to improve scaling speed—providing we have a multi-core machine and have multiple images to scale at the same time—is to use concurrency, as we will see in the next chapter. However, scaling is CPU-bound, so the best speedups we can hope for using concurrency are proportional to the number of processors; for example, on a four core machine the best we could achieve would be slightly less than a 4× speedup. So, in Chapter 5 (§5.3, ➤ 198), we will see how to use Cython to achieve more dramatic speedups.

4 High-Level Concurrency

Interest in concurrent programming has been growing rapidly since the turn of the millennium. This has been accelerated by Java, which has made concurrency much more mainstream; by the near ubiquity of multi-core machines; and by the availability of support for concurrent programming in most modern programming languages.

Writing and maintaining concurrent programs is harder (sometimes *much* harder) than writing and maintaining nonconcurrent programs. Furthermore, concurrent programs can sometimes have worse performance (sometimes *much* worse) than equivalent nonconcurrent programs. Nonetheless, if done well, it is possible to write concurrent programs whose performance compared with their nonconcurrent cousins is so much better as to outweigh the additional effort.

Most modern languages (including C++ and Java) support concurrency directly in the language itself and usually have additional higher-level functionality in their standard libraries. Concurrency can be implemented in a number of ways, with the most important difference being whether shared data is accessed directly (e.g., using shared memory) or indirectly (e.g., using inter-process communication—IPC). Threaded concurrency is where separate concurrent threads of execution operate within the same system process. These threads typically access shared data using serialized access to shared memory, with the serialization enforced by the programmer using some kind of locking mechanism. Process-based concurrency (multiprocessing) is where separate processes execute independently. Concurrent processes typically access shared data using IPC, although they could also use shared memory if the language or its library supported it. Another kind of concurrency is based on "concurrent waiting" rather than concurrent execution; this is the approach taken by implementations of asynchronous I/O.

Python has some low-level support for asynchronous I/O (the asyncore and asynchat modules). High-level support is provided as part of the third-party Twisted framework (twistedmatrix.com). Support for high-level asynchronous I/O—including event loops—is scheduled to be added to Python's standard library with Python 3.4 (www.python.org/dev/peps/pep-3156).

As for the more traditional thread-based and process-based concurrency, Python supports both approaches. Python's threading support is quite conventional, but the multiprocessing support is much higher level than that provided by most other languages or libraries. Furthermore, Python's multiprocessing support uses the same abstractions as threading to make it easy to switch between the two approaches, at least when shared memory isn't used.

Due to the GIL (Global Interpreter Lock), the Python interpreter itself can only execute on one processor core at any one time.* C code can acquire and release the GIL and so doesn't have the same constraint, and much of Python—and quite a bit of its standard library—is written in C. Even so, this means that doing concurrency using threading may not provide the speedups we would hope for.

In general, for CPU-bound processing, using threading can easily lead to worse performance than not using concurrency at all. One solution to this is to write the code in Cython (§5.2, ➤ 187), which is essentially Python with some extra syntax that gets compiled into pure C. This can result in 100× speedups—far more than is likely to be achieved using any kind of concurrency, where the performance improvement will be proportional to the number of processor cores. However, if concurrency is the right approach to take, then for CPU-bound processing it is best to avoid the GIL altogether by using the multiprocessing module. If we use multiprocessing, instead of using separate threads of execution in the same process (and therefore contending for the GIL), we have separate processes each using its own independent instance of the Python interpreter, so there is no contention.

For I/O-bound processing (e.g., networking), using concurrency can produce dramatic speedups. In these cases, network latency is often such a dominant factor that whether the concurrency is done using threading or multiprocessing may not matter.

---

* This limitation doesn't apply to Jython and some other Python interpreters. None of the book's concurrent examples rely on the presence or absence of the GIL.

We recommend that a nonconcurrent program be written first, wherever possible. This will be simpler and quicker to write than a concurrent program, and easier to test. Once the nonconcurrent program is deemed correct, it may turn out to be fast enough as it is. And if it isn't fast enough, we can use it to compare with a concurrent version both in terms of results (i.e., correctness) and in terms of performance. As for what kind of concurrency, we recommend multiprocessing for CPU-bound programs, and either multiprocessing or threading for I/O-bound programs. It isn't only the kind of concurrency that matters, but also the level.

In this book we define three levels of concurrency:

- **Low-Level Concurrency:** This is concurrency that makes explicit use of atomic operations. This kind of concurrency is for library writers rather than for application developers, since it is very easy to get wrong and can be extremely difficult to debug. Python doesn't support this kind of concurrency, although implementations of Python concurrency are typically built using low-level operations.

- **Mid-Level Concurrency:** This is concurrency that does not use any explicit atomic operations but does use explicit locks. This is the level of concurrency that most languages support. Python provides support for concurrent programming at this level with such classes as threading.Semaphore, threading.Lock, and multiprocessing.Lock. This level of concurrency support is commonly used by application programmers, since it is often all that is available.

- **High-Level Concurrency:** This is concurrency where there are no explicit atomic operations and no explicit locks. (Locking and atomic operations may well occur under the hood, but we don't have to concern ourselves with them.) Some modern languages are beginning to support high-level concurrency. Python provides the concurrent.futures module (Python 3.2), and the queue.Queue and multiprocessing queue collection classes, to support high-level concurrency.

Using mid-level approaches to concurrency is easy to do, but it is very error prone. Such approaches are especially vulnerable to subtle, hard-to-track-down problems, as well as to both spectacular crashes and frozen programs, all occurring without any discernable pattern.

The key problem is sharing data. Mutable shared data must be protected by locks to ensure that all accesses to it are serialized (i.e., only one thread or process can access the shared data at a time). Furthermore, when multiple threads or processes are all trying to access the same shared data, then all but one of them will be blocked (that is, idle). This means that while a lock is in force our application could be using only a single thread or process (i.e., as if it were nonconcurrent), with all the others waiting. So, we must be careful to lock as infrequently as possible and for as short a time as possible. The simplest solution is to not share any mutable data at all. Then we don't need explicit locks, and most of the problems of concurrency simply melt away.

Sometimes, of course, multiple concurrent threads or processes need to access the same data, but we can solve this without (explicit) locking. One solution is to use a data structure that supports concurrent access. The queue module provides several thread-safe queues, and for multiprocessing-based concurrency, we can use the multiprocessing.JoinableQueue and multiprocessing.Queue classes. We can use such queues to provide a single source of jobs for all our concurrent threads or processes and as a single destination for results, leaving all the locking to the data structure itself.

If we have data that we want used concurrently for which a concurrency-supporting queue isn't suitable, then the best way to do this without locking is to pass immutable data (e.g., numbers or strings) or to pass mutable data that is only ever read. If mutable data must be used, the safest approach is to deep copy it. Deep copying avoids the overheads and risks of using locks, at the expense of the processing and memory required for the copying itself. Alternatively, for multiprocessing, we can use data types that support concurrent access—in particular multiprocessing.Value for a single mutable value or multiprocessing.Array for an array of mutable values—providing that they are created by a multiprocessing.Manager, as we will see later in the chapter.

In this chapter's first two sections, we will explore concurrency using two applications, one CPU-bound and the other I/O-bound. In both cases we will use Python's high-level concurrency facilities, both the long-established thread-safe queues and the new (Python 3.2) concurrent.futures module. The chapter's third section provides a case study showing how to do concurrent processing in a GUI (graphical user interface) application, while retaining a responsive GUI that reports progress and supports cancellation.

4.1. CPU-Bound Concurrency

In Chapter 3's Image case study (§3.12, 124 ◀) we showed some code for smooth-scaling an image and commented that the scaling was rather slow. Let's imagine that we want to smooth scale a whole bunch of images, and want to do so as fast as possible by taking advantage of multiple cores.

Scaling images is CPU-bound, so we would expect multiprocessing to deliver the best performance, and this is borne out by the timings in Table 4.1.* (In Chapter 5's case study, we will combine multiprocessing with Cython to achieve much bigger speedups; §5.3, ▶ 198.)

---

* The timings were made on a lightly loaded quad-core AMD64 3 GHz machine processing 56 images ranging in size from 1 MiB to 12 MiB, totaling 316 MiB, and resulting in 67 MiB of output.

Table 4.1 *Image scaling speed comparisons*

Program	Concurrency	Seconds	Speedup
imagescale-s.py	*None*	784	*Baseline*
imagescale-c.py	4 coroutines	781	1.00×
imagescale-t.py	4 threads using a thread pool	1339	0.59×
imagescale-q-m.py	4 processes using a queue	206	3.81×
imagescale-m.py	4 processes using a process pool	201	3.90×

The results for the imagescale-t.py program using four threads clearly illustrates that using threading for CPU-bound processing produces worse performance than a nonconcurrent program. This is because all the processing was done in Python on the same core, and in addition to the scaling, Python had to keep context switching between four separate threads, which added a massive amount of overhead. Contrast this with the multiprocessing versions, both of which were able to spread their work over all the machine's cores. The difference between the multiprocessing queue and process pool versions is not significant, and both delivered the kind of speedup we'd expect (that is, in direct proportion to the number of cores).★

All the image-scaling programs accept command-line arguments parsed with argparse. For all versions, the arguments include the size to scale the images down to, whether to use smooth scaling (all our timings do), and the source and target image directories. Images that are less than the given size are copied rather than scaled; all those used for timings needed scaling. For concurrent versions, it is also possible to specify the concurrency (i.e., how many threads or processes to use); this is purely for debugging and timing. For CPU-bound programs, we would normally use as many threads or processes as there are cores. For I/O-bound programs, we would use some multiple of the number of cores (2×, 3×, 4×, or more) depending on the network's bandwidth. For completeness, here is the handle_commandline() function used in the concurrent image scale programs.

```
def handle_commandline():
    parser = argparse.ArgumentParser()
    parser.add_argument("-c", "--concurrency", type=int,
            default=multiprocessing.cpu_count(),
            help="specify the concurrency (for debugging and "
                "timing) [default: %(default)d]")
    parser.add_argument("-s", "--size", default=400, type=int,
```

★ Starting new processes is far more expensive on Windows than on most other operating systems. Fortunately, Python's queues and pools use persistent process pools behind the scenes so as to avoid repeatedly incurring these process startup costs.

```
            help="make a scaled image that fits the given dimension "
                "[default: %(default)d]")
    parser.add_argument("-S", "--smooth", action="store_true",
            help="use smooth scaling (slow but good for text)")
    parser.add_argument("source",
            help="the directory containing the original .xpm images")
    parser.add_argument("target",
            help="the directory for the scaled .xpm images")
    args = parser.parse_args()
    source = os.path.abspath(args.source)
    target = os.path.abspath(args.target)
    if source == target:
        args.error("source and target must be different")
    if not os.path.exists(args.target):
        os.makedirs(target)
    return args.size, args.smooth, source, target, args.concurrency
```

Normally, we would not offer a concurrency option to users, but it can be useful for debugging, timing, and testing, so we have included it. The multiprocessing.cpu_count() function returns the number of cores the machine has (e.g., 2 for a machine with a dual-core processor, 8 for a machine with dual quad-core processors).

The argparse module takes a declarative approach to creating a command line parser. Once the parser is created, we parse the command-line and retrieve the arguments. We perform some basic sanity checks (e.g., to stop the user from writing scaled images over the originals), and we create the target directory if it doesn't already exist. The os.makedirs() function is similar to the os.mkdir() function, except the former can create intermediate directories rather than just a single subdirectory.

Just before we dive into the code, note the following important rules that apply to any Python file that uses the multiprocessing module:

- The file must be an importable module. For example, *my-mod.py* is a legitimate name for a Python *program* but not for a module (since import my-mod is a syntax error); *my_mod.py* or *MyMod.py* are both fine, though.

- The file should have an entry-point function (e.g., main()) and finish with a call to the entry point. For example: if __name__ == "__main__": main().

- On Windows, the Python file and the Python interpreter (python.exe or pythonw.exe) should be on the same drive (e.g., C:).

The following subsections will look at the two multiprocessing versions of the image scale program, imagescale-q-m.py and imagescale-m.py. Both programs report progress (i.e., print the name of each image they scale) and support cancellation (e.g., if the user presses Ctrl+C).

4.1.1. Using Queues and Multiprocessing

The `imagescale-q-m.py` program creates a queue of jobs to be done (i.e., images to scale) and a queue of results.

```
Result = collections.namedtuple("Result", "copied scaled name")
Summary = collections.namedtuple("Summary", "todo copied scaled canceled")
```

The `Result` named tuple is used to store one result. This is a count of how many images were copied and how many scaled—always 1 and 0 or 0 and 1—and the name of the resultant image. The `Summary` named tuple is used to store a summary of all the results.

```
def main():
    size, smooth, source, target, concurrency = handle_commandline()
    Qtrac.report("starting...")
    summary = scale(size, smooth, source, target, concurrency)
    summarize(summary, concurrency)
```

This `main()` function is the same for all the image scale programs. It begins by reading the command line using the custom `handle_commandline()` function we discussed earlier (146 ◄). This returns the size that the images must be scaled to, a Boolean indicating whether smooth scaling should be used, the source directory to read images from, the target directory to write scaled images to, and (for concurrent versions) the number of threads or processes to use (which defaults to the number of cores).

The program reports to the user that it has started and then executes the `scale()` function where all the work is done. When the `scale()` function eventually returns its summary of results, we print the summary using the `summarize()` function.

```
def report(message="", error=False):
    if len(message) >= 70 and not error:
        message = message[:67] + "..."
    sys.stdout.write("\r{:70}{}".format(message, "\n" if error else ""))
    sys.stdout.flush()
```

For convenience, this function is in the `Qtrac.py` module, since it is used by all the console concurrency examples in this chapter. The function overwrites the current line on the console with the given message (truncating it to 70 characters if necessary) and flushes the output so that it is printed immediately. If the message is to indicate an error, a newline is printed so that the error message isn't overwritten by the next message, and no truncation is done.

```
def scale(size, smooth, source, target, concurrency):
    canceled = False
    jobs = multiprocessing.JoinableQueue()
    results = multiprocessing.Queue()
    create_processes(size, smooth, jobs, results, concurrency)
    todo = add_jobs(source, target, jobs)
    try:
        jobs.join()
    except KeyboardInterrupt: # May not work on Windows
        Qtrac.report("canceling...")
        canceled = True
    copied = scaled = 0
    while not results.empty(): # Safe because all jobs have finished
        result = results.get_nowait()
        copied += result.copied
        scaled += result.scaled
    return Summary(todo, copied, scaled, canceled)
```

This function is the heart of the multiprocessing queue-based concurrent image
scaling program, and its work is illustrated in Figure 4.1. The function begins
by creating a joinable queue of jobs to be done. A joinable queue is one that
can be waited for (i.e., until it is empty). It then creates a nonjoinable queue of
results. Next, it creates the processes to do the work: they will all be ready to
work but blocked, since we haven't put any work on the jobs queue yet. Then,
the add_jobs() function is called to populate the jobs queue.

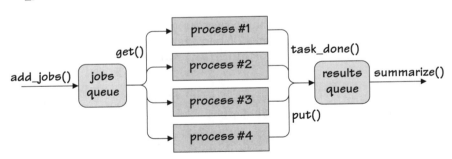

Figure 4.1 *Handling concurrent jobs and results with queues*

With all the jobs in the jobs queue, we wait for the jobs queue to become empty
using the multiprocessing.JoinableQueue.join() method. This is done inside a
try ... except block so that if the user cancels (e.g., by pressing Ctrl+C on Unix),
we can cleanly handle the cancellation.

When the jobs have all been done (or the program has been canceled), we iterate
over the results queue. Normally, using the empty() method on a concurrent
queue is unreliable, but here it works fine, since all the worker processes have

finished and the queue is no longer being updated. This is why we can also use the nonblocking `multiprocessing.Queue.get_nowait()` method, rather than the usual blocking `multiprocessing.Queue.get()` method, to retrieve the results.

Once all the results have been accumulated, we return a `Summary` named tuple with the details. For a normal run, the todo value will be zero, and canceled will be `False`, but for a canceled run, todo will probably be nonzero, and canceled will be `True`.

Although this function is called `scale()`, it is really a fairly generic "do concurrent work" function that provides jobs to processes and accumulates results. It could easily be adapted to other situations.

```
def create_processes(size, smooth, jobs, results, concurrency):
    for _ in range(concurrency):
        process = multiprocessing.Process(target=worker, args=(size,
                smooth, jobs, results))
        process.daemon = True
        process.start()
```

This function creates multiprocessing processes to do the work. Each process is given the same `worker()` function (since they all do the same work), and the details of the work they must do. This includes the shared-jobs queue and the shared results queue. Naturally, we don't have to worry about locking these shared queues since the queues take care of their own synchronization. Once a process is created, we make it a dæmon: when the main process terminates, it cleanly terminates all of its dæmon processes (whereas non-dæmon's are left running, and on Unix, become zombies).

After creating each process and dæmonizing it, we tell it to start executing the function it was given. It will immediately block, of course, since we haven't yet added any jobs to the jobs queue. This doesn't matter, though, since the blocking is taking place in a separate process and doesn't block the main process. Consequently, all the multiprocessing processes are quickly created, after which this function returns. Then, in the caller, we add jobs to the jobs queue for the blocked processes to work on.

```
def worker(size, smooth, jobs, results):
    while True:
        try:
            sourceImage, targetImage = jobs.get()
            try:
                result = scale_one(size, smooth, sourceImage, targetImage)
                Qtrac.report("{} {}".format("copied" if result.copied else
                        "scaled", os.path.basename(result.name)))
                results.put(result)
```

```
            except Image.Error as err:
                Qtrac.report(str(err), True)
        finally:
            jobs.task_done()
```

It is possible to create a multiprocessing.Process subclass (or a threading.Thread subclass) to do concurrent work. But here we have taken a slightly simpler approach and created a function that is passed in as the multiprocessing.Process's target argument. (Exactly the same thing can be done with threading .Threads.)

The worker executes an infinite loop, and in each iteration it tries to retrieve a job of work to do from the shared-jobs queue. It is safe to use an infinite loop, because the process is a dæmon and will therefore be terminated when the program has finished. The multiprocessing.Queue.get() method blocks until it is able to return a job, which in this example is a 2-tuple of the source and target image names.

Once a job is retrieved, we scale (or copy) it using the scale_one() function and report what we did. We also put the result object (of type Result) onto the shared results queue.

It is *essential* when using a joinable queue that, for every job we get, we execute multiprocessing.JoinableQueue.task_done(). This is how the multiprocessing.JoinableQueue.join() method knows when the queue can be joined (i.e., is empty with no more jobs to be done).

```
def add_jobs(source, target, jobs):
    for todo, name in enumerate(os.listdir(source), start=1):
        sourceImage = os.path.join(source, name)
        targetImage = os.path.join(target, name)
        jobs.put((sourceImage, targetImage))
    return todo
```

Once the processes have been created and started, they are all blocked trying to get jobs from the shared-jobs queue.

For every image to be processed, this function creates two strings: sourceImage that has the full path to a source image, and targetImage with the full path to a target image. Each pair of these paths are added as a 2-tuple to the shared-jobs queue. And at the end, the function returns the total number of jobs that need to be done.

As soon as the first job is added to the jobs queue, one of the blocked worker processes will retrieve it and start working on it, just as for the second job that's added, and the third, until all the worker processes have a job to do. Thereafter, the jobs queue is likely to acquire more jobs while the worker processes are working, with a job being retrieved whenever a worker finishes a job. Eventually, all the jobs will have been retrieved, at which point all the worker processes will be blocked waiting for more work, and they will be terminated when the program finishes.

```
def scale_one(size, smooth, sourceImage, targetImage):
    oldImage = Image.from_file(sourceImage)
    if oldImage.width <= size and oldImage.height <= size:
        oldImage.save(targetImage)
        return Result(1, 0, targetImage)
    else:
        if smooth:
            scale = min(size / oldImage.width, size / oldImage.height)
            newImage = oldImage.scale(scale)
        else:
            stride = int(math.ceil(max(oldImage.width / size,
                                       oldImage.height / size)))
            newImage = oldImage.subsample(stride)
        newImage.save(targetImage)
        return Result(0, 1, targetImage)
```

This function is where the actual scaling (or copying) takes place. It uses the cyImage module (see §5.3, ➤ 198) or falls back to the Image module (see §3.12, 124 ◄) if cyImage isn't available. If the image is already smaller than the given size, it is simply saved to the target and a Result is returned that says that one image was copied, that none were scaled, and the name of the target image. Otherwise, the image is smooth scaled or subsampled with the resultant image being saved. In this case, the returned Result says that no image was copied, that one was scaled, and again the name of the target image.

```
def summarize(summary, concurrency):
    message = "copied {} scaled {} ".format(summary.copied, summary.scaled)
    difference = summary.todo - (summary.copied + summary.scaled)
    if difference:
        message += "skipped {} ".format(difference)
    message += "using {} processes".format(concurrency)
    if summary.canceled:
        message += " [canceled]"
    Qtrac.report(message)
    print()
```

Once all the images have been processed (i.e., once the jobs queue has been joined), the Summary is created (in the scale() function; 148 ◄) and passed to this function. A typical run with the summary produced by this function shown on the second line might look like this:

```
$ ./imagescale-m.py -S /tmp/images /tmp/scaled
copied 0 scaled 56 using 4 processes
```

For timings on Linux, simply precede the command with time. On Windows, there is no built-in command for this, but there are solutions.* (Doing timings *inside* programs that use multiprocessing doesn't seem to work. In our experiments, we found that timings reported the runtime of the main process but excluded that of the worker processes. Note that Python 3.3's time module has several new functions to support accurate timing.)

The three-second timing difference between imagescale-q-m.py and imagescale-m.py is insignificant and could easily be reversed on a different run. So, in effect, these two versions are equivalent.

4.1.2. Using Futures and Multiprocessing

Python 3.2 introduced the concurrent.futures module that offers a nice, high-level way to do concurrency with Python using multiple threads and multiple processes. In this subsection, we will review three functions from the imagescale-m.py program (all the rest being the same as those in the imagescale-q-m.py program we reviewed in the previous subsection). The imagescale-m.py program uses *futures*. According to the documentation, a concurrent.futures.Future is an object that "encapsulates the asynchronous execution of a callable" (see docs.python.org/dev/library/concurrent.futures.html#future-objects). Futures are created by calling the concurrent.futures.Executor.submit() method, and they can report their state (canceled, running, done) and the result or exception they produced.

The concurrent.futures.Executor class cannot be used directly, because it is an abstract base class. Instead, one of its two concrete subclasses must be used. The concurrent.futures.ProcessPoolExecutor() achieves concurrency by using multiple processes. Using a process pool means that any Future used with it may only execute or return pickleable objects, which includes nonnested functions, of course. This restriction does not apply to the concurrent.futures.ThreadPoolExecutor, which provides concurrency using multiple threads.

Conceptually, using a thread or process pool is simpler than using queues, as Figure 4.2 illustrates.

Figure 4.2 *Handling concurrent jobs and results with a pool executor*

---

* See, for example, stackoverflow.com/questions/673523/how-to-measure-execution-time-of-command-in-windows-command-line.

```
def scale(size, smooth, source, target, concurrency):
    futures = set()
    with concurrent.futures.ProcessPoolExecutor(
            max_workers=concurrency) as executor:
        for sourceImage, targetImage in get_jobs(source, target):
            future = executor.submit(scale_one, size, smooth, sourceImage,
                    targetImage)
            futures.add(future)
        summary = wait_for(futures)
        if summary.canceled:
            executor.shutdown()
        return summary
```

This function has the same signature, and does the same work, as the same function in the `imagescale-q-m.py` program, but it works in a radically different way. We begin by creating an empty set of futures. Then we create a process pool executor. Behind the scenes, this will create a number of worker processes. The exact number is determined by a heuristic, but here we have overridden this to specify the number ourselves, purely for debugging and timing convenience.

Once we have a process pool executor, we iterate over the jobs returned by the `get_jobs()` function and submit each one to the pool. The `concurrent.futures.ProcessPoolExecutor.submit()` method accepts a worker function and optional arguments and returns a `Future` object. We add each future to our set of futures. The pool starts work as soon as it has at least one future to work on. When all the futures have been created, we call a custom `wait_for()` function, passing it the set of futures. This function will block until all the futures have been done (or until the user cancels). If the user cancels, we manually shutdown the process pool executor.

```
def get_jobs(source, target):
    for name in os.listdir(source):
        yield os.path.join(source, name), os.path.join(target, name)
```

This function performs the same service as the previous subsection's `add_jobs()` function, only instead of adding jobs to a queue, it is a generator function that yields jobs on demand.

```
def wait_for(futures):
    canceled = False
    copied = scaled = 0
    try:
        for future in concurrent.futures.as_completed(futures):
            err = future.exception()
            if err is None:
```

```
                    result = future.result()
                    copied += result.copied
                    scaled += result.scaled
                    Qtrac.report("{} {}".format("copied" if result.copied else
                            "scaled", os.path.basename(result.name)))
                elif isinstance(err, Image.Error):
                    Qtrac.report(str(err), True)
                else:
                    raise err # Unanticipated
        except KeyboardInterrupt:
            Qtrac.report("canceling...")
            canceled = True
            for future in futures:
                future.cancel()
    return Summary(len(futures), copied, scaled, canceled)
```

Once all the futures have been created, we call this function to wait for the futures to complete. The concurrent.futures.as_completed() function blocks until a future has finished (or been canceled) and then returns that future. If the worker callable that the future executed raised an exception, the Future.exception() method will return it; otherwise, it returns None. If no exception occurred, we retrieve the future's result and report progress to the user. If an exception occurred of a kind we might reasonably expect (i.e., from the Image module), again, we report it to the user. But if we get an unexpected exception, we raise it since it either means we have a logical error in our program or the user canceled with Ctrl+C.

If the user cancels by pressing Ctrl+C, we iterate over all the futures and cancel each one. At the end, we return a summary of the work that was done.

Using concurrent.futures is clearer and more robust than using queues, although either approach is far easier and better than one that involves the use of explicit locks when using multithreading. It is also easy to switch between using multithreading and multiprocessing: we just have to use a concurrent.futures.ThreadPoolExecutor instead of a concurrent.futures.ProcessPoolExecutor. When using multithreading of any kind, if we need to access shared data, we must use immutable types or deep copy (e.g., for read-only access), or use locks (e.g., to serialize read-write accesses), or use a thread-safe type (e.g., a queue.Queue). Similarly, when using multiprocessing, to access shared data we must use immutable types or deep copy, and for read-write access we must use managed multiprocessing.Values or multiprocessing.Arrays, or use multiprocessing.Queues. Ideally, we should avoid using any shared data at all. Failing that, we should only share read-only data (e.g., by using immutable types or by deep copying) or use concurrency-safe queues, so that no explicit locks are required, and our code is straightforward to understand and maintain.

4.2. I/O-Bound Concurrency

A common requirement is to download a bunch of files or web pages from the Internet. Due to network latency, it is usually possible to do many downloads concurrently and thereby finish much more quickly than would be the case if we downloaded each file one at a time.

In this section, we will review the whatsnew-q.py and whatsnew-t.py programs. These programs download RSS feeds: small XML documents summarizing technology news stories. The feeds come from various web sites, and the program uses them to produce a single HTML page with links to all the stories. Figure 4.3 shows part of a "what's new"-generated HTML page. Table 4.2 (➤ 156) shows the timings for various versions of the program.* Although the "what's new" programs' speedups look proportional to the number of cores, this is a coincidence; the cores were all underutilized, and most of the time was spent waiting for network I/O.

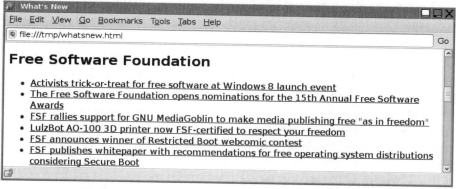

Figure 4.3 *Some technology news links from an RSS feed*

The table also shows timings for versions of a gigapixel program (not shown in the book). These programs access the www.gigapan.org web site and retrieve nearly 500 JSON-format files, totaling 1.9 MiB, that contain metadata about gigapixel images. The code for the versions of this program mirrors that of the "what's new" programs, although the gigapixel programs achieve much greater speedups. The better performance is because the gigapixel programs access a single high-bandwidth site, whereas the "what's new" programs must access lots of different sites with varying bandwidths.

Because network latency varies so much, the speedups could easily change, with concurrent versions achieving improvements from as little as 2× to as much as 10×, or even better, depending on the sites accessed, the amount of

---

* The timings were made on a lightly loaded quad-core AMD64 3 GHz machine, downloading from almost 200 web sites on a domestic broadband connection.

Table 4.2 *Download speed comparisons*

Program	Concurrency	Seconds	Speedup
whatsnew.py	*None*	172	*Baseline*
whatsnew-c.py	16 coroutines	180	0.96×
whatsnew-q-m.py	16 processes using a queue	45	3.82×
whatsnew-m.py	16 processes using a process pool	50	3.44×
whatsnew-q.py	16 threads using a queue	50	3.44×
whatsnew-t.py	16 threads using a thread pool	48	3.58×
gigapixel.py	*None*	238	*Baseline*
gigapixel-q-m.py	16 processes using a queue	35	6.80×
gigapixel-m.py	16 processes using a process pool	42	5.67×
gigapixel-q.py	16 threads using a queue	37	6.43×
gigapixel-t.py	16 threads using a thread pool	37	6.43×

data downloaded, and the bandwidth of the network connection. In view of this, the differences between the multiprocessing and multithreading versions are insignificant and could easily be reversed on a different run.

The key thing to remember from Table 4.2 is that we will achieve much faster downloading using a concurrent approach, although the actual speedup will vary from run to run and is sensitive to circumstances.

4.2.1. Using Queues and Threading

We will begin by looking at the whatsnew-q.py program, which uses multiple threads and two thread-safe queues. One queue is a jobs queue, where each job to do is a URL. The other queue is a results queue, where each result is a 2-tuple holding either True and an HTML fragment to go into the HTML page being built up, or False and an error message.

```
def main():
    limit, concurrency = handle_commandline()
    Qtrac.report("starting...")
    filename = os.path.join(os.path.dirname(__file__), "whatsnew.dat")
    jobs = queue.Queue()
    results = queue.Queue()
    create_threads(limit, jobs, results, concurrency)
    todo = add_jobs(filename, jobs)
    process(todo, jobs, results, concurrency)
```

The `main()` function orchestrates all the work. It begins by processing the command line and getting a limit (the maximum number of news items to read from a given URL) and a concurrency level for debugging and timing. The program then reports to the user that it has started and gets the filename with the full path of the data file that holds the URLs and their one-line titles.

Next, the function creates the two thread-safe queues and the worker threads. Once all the worker threads have been started (and, of course, they are all blocked because there is no work yet), we add all the jobs to the job queue. Finally, in the `process()` function, we wait for the jobs to be done and then output the results. The program's overall concurrency structure is illustrated in Figure 4.4 (➤ 158).

Incidentally, if we had a lot of jobs to add, or if adding each job was time-consuming, we might be better off adding the jobs in a separate thread (or process if using multiprocessing).

```python
def handle_commandline():
    parser = argparse.ArgumentParser()
    parser.add_argument("-l", "--limit", type=int, default=0,
            help="the maximum items per feed [default: unlimited]")
    parser.add_argument("-c", "--concurrency", type=int,
            default=multiprocessing.cpu_count() * 4,
            help="specify the concurrency (for debugging and "
                "timing) [default: %(default)d]")
    args = parser.parse_args()
    return args.limit, args.concurrency
```

Since the "what's new" programs are I/O-bound, we give them a default concurrency level that is a multiple of the number of cores—in this case, 4×.[*]

```python
def create_threads(limit, jobs, results, concurrency):
    for _ in range(concurrency):
        thread = threading.Thread(target=worker, args=(limit, jobs,
                results))
        thread.daemon = True
        thread.start()
```

This function creates as many worker threads as the `concurrency` variable specifies and gives each one a worker function to execute and the arguments the function must be called with.

Just as with the processes we saw in the previous section, we dæmonize each thread to ensure that it will be terminated when the program finishes. We start

---

[*] This multiple was chosen because it worked best in our tests. We recommend experimenting, since setups differ.

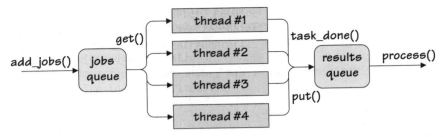

Figure 4.4 *Handling concurrent jobs and results with queues*

each thread, and it is immediately blocked because there are no jobs to do, but it is only the worker threads that are blocked, not the program's main thread.

```
def worker(limit, jobs, results):
    while True:
        try:
            feed = jobs.get()
            ok, result = Feed.read(feed, limit)
            if not ok:
                Qtrac.report(result, True)
            elif result is not None:
                Qtrac.report("read {}".format(result[0][4:-6]))
                results.put(result)
        finally:
            jobs.task_done()
```

We have made the worker function execute an infinite loop, since it is a dæmon, and therefore it will be terminated by the program when the program has finished.

The function blocks waiting to get a job from the jobs queue. As soon as it gets a job it uses the custom Feed.py module's Feed.read() function to read the file identified by the URL. All the "what's new" programs rely on a custom Feed.py module to provide an iterator for the jobs file and a reader for each RSS feed. If the read fails, ok is False and we print the result (which is an error message). Otherwise, providing we got a result (a list of HTML strings), we print the first item (stripping off the HTML tags) and add the result to the results queue.

For queues that we plan to join, it is essential that for every queue.Queue.get() call, we have a corresponding queue.Queue.task_done() call. We have ensured that this will happen by using a try ... finally block.*

---

* Note that although the queue.Queue class is a thread-safe joinable queue, the multiprocessing equivalent is the multiprocessing.JoinableQueue class, not the multiprocessing.Queue class.

```
def read(feed, limit, timeout=10):
    try:
        with urllib.request.urlopen(feed.url, None, timeout) as file:
            data = file.read()
        body = _parse(data, limit)
        if body:
            body = ["<h2>{}</h2>\n".format(escape(feed.title))] + body
            return True, body
        return True, None
    except (ValueError, urllib.error.HTTPError, urllib.error.URLError,
            etree.ParseError, socket.timeout) as err:
        return False, "Error: {}: {}".format(feed.url, err)
```

The Feed.read() function reads a given URL (feed) and attempts to parse it. If the parse is successful, it returns True and a list of HTML fragments (a title and one or more links); otherwise, it returns False and None or an error message.

```
def _parse(data, limit):
    output = []
    feed = feedparser.parse(data) # Atom + RSS
    for entry in feed["entries"]:
        title = entry.get("title")
        link = entry.get("link")
        if title:
            if link:
                output.append('<li><a href="{}">{}</a></li>'.format(
                        link, escape(title)))
            else:
                output.append('<li>{}</li>'.format(escape(title)))
        if limit and len(output) == limit:
            break
    if output:
        return ["<ul>"] + output + ["</ul>"]
```

The Feed.py module contains two versions of the private _parse() function. The one shown here uses the third-party feedparser module (pypi.python.org/pypi/feedparser), which can handle both Atom and RSS format news feeds. The other one (not shown) is a fallback if feedparser isn't available and can handle only RSS format feeds.

The feedparser.parse() function does all the hard work of parsing the news feed. We just need to iterate over the entries it produces and retrieve the title and link for each news story, building up an HTML list to represent them.

```
def add_jobs(filename, jobs):
    for todo, feed in enumerate(Feed.iter(filename), start=1):
        jobs.put(feed)
    return todo
```

Each feed is returned by the `Feed.iter()` function as a (*title*, *url*) 2-tuple that is added to the jobs queue. And at the end, the total number of jobs to do is returned.

In this case, we could have safely returned *jobs*.qsize() rather than kept track of the total to do ourselves. However, if we were to execute add_jobs() in its own thread, using `queue.Queue.qsize()` would not be reliable, since jobs would be taken off at the same time as they were added.

```
Feed = collections.namedtuple("Feed", "title url")

def iter(filename):
    name = None
    with open(filename, "rt", encoding="utf-8") as file:
        for line in file:
            line = line.rstrip()
            if not line or line.startswith("#"):
                continue
            if name is None:
                name = line
            else:
                yield Feed(name, line)
                name = None
```

This is the `Feed.py` module's `Feed.iter()` function. The `whatsnew.dat` file is expected to be a UTF-8-encoded plain-text file that contains two lines per feed: a title line (e.g., The Guardian – Technology) and, on the next line, the URL (e.g., `http://feeds.pinboard.in/rss/u:guardiantech/`). Blank lines and comment lines (i.e., lines starting with #) are ignored.

```
def process(todo, jobs, results, concurrency):
    canceled = False
    try:
        jobs.join() # Wait for all the work to be done
    except KeyboardInterrupt: # May not work on Windows
        Qtrac.report("canceling...")
        canceled = True
    if canceled:
        done = results.qsize()
    else:
        done, filename = output(results)
```

```
    Qtrac.report("read {}/{} feeds using {} threads{}".format(done, todo,
            concurrency, " [canceled]" if canceled else ""))
    print()
    if not canceled:
        webbrowser.open(filename)
```

Once all the threads have been created and the jobs added, this function is called. It calls queue.Queue.join(), which blocks until the queue is empty (i.e., when all the jobs are done) or until the user cancels. If the user did not cancel, the output() function is called to write the HTML file with all the lists of links, and then a summary is printed. Finally, the webbrowser module's open() function is called on the HTML file to open it in the user's default web browser (see Figure 4.3; 155 ◀).

```
def output(results):
    done = 0
    filename = os.path.join(tempfile.gettempdir(), "whatsnew.html")
    with open(filename, "wt", encoding="utf-8") as file:
        file.write("<!doctype html>\n")
        file.write("<html><head><title>What's New</title></head>\n")
        file.write("<body><h1>What's New</h1>\n")
        while not results.empty(): # Safe because all jobs have finished
            result = results.get_nowait()
            done += 1
            for item in result:
                file.write(item)
        file.write("</body></html>\n")
    return done, filename
```

After all the jobs are done, this function is called with the results queue. Each result contains a list of HTML fragments (a title followed by one or more links). This function creates a new whatsnew.html file and populates it with all the news feed titles and their links. At the end, the function returns the number of results (i.e., the count of those jobs that were successfully done) and the name of the HTML file it wrote. This information is used by the process() function to print its summary and to open the HTML file in the user's web browser.

4.2.2. Using Futures and Threading

If we are using Python 3.2 or later, we can take advantage of the concurrent.futures module to implement this program without the need for queues (or explicit locks). In this subsection, we will review the whatsnew-t.py program, which makes use of this module, although we will omit those functions that are identical to those we saw in the previous subsection (e.g., handle_commandline() and the Feed.py module's functions).

```
def main():
    limit, concurrency = handle_commandline()
    Qtrac.report("starting...")
    filename = os.path.join(os.path.dirname(__file__), "whatsnew.dat")
    futures = set()
    with concurrent.futures.ThreadPoolExecutor(
            max_workers=concurrency) as executor:
        for feed in Feed.iter(filename):
            future = executor.submit(Feed.read, feed, limit)
            futures.add(future)
        done, filename, canceled = process(futures)
        if canceled:
            executor.shutdown()
    Qtrac.report("read {}/{} feeds using {} threads{}".format(done,
            len(futures), concurrency, " [canceled]" if canceled else ""))
    print()
    if not canceled:
        webbrowser.open(filename)
```

This function creates an initially empty set of futures and then creates a thread pool executor that works just the same as a process pool executor, except that it uses separate threads rather than separate processes. Within the context of the executor, we iterate over the data file, and for each feed, we create a new future (using the concurrent.futures.ThreadPoolExecutor.submit() method) that will execute the Feed.read() function on the given feed URL, returning at most limit links. We then add the future to the set of futures.

Once all the futures have been created, we call a custom process() function that will wait until all the futures have finished (or until the user cancels). Then, a summary of results is printed, and if the user didn't cancel, the generated HTML page is opened in the user's web browser.

```
def process(futures):
    canceled = False
    done = 0
    filename = os.path.join(tempfile.gettempdir(), "whatsnew.html")
    with open(filename, "wt", encoding="utf-8") as file:
        file.write("<!doctype html>\n")
        file.write("<html><head><title>What's New</title></head>\n")
        file.write("<body><h1>What's New</h1>\n")
        canceled, results = wait_for(futures)
        if not canceled:
            for result in (result for ok, result in results if ok and
                    result is not None):
                done += 1
```

```
            for item in result:
                    file.write(item)
        else:
            done = sum(1 for ok, result in results if ok and result is not
                    None)
        file.write("</body></html>\n")
    return done, filename, canceled
```

This function writes the start of the HTML file and then calls a custom
wait_for() function to wait for all the work to be done. If the user didn't cancel,
the function iterates over the results (which are True, list or False, str or False,
None 2-tuples), and for those with lists (which consist of a title followed by one or
more links), the items are written to the HTML file.

If the user canceled, we simply calculate how many feeds were successfully
read. In either case, we return the number of feeds read, the HTML file's
filename, and whether the user canceled.

```
def wait_for(futures):
    canceled = False
    results = []
    try:
        for future in concurrent.futures.as_completed(futures):
            err = future.exception()
            if err is None:
                ok, result = future.result()
                if not ok:
                    Qtrac.report(result, True)
                elif result is not None:
                    Qtrac.report("read {}".format(result[0][4:-6]))
                results.append((ok, result))
            else:
                raise err # Unanticipated
    except KeyboardInterrupt:
        Qtrac.report("canceling...")
        canceled = True
        for future in futures:
            future.cancel()
    return canceled, results
```

This function iterates over the futures, blocking until one is finished or canceled.
Once a future is received, the function reports an error or a successfully read
feed as appropriate, and in either case appends the Boolean and the result (a list
of strings or an error string) to a list of results.

If the user cancels (by pressing Ctrl+C), we cancel all of the futures. At the end, we return whether the user canceled and the list of results.

Using concurrent.futures is just as convenient when using multiple threads as when using multiple processes. And in terms of performance, it is clear that when used in the right circumstances—I/O-based rather than CPU-based processing—and with due care, multithreading provides the improved performance that we would expect.

4.3. Case Study: A Concurrent GUI Application

Writing concurrent GUI (graphical user interface) applications can be tricky, especially using Tkinter, Python's standard GUI toolkit. A short introduction to GUI programming with Tkinter is given in Chapter 7 (➤ 231); readers with no Tkinter experience are recommended to read that chapter first and then return here.

One obvious approach to achieving concurrency in a GUI application is to use multithreading, but in practice this can lead to a slow or even frozen GUI when lots of processing is taking place; after all, GUIs are CPU-bound. An alternative approach is to use multiprocessing, but this can still result in very poor GUI responsiveness.

In this section, we will review the ImageScale application (in the example's imagescale directory). The application is shown in Figure 4.5. This application takes a sophisticated approach that combines concurrent processing with a responsive GUI that reports progress and supports cancellation.

As Figure 4.6 illustrates, the application combines multithreading and multiprocessing. It has two threads of execution—the main GUI thread and a worker thread—and the worker thread hands off its work to a pool of processes. This architecture produces a GUI that is always responsive, because the GUI gets most of the processor time for the core shared by the two threads, with the worker (which does almost no work itself) getting the rest. And the worker's processes end up executing on their own cores (on a multi-core machine), so they don't contend with the GUI at all.

A comparable console program, imagescale-m.py, is around 130 lines of code. (We reviewed this earlier; §4.1, 144 ◄.) By comparison, the ImageScale GUI application is spread over five files (see Figure 4.7, ➤ 166), amounting to nearly 500 lines of code. The image scaling code is only around 60 lines; most of the rest is GUI code.

In this section's subsections we will review the code that is most relevant to concurrent GUI programming and some of the other code to provide sufficient context for understanding.

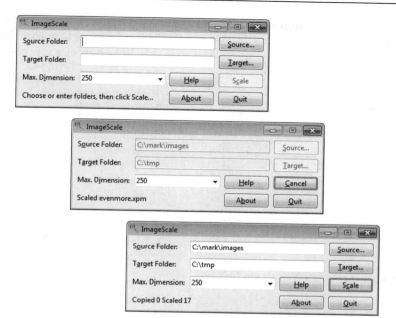

Figure 4.5 *The ImageScale application before, during, and after scaling some images*

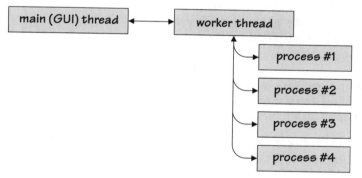

Figure 4.6 *The ImageScale application's concurrency model (arrows indicate communication)*

4.3.1. Creating the GUI

In this subsection we will review the most important code relating to the creation of the GUI and the GUI's concurrency support, quoting from the image-scale/imagescale.pyw and imagescale/Main.py files.

```
import tkinter as tk
import tkinter.ttk as ttk
import tkinter.filedialog as filedialog
import tkinter.messagebox as messagebox
```

These are the GUI-related imports in the `Main.py` module. Some Tkinter users import using `from tkinter import *`, but we prefer these imports both to keep the GUI names in their own namespaces and to make those namespaces convenient —hence `tk` rather than `tkinter`.

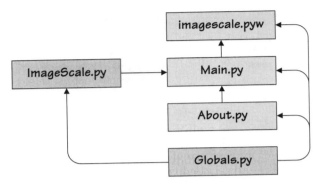

Figure 4.7 *The ImageScale application's files in context (arrows indicate imports)*

```
def main():
    application = tk.Tk()
    application.withdraw() # hide until ready to show
    window = Main.Window(application)
    application.protocol("WM_DELETE_WINDOW", window.close)
    application.deiconify() # show
    application.mainloop()
```

This is the application's entry point in `imagescale.pyw`. The actual function has some additional code that isn't shown, concerned with user preferences and setting the application's icon.

The key points to note here are that we must always create a top-level, normally invisible `tkinter.Tk` object (the ultimate parent). Then we create an instance of a window (in this case a custom `tkinter.ttk.Frame` subclass), and finally, we start off the Tkinter event loop.

To avoid flicker or the appearance of an incomplete window, we hide the application as soon as it is created (so the user never sees it at this point), and only when the window has been fully created do we show it.

The `tkinter.Tk.protocol()` call is used to tell Tkinter that if the user clicks the window's ✕ close button, the custom `Main.Window.close()` method should be called.* This method is discussed later (§4.3.4, ➤ 177).

---

* On OS X, the close button is usually a circular red button, with a black dot in the center if the application has unsaved changes.

GUI programs have a similar processing structure to some server programs, in that once started, they simply wait for events to occur, to which they then respond. In a server, the events might be network connections and communications, but in a GUI application, the events are either user-generated (such as key presses and mouse clicks) or system-generated (such as a timer timing out or a message saying that the window has been shown; for example, after another application's window that was on top of it is moved or closed). The GUI event loop is illustrated in Figure 4.8. We saw examples of event handling in Chapter 3 (§3.1, 74 ◀.)

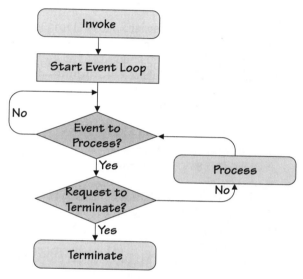

Figure 4.8 *A classic GUI event loop*

```
PAD = "0.75m"
WORKING, CANCELED, TERMINATING, IDLE = ("WORKING", "CANCELED",
        "TERMINATING", "IDLE")
class Canceled(Exception): pass
```

Here are some of the constants that are imported by ImageScale's GUI modules using from Globals import *. The PAD is a padding distance of 0.75 mm used for laying out the widgets (and for which the code isn't shown). The other constants are just enumerations identifying what state the application is in: WORKING, CANCELED, TERMINATING, or IDLE. We will see how the Canceled exception is used later on.

```
class Window(ttk.Frame):
    def __init__(self, master):
```

```
        super().__init__(master, padding=PAD)
        self.create_variables()
        self.create_ui()
        self.sourceEntry.focus()
```

When a `Window` is created, it must call its base class's `__init__()` method. Here, we also create the variables that the program will use and the user interface itself. At the end, we give the keyboard focus to the text entry box for the source directory. This means that the user can type in the directory immediately, or they could, of course, click the Source button to invoke a directory chooser dialog, and set it that way.

We won't show the `create_ui()` method, nor the `create_widgets()`, `layout_widgets()`, and `create_bindings()` methods that it calls, since they are concerned only with creating the GUI and have nothing to do with concurrent programming. (Of course, we will see examples of creating GUIs in Chapter 7 when we introduce Tkinter programming.)

```
    def create_variables(self):
        self.sourceText = tk.StringVar()
        self.targetText = tk.StringVar()
        self.statusText = tk.StringVar()
        self.statusText.set("Choose or enter folders, then click Scale...")
        self.dimensionText = tk.StringVar()
        self.total = self.copied = self.scaled = 0
        self.worker = None
        self.state = multiprocessing.Manager().Value("i", IDLE)
```

We have shown only the most relevant lines of this method. The `tkinter.String-Var` variables hold strings that are associated with user interface widgets. The total, copied, and scaled variables are used to keep counts. The worker, initially None, is set to be a second thread once the user requests some processing to be done.

If the user cancels (i.e., by clicking the Cancel button), as we will see later, the `scale_or_cancel()` method is invoked. This method sets the application's state (which can be WORKING, CANCELED, TERMINATING, or IDLE). Similarly, if the user quits the application (i.e., by clicking the Quit button), the `close()` method is called. Naturally, if the user cancels the scaling or terminates the application in the middle of scaling, we want to respond as quickly as possible. This means changing the Cancel button's text to Canceling... and disabling the button, and stopping the worker thread's processes from doing any more work. Once work has stopped, the Scale button must be reenabled. This means that both threads and all the worker processes must be able to regularly check the application's state to see if the user has canceled or quit.

One way to make the application's state accessible would be to use a state variable and a lock. But this would mean that we would have to acquire the lock before every access to the state variable and then release the lock. This isn't difficult using a context manager, but it is easy to forget to use the lock. Fortunately, the multiprocessing module provides the multiprocessing.Value class, which can hold a single value of a specific type that can be safely accessed because it does its own locking (just like the thread-safe queues do). To create a Value, we must pass it a type identifier—here, we have used "i" to signify an int—and an initial value, in this case the IDLE constant since the application begins in the IDLE state.

One point to notice is that instead of creating a multiprocessing.Value directly, we created a multiprocessing.Manager and got that to create a Value for us. This is essential for the correct working of the Value. (If we had more than one Value or Array, we would create a multiprocessing.Manager instance and use it for each one, but there was no need in this example.)

```python
def create_bindings(self):
    if not TkUtil.mac():
        self.master.bind("<Alt-a>", lambda *args:
                self.targetEntry.focus())
        self.master.bind("<Alt-b>", self.about)
        self.master.bind("<Alt-c>", self.scale_or_cancel)
        ...
    self.sourceEntry.bind("<KeyRelease>", self.update_ui)
    self.targetEntry.bind("<KeyRelease>", self.update_ui)
    self.master.bind("<Return>", self.scale_or_cancel)
```

When we create a tkinter.ttk.Button, we can associate a command (i.e., a function or method) that Tkinter should execute when the button is clicked. This has been done in the create_widgets() method (which isn't shown). We also want to provide support for keyboard users. So, for example, if the user clicks the Scale button, or—on non-OS X platforms—presses Alt+C or Enter, the scale_or_cancel() method will be invoked.

When the application starts up, the Scale button is initially disabled since there is no source or target folder. But once these folders have been set—either typed in or set via a directory chooser dialog invoked by the Source and Target buttons—the Scale button must be enabled. To achieve this, we have an update_ui() method that enables or disables widgets depending on the situation, and we call this method whenever the user types in the source or target text entry boxes.

The TkUtil module is provided with the book's examples. It contains various utility functions—such as TkUtil.mac(), which reports whether the operating system is OS X—plus generic support for about boxes and modal dialogs, and some other helpful functionality.*

```
def update_ui(self, *args):
    guiState = self.state.value
    if guiState == WORKING:
        text = "Cancel"
        underline = 0 if not TkUtil.mac() else -1
        state = "!" + tk.DISABLED
    elif guiState in {CANCELED, TERMINATING}:
        text = "Canceling..."
        underline = -1
        state = tk.DISABLED
    elif guiState == IDLE:
        text = "Scale"
        underline = 1 if not TkUtil.mac() else -1
        state = ("!" + tk.DISABLED if self.sourceText.get() and
                 self.targetText.get() else tk.DISABLED)
    self.scaleButton.state((state,))
    self.scaleButton.config(text=text, underline=underline)
    state = tk.DISABLED if guiState != IDLE else "!" + tk.DISABLED
    for widget in (self.sourceEntry, self.sourceButton,
            self.targetEntry, self.targetButton):
        widget.state((state,))
    self.master.update() # Make sure the GUI refreshes
```

This method is called whenever a change occurs that might affect the user interface. It could be invoked directly or in response to an event—a key press or button click that has been bound to it—in which case one or more additional arguments are passed, which we ignore.

We begin by retrieving the GUI's state (WORKING, CANCELED, TERMINATING, or IDLE). Instead of creating a variable, we could have used self.state.value directly in each if statement, but under the hood this must lock, so we are better off calling it once to minimize the amount of time it is locked. It doesn't matter if the state changes during the course of this method's execution, because such a change would result in this method being reinvoked anyway.

If the application is working, then we want the scale button's text to be Cancel (since we are using this button as a start and a stop button), and to enable it. On most platforms, an underlined letter indicates a keyboard accelerator (e.g., the Cancel button can be invoked by pressing Alt+C), but this functionality

---

* Tkinter—or rather, the underlying Tcl/Tk 8.5—does account for some of the cross-platform differences between Linux, OS X, and Windows. However, we are still left to handle many of the differences—especially for OS X—ourselves.

isn't supported on OS X, so on that platform we set underlining off by using an invalid index position.

Once we know the application's state, we update the scale button's text and underline, and enable or disable some of the widgets as appropriate. And at the end, we call the update() method to force Tkinter to repaint the window to reflect any changes that we have made.

```
def scale_or_cancel(self, event=None):
    if self.scaleButton.instate((tk.DISABLED,)):
        return
    if self.scaleButton.cget("text") == "Cancel":
        self.state.value = CANCELED
        self.update_ui()
    else:
        self.state.value = WORKING
        self.update_ui()
        self.scale()
```

The scale button is used to start scaling, or to cancel scaling since we change its text depending on the application's state. If the user presses Alt+C (on non-OS X platforms) or Enter, or clicks the Scale or Cancel button (i.e., the scale button), this method is called.

If the button is disabled, we safely do nothing and return. (A disabled button cannot be clicked, of course, but the user could still invoke this method if they used a keyboard accelerator such as Alt+C.)

If the button is enabled and its text is Cancel, we change the application's state to CANCELED and update the user interface. In particular, the scale button will be disabled and its text changed to Canceling.... As we will see, during processing we regularly check to see if the application's state has changed, so we will soon detect the cancellation and stop any further processing. When the cancel is complete, the scale button will be enabled and have its text set to Scale. Figure 4.5 (165 ◄) shows the application before, during, and after scaling some images. Figure 4.9 (► 172) shows the application before, during, and after canceling.

If the button's text is Scale, we set the state to WORKING, update the user interface (so now the button's text is Cancel), and start scaling.

```
def scale(self):
    self.total = self.copied = self.scaled = 0
    self.configure(cursor="watch")
    self.statusText.set("Scaling...")
    self.master.update() # Make sure the GUI refreshes
    target = self.targetText.get()
    if not os.path.exists(target):
```

```
        os.makedirs(target)
    self.worker = threading.Thread(target=ImageScale.scale, args=(
            int(self.dimensionText.get()), self.sourceText.get(),
            target, self.report_progress, self.state,
            self.when_finished))
    self.worker.daemon = True
    self.worker.start() # returns immediately
```

We begin by setting all the counts to zero and changing the application's cursor to be a "busy" indicator. Then we update the status label and refresh the GUI so that the user can see that scaling has begun. Next, we create the target directory if it doesn't already exist, including any missing intermediate directories.

With everything prepared, we now create a new worker thread. (Any previous worker thread is no longer referenced so is available for garbage collection.) We create the worker thread using the threading.Thread() function, passing it the function we want it to execute in the thread and the arguments to pass to the function. The arguments are the maximum dimension of the scaled images; the source and target directories; a callable (in this case the bound self .report_progress() method) to be called when each job is done; the application's state Value so that worker processes can regularly check to see if the user has canceled; and a callable (here, the bound self.when_finished() method) to call when processing has finished (or been canceled).

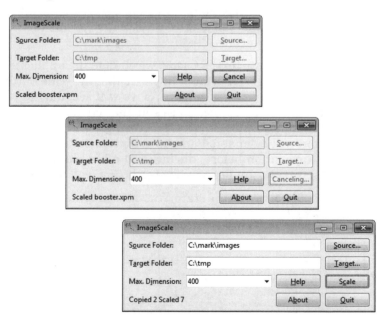

Figure 4.9 *The ImageScale application before, during, and after canceling*

Once the thread has been created, we make it a dæmon to ensure that it is cleanly terminated if the user quits the application, and we start it running.

As we will see, the worker thread itself does almost no work so as to give the GUI thread as much time on the core they share as possible. The `ImageScale.scale()` function delegates all the worker's work to multiple processes to execute on other cores (on a multi-core machine) and leave the GUI responsive (although with this architecture the GUI is still responsive, even on a single-core machine, because the GUI thread still gets as much CPU time as the worker thread).

4.3.2. The ImageScale Worker Module

We have separated out the functions called by the worker thread into their own module, `imagescale/ImageScale.py`, from which this subsection's code quotes are taken. This is not just a matter of organizational convenience but a necessity, since we want these functions to be usable by the `multiprocessing` module, and this means that they must be importable and any module data must be pickleable. Modules that contain GUI widgets or widget subclasses may not—and certainly should not—be imported in this way, since doing so can confuse the windowing system.

The module has three functions, the first of which, `ImageScale.scale()`, is the one executed by the worker thread.

```
def scale(size, source, target, report_progress, state, when_finished):
    futures = set()
    with concurrent.futures.ProcessPoolExecutor(
            max_workers=multiprocessing.cpu_count()) as executor:
        for sourceImage, targetImage in get_jobs(source, target):
            future = executor.submit(scale_one, size, sourceImage,
                    targetImage, state)
            future.add_done_callback(report_progress)
            futures.add(future)
            if state.value in {CANCELED, TERMINATING}:
                executor.shutdown()
                for future in futures:
                    future.cancel()
                break
        concurrent.futures.wait(futures) # Keep working until finished
    if state.value != TERMINATING:
        when_finished()
```

This function is executed by the `self.worker` thread created in the `Main.Window.scale()` method. It uses a process pool (i.e., multiprocessing rather than multithreading) of processes to do the actual work. This ensures that the worker thread only has to call this function, while all the actual work is delegated to separate processes.

For each source and target image retrieved from the ImageScale.get_jobs() function, a future is created to execute the ImageScale.scale_one() function with the maximum dimension (size), the source and the target images, and the application's state Value.

In the previous section, we waited for futures to finish using the concurrent.futures.as_completed() function, but here we add a callback function to each future (the Main.Window.report_progress() method) and use concurrent.futures.wait() instead.

After each future is added we check to see if the user has canceled or quit, and if they have we shut down the process pool and cancel all the futures. By default, the concurrent.futures.Executor.shutdown() function returns immediately and will only take effect once all the futures are finished or canceled.

Once all the futures have been created, this function blocks (the worker thread, not the GUI thread) at the concurrent.futures.wait() call. This means that if the user cancels after the futures have been created, we must now check for cancellation when executing each future's callable (i.e., inside the ImageScale.scale_one() function).

Once the processing has been finished or canceled, and so long as we aren't quitting, we call the when_finished() callback that was passed in. Once the end of the scale() method is reached, the thread is finished.

```
def get_jobs(source, target):
    for name in os.listdir(source):
        yield os.path.join(source, name), os.path.join(target, name)
```

This little generator function yields 2-tuples of source and target image names with full paths.

```
Result = collections.namedtuple("Result", "name copied scaled")

def scale_one(size, sourceImage, targetImage, state):
    if state.value in {CANCELED, TERMINATING}:
        raise Canceled()
    oldImage = Image.Image.from_file(sourceImage)
    if state.value in {CANCELED, TERMINATING}:
        raise Canceled()
    if oldImage.width <= size and oldImage.height <= size:
        oldImage.save(targetImage)
        return Result(targetImage, 1, 0)
    else:
        scale = min(size / oldImage.width, size / oldImage.height)
```

```
    newImage = oldImage.scale(scale)
    if state.value in {CANCELED, TERMINATING}:
        raise Canceled()
    newImage.save(targetImage)
    return Result(targetImage, 0, 1)
```

This is the function that does the actual scaling (or copying); it uses the cyImage module (see §5.3, ➤ 198) or falls back to the Image module (see §3.12, 124 ◄). For each job, it returns a Result named tuple, or it raises the custom Canceled exception if the user has canceled or quit.

If the user cancels or quits in the middle of loading, scaling, or saving, the function won't stop until the loading, scaling, or saving has finished. This means that when the user cancels or quits, they might have to wait for *n* images to complete loading, scaling, or saving, where *n* is the number of processes in the process pool, before the cancellation will take effect. Checking for cancellation or termination before each expensive non-cancelable computation (loading the source image, scaling, saving) is the best we can do to make the application as responsive as possible.

Whenever a result is returned (or a Canceled exception raised), the associated future finishes. And because we associated a callable with each future, that callable is called, which in this case is the Main.Window.report_progress() method.

4.3.3. How the GUI Handles Progress

In this subsection, we will review the GUI methods that report progress to the user. These methods are in imagescale/Main.py.

Since we have multiple processes executing futures, it is possible that two or more might call report_progress() at the same time. In fact, this should never happen, because the callable associated with a future is called in the thread in which the association was created—in this case, the worker thread—and since we have only one such thread, in theory the method cannot be called more than once at the same time. However, this is an implementation detail, and as such, it would be poor practice to rely on it. So, much as we want to do high-level concurrency and avoid mid-level features like locks, in this case we have no real choice. Therefore, we have created a lock to ensure that the report_progress() method's work is always serialized.

```
ReportLock = threading.Lock()
```

The lock is in Main.py, and it is used only in a single method.

```
def report_progress(self, future):
    if self.state.value in {CANCELED, TERMINATING}:
        return
    with ReportLock:    # Serializes calls to Window.report_progress()
        self.total += 1 # and accesses to self.total, etc.
        if future.exception() is None:
            result = future.result()
            self.copied += result.copied
            self.scaled += result.scaled
            name = os.path.basename(result.name)
            self.statusText.set("{} {}".format(
                    "Copied" if result.copied else "Scaled", name))
            self.master.update() # Make sure the GUI refreshes
```

This method is called whenever a future finishes, whether normally or by raising an exception. If the user has canceled, we bail out, since the user interface will be updated by the when_finished() method anyway. And if the user has quit, there is no point in updating the user interface, since it will go away when the application terminates.

Most of the method's body is serialized by a lock, so if two or more futures finish at the same time, only one will get to execute this part of the method at any one time; the others will be blocked until the lock is released. (We don't have to worry about the self.state Value, since it is a synchronized type.) Since we are in the context of a lock, we want to do as little work as possible to minimize any blocking.

We begin by incrementing the total count of jobs. If the future raised an exception (e.g., Canceled), we do nothing more. Otherwise, we increment the copied and scaled counts (by 0 and 1 or 1 and 0) and update the GUI's status label. It is very important that we do the GUI updates in the context of the lock. This is to avoid the risk of the undefined behavior that might occur if two or more GUI updates are made concurrently.

```
def when_finished(self):
    self.state.value = IDLE
    self.configure(cursor="arrow")
    self.update_ui()
    result = "Copied {} Scaled {}".format(self.copied, self.scaled)
    difference = self.total - (self.copied + self.scaled)
    if difference: # This will kick in if the user canceled
        result += " Skipped {}".format(difference)
    self.statusText.set(result)
    self.master.update() # Make sure the GUI refreshes
```

This method is called by the worker thread once it has finished, whether by completing the processing or due to cancellation, but not in the case of termination. Since this method is called only when the worker and its processes are finished, there is no need to use the ReportLock. The method sets the application's state back to IDLE, restores the normal arrow cursor, and sets the status label's text to show the work done and whether the user canceled.

4.3.4. How the GUI Handles Termination

Terminating a concurrent GUI program isn't simply a matter of quitting. We must first attempt to stop any worker threads—and especially processes—so that we terminate cleanly and don't leave any zombie processes that tie up resources (e.g., memory).

We handle termination in the imagescale/Main.py module's close() method.

```
def close(self, event=None):
    ...
    if self.worker is not None and self.worker.is_alive():
        self.state.value = TERMINATING
        self.update_ui()
        self.worker.join() # Wait for worker to finish
    self.quit()
```

If the user clicks the Quit button or the window's ✕ close button (or presses Alt+Q on non-OS X platforms), this method is called. It saves some user settings (not shown) and then checks to see if the worker thread is still working (i.e., if the user has quit while scaling is in progress). If this is the case, the method sets the application's state to TERMINATING and updates the user interface so that the user can see that the processing is being canceled. The change of state will be detected by the worker thread's processes (since they regularly check the state Value), and as soon as they detect termination, they stop work. The call to threading.Thread.join() blocks until the worker thread (and its processes) are finished. If we didn't wait, we might leave some zombie processes behind (i.e., processes that consume memory but are not doing anything useful). At the end, we call tkinter.ttk.Frame.quit() to terminate the application.

The ImageScale application shows that it is possible to combine multithreading and multiprocessing to produce a GUI application that does its work concurrently, while still remaining responsive to the user. Furthermore, the application's architecture supports progress reporting and cancelation.

Writing concurrent programs using high-level concurrency features such as thread-safe queues and futures—and avoiding mid-level features such as locks —is much easier than using low- and mid-level features. Nonetheless, we must be careful to make sure that our concurrent program actually outperforms a nonconcurrent equivalent. For example, in Python, we should avoid using multithreading for CPU-bound processing.

We must also be sure that we don't accidentally mutable shared data. So, we must always pass immutable data (e.g., numbers and strings), or pass mutable data that is only ever read (e.g., it was written before the concurrency began), or deep copy mutable data. However, as the ImageScale case study showed, sometimes we really do need to share data. Fortunately, by using a managed `multiprocessing.Value` (or `multiprocessing.Array`), we are able to do this without explicit locking. Alternatively, we can create our own thread-safe classes. We will see an example of this in Chapter 6 (§6.2.1.1, ➤ 221).

5 Extending Python

Python is fast enough for the vast majority of programs. And in those cases where it isn't, we can often achieve sufficient speedups by using concurrency, as we saw in the previous chapter. Sometimes, though, we really do need to do faster processing. There are three key ways we can make our Python programs run faster: we can use PyPy (pypy.org), which has a built-in JIT (Just in Time compiler); we can use C or C++ code for time-critical processing; or we can compile our Python (or Cython) code into C using Cython.★

Once PyPy is installed, we can execute our Python programs using the PyPy interpreter rather than the standard CPython interpreter. This will give us a significant speedup for long-running programs, since the cost of the JIT compiling will be outweighed by the reduced runtime, but might produce slower execution for programs with very short runtimes.

To use C or C++, whether our own code or third-party libraries, we must make the code available to our Python program so that it can benefit from the C or C++ code's fast execution. For those who want to write their own C or C++ code, a sensible approach is to make direct use of the Python C interface (docs.python.org/3/extending). For those who want to make use of existing C or C++ code, there are several possible approaches. One option is to use a wrapper that will take the C or C++ and produce a Python interface for it. Two popular tools for this are SWIG (www.swig.org) and SIP (www.riverbank-computing.co.uk/software/sip). Another option for C++ is to use boost::python (www.boost.org/libs/python/doc/). A newer entry into this field is CFFI (C Foreign Function Interface for Python), which despite its newness is being used by the well-established PyPy (bitbucket.org/cffi/cffi).

★New Python compilers are becoming available; for example, Numba (numba.pydata.org) and Nuitka (nuitka.net).

> ### Extending Python on OS X and Windows
>
> Although the examples in this chapter have been tested only on Linux, they should all work fine on both OS X and Windows. (For many ctypes and Cython programmers, these are their primary development platforms.) However, some platform-specific tweaks may be necessary. This is because whereas most Linux systems use a packaged GCC compiler and system-wide libraries with the appropriate word size for the machine they are running on, the situation for OS X and Windows systems is usually more complicated, or at least a bit different.
>
> On OS X and Windows, it is generally necessary to match the compiler and word size (32- or 64-bit) used to build Python with that used for any external shared libraries (.dylib or .DLL files) or to build Cython code. On OS X, the compiler might be GCC but nowadays is most likely to be Clang; on Windows it could be some form of GCC or a commercial compiler such as those sold by Microsoft. Furthermore, OS X and Windows often have shared libraries in application directories rather than system wide, and header files may need to be obtained separately. So, rather than giving lots of platform- and compiler-specific configuration information (which might quickly become outdated with new compiler and operating system versions), we focus instead on how to *use* ctypes and Cython, leaving readers on non-Linux systems to determine their own system's particular requirements when they are ready to use these technologies.

All of the possibilities described so far are worth exploring, but in this chapter we will focus on two other technologies: the ctypes package that comes as part of Python's standard library (docs.python.org/3/library/ctypes.html) and Cython (cython.org). Both of these can be used to provide Python interfaces for our own or for third-party C and C++ code, and Cython can also be used to compile both Python and Cython code into C to improve its performance—sometimes with dramatic results.

5.1. Accessing C Libraries with ctypes

The standard library's ctypes package provides access to our own or third-party functionality written in C or C++ (or indeed any compiled language that uses the C calling convention) and that has been compiled into a stand-alone shared library (.so on Linux, .dylib on OS X, or .DLL on Windows).

For this section, and for the following section's first subsection (§5.2.1, ➤ 188), we will create a module that provides Python access to some C functions in a shared library. The library we will use is libhyphen.so, or, on some systems, libhyphen.uno.so. (See the "Extending Python on OS X and Windows" sidebar.) This library usually comes with OpenOffice.org or LibreOffice and provides a function that, when given a word, produces a copy of the word with hyphens inserted wherever they are valid. Although the function does what sounds like a simple task, the function's signature is quite complicated (which makes it ideal as a ctypes example). And, in fact, there are three functions that we will need to use: one for loading in a hyphenation dictionary, one for doing the hyphenation, and one for freeing up resources when we have finished.

A typical pattern of use for ctypes is to load the library into memory, take references to the functions we want to use, then call the functions as required. The Hyphenate1.py module follows this pattern. First, let's see how the module is used. Here is an interactive session done at a Python prompt (e.g., in IDLE):

```
>>> import os
>>> import Hyphenate1 as Hyphenate
>>>
>>> # Locate your hyph*.dic files
>>> path = "/usr/share/hyph_dic"
>>> if not os.path.exists(path): path = os.path.dirname(__file__)
>>> usHyphDic = os.path.join(path, "hyph_en_US.dic")
>>> deHyphDic = os.path.join(path, "hyph_de_DE.dic")
>>>
>>> # Create wrappers so you don't have to keep specifying the dictionary
>>> hyphenate = lambda word: Hyphenate.hyphenate(word, usHyphDic)
>>> hyphenate_de = lambda word: Hyphenate.hyphenate(word, deHyphDic)
>>>
>>> # Use your wrappers
>>> print(hyphenate("extraordinary"))
ex-traor-di-nary
>>> print(hyphenate_de("außergewöhnlich"))
außerge-wöhn-lich
```

The only function we use outside the module is Hyphenate1.hyphenate(), which uses the library's hyphenation function. Inside the module there are a couple of private functions that access another couple of functions from the library. Incidentally, the hyphenation dictionaries are in the format used by the open-source TeX typesetting system.

All the code is in the Hyphenate1.py module. The three functions we need from the library are:

```
HyphenDict *hnj_hyphen_load(const char *filename);

void hnj_hyphen_free(HyphenDict *hdict);

int hnj_hyphen_hyphenate2(HyphenDict *hdict, const char *word,
    int word_size, char *hyphens, char *hyphenated_word, char ***rep,
    int **pos, int **cut);
```

These signatures are taken from the hyphen.h header file. A * in C and C++ signifies a *pointer*. A pointer holds the memory address of a block of memory; that is, of a contiguous block of bytes. The block may be as small as a single byte but could be of any size; for example, 8 bytes for a 64-bit integer. Strings typically take between 1 and 4 bytes per character (depending on the in-memory encoding) plus some fixed overhead.

The first function, hnj_hyphen_load(), takes a filename passed as a pointer to a block of chars (bytes). This file must be a hyphenation dictionary in TEX format. The hnj_hyphen_load() function returns a pointer to a HyphenDict struct—a complex aggregate object (rather like a Python class instance). Fortunately, we don't need to know anything about the internals of a HyphenDict, since we only ever need to pass around pointers to them.

In C, functions that accept *C-strings*—that is, pointers to blocks of characters or bytes—normally take one of two approaches: either they require just a pointer, in which case they expect the last byte to be 0x00 ('\0') (that is, for the C-string to be null-terminated), or they take a pointer and a byte count. The hnj_hyphen_load() function takes only a pointer, so the given C-string must be null terminated. As we will see, if the ctypes.create_string_buffer() function is passed a str, it returns an equivalent null-terminated C-string.

For every hyphenation dictionary that we load, we must eventually free it. (If we don't do this, the hyphenation library will stay in memory needlessly.) The second function, hnj_hyphen_free(), takes a HyphenDict pointer and frees the resources associated with it. The function has no return value. Once freed, such a pointer must never be reused, just as we would never use a variable after it has been deleted with del in Python.

The third function, hnj_hyphen_hyphenate2(), is the one that performs the hyphenation service. The hdict argument is a pointer to a HyphenDict that has been returned by the hnj_hyphen_load() function (and that has not yet been freed with the hnj_hyphen_free() function). The word is the word we want to hyphenate provided as a pointer to a block of UTF-8-encoded bytes. The word_size is the number of bytes in the block. The hyphens is a pointer to a block of bytes that we don't want to use, but we must still pass a valid pointer for it for the function to work correctly. The hyphenated_word is a pointer to a block of bytes long enough to hold the original UTF-8-encoded word with hyphens inserted. (The library actually inserts = characters as hyphens.) Initially, this block should hold all 0x00 bytes. The rep is a pointer to a pointer to a pointer to a block of bytes; we don't need this, but we must still pass a valid pointer for it. Similarly, pos and cut are pointers to pointers to ints that we aren't interested in, but we must still pass valid pointers for them. The function's return value is a Boolean flag, with 1 signifying failure and 0 signifying success.

Now that we know what we want to wrap, we will review the Hyphenate1.py module's code (as usual, omitting the imports), starting with finding and loading the hyphenation shared library.

```
class Error(Exception): pass

_libraryName = ctypes.util.find_library("hyphen")
if _libraryName is None:
    _libraryName = ctypes.util.find_library("hyphen.uno")
if _libraryName is None:
    raise Error("cannot find hyphenation library")

_LibHyphen = ctypes.CDLL(_libraryName)
```

We begin by creating an exception class, Hyphenate1.Error, so that users of our module can distinguish between module-specific exceptions and more general ones like ValueError. The ctypes.util.find_library() function looks for a shared library. On Linux it will prefix the given name with lib and add an extension of .so, so the first call will look for libhyphen.so in various standard locations. On OS X, it will look for hyphen.dylib, and on Windows, for hyphen.dll. This library is sometimes called libhyphen.uno.so, so we search for this if it wasn't found under the original name. And if we can't find it, we give up by raising an exception.

If the library is found, we load it into memory using the ctypes.CDLL() function and set the private _LibHyphen variable to refer to it. For those wanting to write Windows-only programs that access Windows-specific interfaces, the ctypes.OleDLL() and ctypes.WinDLL() functions can be used to load Windows API libraries.

Once the library is loaded, we can create Python wrappers for the library functions we are interested in. A common pattern for this is to assign a library function to a Python variable, and then specify the types of the arguments (as a list of ctypes types) and the return type (as a single ctypes type) that the function uses.

If we specify the wrong number or types of arguments, or the wrong return type, our program will crash! The CFFI package (bitbucket.org/cffi/cffi) is more robust in this respect and also works much better with the PyPy interpreter (pypy.org) than ctypes.

```
_load = _LibHyphen.hnj_hyphen_load
_load.argtypes = [ctypes.c_char_p]   # const char *filename
_load.restype = ctypes.c_void_p      # HyphenDict *
```

Here, we have created a private module function, _load(), that when called will actually call the underlying hyphenation library's hnj_hyphen_load() function. Once we have a reference to the library function, we must specify its argument

and return types. Here, there is just one argument (of C type const char *),
which we can represent directly with ctypes.c_char_p ("C character pointer").
The function returns a pointer to a HyphenDict struct. One way to handle this
would be to create a class that inherits ctypes.Structure to represent the type.
However, since we only ever have to pass this pointer around and never access
what it points to ourselves, we can simply declare that the function returns a
ctypes.c_void_p ("C void pointer"), which can point to any type at all.

These three lines (in addition to finding and loading the library in the first
place) are all we need to provide a _load() method that will load a hyphenation
dictionary.

```
_unload = _LibHyphen.hnj_hyphen_free
_unload.argtypes = [ctypes.c_void_p]   # HyphenDict *hdict
_unload.restype = None
```

The code here follows the same pattern as before. The hnj_hyphen_free()
function takes a single argument, a pointer to a HyphenDict struct, but since we
only ever pass such pointers, we can safely specify a void pointer—providing we
always actually pass in a HyphenDict struct pointer. This function has no return
value; this is signified by setting its restype to None. (If we don't specify a restype,
it is assumed that the function returns an int.)

```
_int_p = ctypes.POINTER(ctypes.c_int)
_char_p_p = ctypes.POINTER(ctypes.c_char_p)

_hyphenate = _LibHyphen.hnj_hyphen_hyphenate2
_hyphenate.argtypes = [
        ctypes.c_void_p,    # HyphenDict *hdict
        ctypes.c_char_p,    # const char *word
        ctypes.c_int,       # int word_size
        ctypes.c_char_p,    # char *hyphens [not needed]
        ctypes.c_char_p,    # char *hyphenated_word
        _char_p_p,          # char ***rep   [not needed]
        _int_p,             # int **pos     [not needed]
        _int_p]             # int **cut     [not needed]
_hyphenate.restype = ctypes.c_int # int
```

This is the most complicated function we need to wrap. The hdict argument
is a pointer to a HyphenDict struct, which we specify as a C void pointer. Then
we have the word to be hyphenated, passed as a pointer to a block of bytes for
which we use a C character pointer. This is followed by the word_size, a count
of the bytes that we specify as an integer (ctypes.c_int). Next, we have the
hyphens buffer that we don't need, then the hyphenated_word, again specified as
a C character pointer. There is no built-in ctypes type for a pointer to a pointer
to a character (byte), so we have created our own type, _char_p_p, specifying it

as a pointer to a C character pointer. We have done a similar thing for the two pointers to pointer to integers.

Strictly speaking, we don't have to specify a `restype`, since the function's return type is an integer, but we prefer to be explicit.

We have created private wrapper functions for the hyphenation library's functions, since we want to insulate users of our module from the low-level details. To this end, we will provide a single public function, `hyphenate()`, which will accept a word to be hyphenated, a hyphenation dictionary to use, and the hyphenation character to use. For efficiency, we will only ever load any particular hyphenation dictionary once. And, of course, we will make sure that all hyphenation dictionaries that have been loaded are freed at program termination.

```
def hyphenate(word, filename, hyphen="-"):
    originalWord = word
    hdict = _get_hdict(filename)
    word = word.encode("utf-8")
    word_size = ctypes.c_int(len(word))
    word = ctypes.create_string_buffer(word)
    hyphens = ctypes.create_string_buffer(len(word) + 5)
    hyphenated_word = ctypes.create_string_buffer(len(word) * 2)
    rep = _char_p_p(ctypes.c_char_p(None))
    pos = _int_p(ctypes.c_int(0))
    cut = _int_p(ctypes.c_int(0))
    if _hyphenate(hdict, word, word_size, hyphens, hyphenated_word, rep,
            pos, cut):
        raise Error("hyphenation failed for '{}'".format(originalWord))
    return hyphenated_word.value.decode("utf-8").replace("=", hyphen)
```

The function begins by storing a reference to the word passed in to be hyphenated so that we can use it in an error message, if necessary. Then, we get the hyphenation dictionary: the private `_get_hdict()` function returns a pointer to the `HyphenDict` struct that corresponds to the given filename. If the dictionary has already been loaded, the pointer created at that time is returned; otherwise, the dictionary is loaded for the first and only time, its pointer stored for later use, and returned.

The word must be passed to the hyphenation function as a block of UTF-8-encoded bytes, which is easily achieved using the `str.encode()` method. We also need to pass the number of bytes the word occupies: we compute this and convert the Python `int` into a C int. We can't pass a raw Python `bytes` object to a C function, so we create a string buffer (really a block of C `chars`) that contains the word's bytes. The `ctypes.create_string_buffer()` creates a block of C `chars` based on a bytes object or of the given size. Although we don't want to use the hyphens argument, we must still properly prepare it, and the documentation says that it must be a pointer to a block of C chars whose length is five more than the length of the word (in bytes). So, we create a suitable block of chars. The hyphenated word will be put into a block of C chars that is passed to the function, so we must make a block of sufficient size. The documentation recommends a size twice that of the word's size.

We don't want to use the rep, pos, or cut arguments, but we must pass correct values for them or the function won't work. The rep is a pointer to a pointer to a pointer to a block of C chars, so we have created a pointer to an empty block (a null pointer in C, i.e., a pointer that points to nothing) and then assigned a pointer to a pointer to this pointer to the rep variable. For the pos and cut arguments, we have created pointers to pointers to integers of value 0.

Once all the arguments have been set up, we call the private _hyphenate() function (under the hood, we are really calling the hyphenation library's hnj_hyphen_hyphenate2() function) and raise an error if the function returns a nonzero (i.e., failure) result. Otherwise, we extract the raw bytes from the hyphenated word using the value property (which returns a null-terminated bytes, i.e., one whose last byte is 0x00). Then we decode the bytes using the UTF-8 encoding into a str and replace the hyphenation library's = hyphens with the user's preferred hyphen (which defaults to -). This string is then returned as the hyphenate() function's result.

Note that for C functions that use char * and sizes rather than null-terminated strings, we can access the bytes using the raw property rather than the value property.

```
_hdictForFilename = {}

def _get_hdict(filename):
    if filename not in _hdictForFilename:
        hdict = _load(ctypes.create_string_buffer(
                filename.encode("utf-8")))
        if hdict is None:
            raise Error("failed to load '{}'".format(filename))
        _hdictForFilename[filename] = hdict
    hdict = _hdictForFilename.get(filename)
    if hdict is None:
        raise Error("failed to load '{}'".format(filename))
    return hdict
```

This private helper function returns a pointer to a HyphenDict struct, reusing pointers to dictionaries that have already been loaded.

If the filename is not in the _hdictForFilename dict, it is a new hyphenation dictionary and must be loaded. Because the filename is passed as a C const char * (i.e., is immutable), we can create and pass it as a ctypes string buffer directly. If the _load() function returns None the loading failed, and we report this by raising an exception. Otherwise, we store the pointer for later use.

At the end, whether or not we loaded the hyphenation dictionary on this occasion, we try to retrieve the corresponding pointer to it, which we then return.

```
def _cleanup():
    for hyphens in _hdictForFilename.values():
        _unload(hyphens)


atexit.register(_cleanup)
```

The _hdictForFilename dict holds pointers to all the hyphenation dictionaries that we have loaded as its values. We must be sure to free all these before our program terminates. We do this by creating a private _cleanup() function that calls our private _unload() function for every hyphenation dictionary pointer (and which itself calls the hyphenation library's hnj_hyphen_free() function under the hood). We don't bother to clear the _hdictForFilename dict at the end, since _cleanup() is only ever called on program termination (so the dict will be deleted anyway). We ensure that _cleanup() is called by registering it as an "at exit" function using the standard library's atexit module's register() function.

We have now reviewed all the code needed to provide a hyphenate() function in a module that accesses the hyphen library's functions. Using ctypes takes some care (e.g., setting argument types and initializing arguments) but opens up the world of C and C++ functionality to our Python programs. One practical use of ctypes is when we want to write some speed-critical code in C or C++ that we also want to be in a shared library, so that it can be used both by Python (via ctypes) and directly in our own C and C++ programs. The other main use is to access C and C++ functionality in third-party shared libraries, although in most cases we should be able to find a standard library or third-party module that already wraps the shared library we are interested in.

The ctypes module offers a lot more sophistication and functionality than we have the space to present here. And although it is harder to use than CFFI or Cython, it may prove to be more convenient, since it comes standard with Python.

5.2. Using Cython

Cython (cython.org) is described on its web site as a programming language "that makes writing C extensions for the Python language as easy as Python itself". Cython can be used in three different ways. The first way is to use it to wrap C or C++ code, just like ctypes, although arguably using Cython is easier, especially for those familiar with C or C++. The second way is to compile our Python code into fast C. This can be done in essence by changing a module's extension from `.py` to `.pyx` and compiling it. This alone should be sufficient to achieve a 2× speedup for CPU-bound code. The third way is like the second, only instead of leaving the code as is in the `.pyx` file, we *Cythonize* it; that is, we take advantage of the language extensions offered by Cython so that it compiles down to much more efficient C code. This can deliver 100× or better speedups for CPU-bound processing.

5.2.1. Accessing C Libraries with Cython

In this subsection, we will create the Hyphenate2 module, which provides exactly the same functionality as the Hyphenate1.py module created in the previous section, only this time we will use Cython rather than ctypes. The ctypes version used a single file, Hyphenate1.py, but for Cython we need to create a directory into which we will put four files.

The first file we need is Hyphenate2/setup.py. This tiny infrastructure file contains a single statement that tells Cython where to find the hyphenation library and what to build. The second file is Hyphenate2/ __init__.py. This file is an optional convenience that contains a single statement that exports the public Hyphenate2.hyphenate() function and the Hyphenate2.Error exception. The third file is Hyphenate2/chyphenate.pxd. This very small file is used to tell Cython about the hyphenation library and the functions within it we wish to access. The fourth file is Hyphenate2/Hyphenate.pyx. This is a Cython module that we will use to implement the public hyphenate() function and its private helper functions. We will review each of these files in turn.

```
distutils.core.setup(name="Hyphenate2",
        cmdclass={"build_ext": Cython.Distutils.build_ext},
        ext_modules=[distutils.extension.Extension("Hyphenate",
                ["Hyphenate.pyx"], libraries=["hyphen"])])
```

Here is the content of the Hyphenate2/setup.py file, excluding the imports. It makes use of Python's distutils package.* The name is optional. The cmdclass must be given as shown. The first string given to the Extension() is the name we want our compiled module to have (e.g., Hyphenate.so). This is followed by a list of .pyx files that contain the code to compile and, optionally, a list of external C or C++ libraries. For this example, the hyphen library is required, of course.

To build the extension, execute the following in the directory containing all the files (e.g., Hyphenate2):

---

* It is probably best to install the Python distribute package ≥ 0.6.28 or, better still, the setuptools package ≥ 0.7 (python-packaging-user-guide.readthedocs.org). A modern package tool is needed to install many third-party packages, including some of those used in this book.

```
$ cd pipeg/Hyphenate2
$ python3 setup.py build_ext --inplace
running build_ext
cythoning Hyphenate.pyx to Hyphenate.c
building 'Hyphenate' extension
creating build
creating build/temp.linux-x86_64-3.3
...
```

If we have multiple Python interpreters installed, we should give the full path to the particular one we want to use. For Python 3.1, this will produce Hyphenate.so, but for later versions a version-specific shared library will be created; for example, Hyphenate.cpython-33m.so for Python 3.3.

```
from Hyphenate2.Hyphenate import hyphenate, Error
```

This is the complete Hyphenate2/__init__.py file. We provide it as a small convenience to the user so that they can write, say, import Hyphenate2 as Hyphenate, and then call Hyphenate.hyphenate(). Otherwise, the import would be, say, import Hyphenate2.Hyphenate as Hyphenate.

```
cdef extern from "hyphen.h":
    ctypedef struct HyphenDict:
        pass

    HyphenDict *hnj_hyphen_load(char *filename)
    void hnj_hyphen_free(HyphenDict *hdict)
    int hnj_hyphen_hyphenate2(HyphenDict *hdict, char *word,
            int word_size, char *hyphens, char *hyphenated_word,
            char ***rep, int **pos, int **cut)
```

This is the Hyphenate2/chyphenate.pxd file. A .pxd file is required whenever we want to access external shared C or C++ libraries inside Cython code.

The first line declares the name of the C or C++ header file that contains the declarations of the functions and types we want to access. Then the body declares these functions and types. Cython provides a convenient way to refer to a C or C++ struct without having to declare all of its details. This is only allowed if we only ever pass pointers to the struct and never access its fields directly ourselves; this is commonly the case and certainly applies to the hyphenation library. The function declarations are essentially just copied from the C or C++ header file, although we should drop the statement-terminating semicolons from the end of each declaration.

Cython uses this .pxd file to create a bridge of C code between our compiled Cython and the external library to which the .pxd file refers.

Now that we have created the setup.py file, the __init__.py file, and the chyphen-ate.pxd file, we are ready to create the last file: Hyphenate.pyx. This file contains Cython code; that is, Python with Cython extensions. We will start with the imports and then look at each of the functions in turn.

```
import atexit
cimport chyphenate
cimport cpython.pycapsule as pycapsule
```

We need the standard library's atexit module to ensure that loaded hyphenation dictionaries are freed when the program terminates.

Cython files can import normal Python modules using import and, also, Cython .pxd files (i.e., wrappers for external C libraries) using cimport. So, here, we import chyphenate.pxd as the chyphenate module, and this provides us with the chyphenate.HyphenDict type and the three functions in the hyphenation library.

We want to create a Python dict whose keys are hyphenation dictionary file-names and whose values are pointers to chyphenate.HyphenDicts. However, Python dicts can't store pointers (they aren't a Python type). Fortunately, Cython provides us with a solution: pycapsule. This Cython module can encapsu-late a pointer in a Python object, and the encapsulating object can, of course, be stored in any Python collection. As we will see, pycapsule also provides a way of extracting the pointer from the Python object.

```
def hyphenate(str word, str filename, str hyphen="-"):
    cdef chyphenate.HyphenDict *hdict = _get_hdict(filename)
    cdef bytes bword = word.encode("utf-8")
    cdef int word_size = len(bword)
    cdef bytes hyphens = b"\x00" * (word_size + 5)
    cdef bytes hyphenated_word = b"\x00" * (word_size * 2)
    cdef char **rep = NULL
    cdef int *pos = NULL
    cdef int *cut = NULL
    cdef int failed = chyphenate.hnj_hyphen_hyphenate2(hdict, bword,
            word_size, hyphens, hyphenated_word, &rep, &pos, &cut)
    if failed:
        raise Error("hyphenation failed for '{}'".format(word))
    end = hyphenated_word.find(b"\x00")
    return hyphenated_word[:end].decode("utf-8").replace("=", hyphen)
```

This function is structurally the same as the ctypes version we created in the pre-vious section (185 ◄). The most obvious difference is that we give explicit types to all the arguments and to all the variables. This isn't *required* by Cython, but it does allow Cython to perform some optimizations to improve performance.

The hdict is a pointer to a HyphenDict struct, and bword holds the UTF-8-encoded bytes of the word we want to hyphenate. The word_size int is easily created. For the hyphens that we don't actually use, we must still create a buffer (i.e., a block of C chars) sufficiently large, and we do so very naturally by multiplying a null byte by the required size. We use the same technique to create the hyphenated_word buffer.

We don't use the rep, pos, or cut arguments, but it is essential that they are passed correctly, or the function won't work. In all three cases, we create them using C pointer syntax (i.e., cdef char **rep) using one less level of indirection (one less pointer, i.e., one less *) than is actually needed. Then, in the call to the function, we use the C address of operator (&) to pass their address, and this gives us the one extra level of indirection. We can't just pass a C null pointer (NULL) for these arguments, because all of them are expected to be non-null pointers, even if what they ultimately point to is null. Recall that, in C, NULL is a pointer that points to nothing.

With all the arguments properly initialized, we call the function that is exported by the Cython chyphenate module (in effect, from the chyphenate.pxd file). If the hyphenation fails, we raise a normal Python exception. If the hyphenation succeeds, we return the hyphenated word. To do this, we must slice the hyphenated_word buffer up to the first null byte, then decode the sliced bytes as UTF-8 into a str, and finally, replace the hyphenation library's = hyphens with the hyphen character the user specified (or the default of –).

```
_hdictForFilename = {}

cdef chyphenate.HyphenDict *_get_hdict(
        str filename) except <chyphenate.HyphenDict*>NULL:
    cdef bytes bfilename = filename.encode("utf-8")
    cdef chyphenate.HyphenDict *hdict = NULL
    if bfilename not in _hdictForFilename:
        hdict = chyphenate.hnj_hyphen_load(bfilename)
        if hdict == NULL:
            raise Error("failed to load '{}'".format(filename))
        _hdictForFilename[bfilename] = pycapsule.PyCapsule_New(
                <void*>hdict, NULL, NULL)
    capsule = _hdictForFilename.get(bfilename)
    if not pycapsule.PyCapsule_IsValid(capsule, NULL):
        raise Error("failed to load '{}'".format(filename))
    return <chyphenate.HyphenDict*>pycapsule.PyCapsule_GetPointer(capsule,
        NULL)
```

This private function is defined using cdef rather than def; this means it is a Cython function, not a Python function. After the cdef we specify the function's return type, in this case a pointer to a chyphenate.HyphenDict. Then we give the name of the function as usual, followed by its arguments, usually with their types. In this case there is just one string argument, the filename.

Since the return type is a pointer rather than a Python object (i.e., object), it would not normally be possible to report exceptions to the caller. In fact, any exception would simply result in a warning message being printed, but otherwise the exception would be ignored. But we would like this function to be able to raise Python exceptions. We have done this by specifying a return value that indicates when an exception has occurred; in this case, a null pointer to a chyphenate.HyphenDict.

The function begins by declaring a pointer to a chyphenate.HyphenDict whose value is null (i.e., it safely points to nothing). We then see if the hyphenation dictionary's filename is in the _hdictForFilename dict. If it isn't, we must load in a new hyphenation dictionary using the hyphen library's hnj_hyphen_load() function that is available via our chyphenate module. If the load succeeds, a non-null chyphenate.HyphenDict pointer is returned, and we cast this pointer to be a void pointer (which can point to anything) and create a new pycapsule.PyCapsule to store it in. The *<type>* Cython syntax is used to cast a value of one type to a different C type in Cython. For example, the Cython <int>(*x*) converts an *x* value (which must be a number or a C char) to a C int. This is similar to Python's int(*x*) syntax, except that in Python the *x* could be a Python int or float—or a str that held an integer (e.g., "123")—and returns a Python int.

The second argument to pycapsule.PyCapsule_New() is a name to give to the encapsulated pointer (as a C char *), and the third argument is a pointer to a destructor function. We don't want to set either, so we pass null pointers for both of them. We then store the encapsulated pointer in the dict with the filename as its key.

At the end, whether or not we loaded the hyphenation dictionary in this call, we try to retrieve the capsule that contains a pointer to it. We must check that the capsule contains a valid (i.e., not-null) pointer by passing the capsule and its associated name to pycapsule.PyCapsule_IsValid(). We pass null for the name, because we didn't name any of our capsules. If the capsule is valid, we extract the pointer using the pycapsule.PyCapsule_GetPointer() function—again, passing the capsule and null for its name—and cast the pointer from a void pointer back to being a chyphenate.HyphenDict pointer, which we then return.

```
def _cleanup():
    cdef chyphenate.HyphenDict *hdict = NULL
    for capsule in _hdictForFilename.values():
        if pycapsule.PyCapsule_IsValid(capsule, NULL):
            hdict = (<chyphenate.HyphenDict*>
                    pycapsule.PyCapsule_GetPointer(capsule, NULL))
            if hdict != NULL:
                chyphenate.hnj_hyphen_free(hdict)
```

```
atexit.register(_cleanup)
```

When the program terminates, all functions registered with the atexit.register() function are called. In this case, the function calls our module's private _cleanup() function. This function begins by declaring a pointer to a chyphenate.HyphenDict whose value is null. Then it iterates over all the _hdictForFilename dict's values, each of which is a capsule containing a pointer to an unnamed chyphenate.HyphenDict. For each valid capsule that has a not-null pointer, the chyphenate.hnj_hyphen_free() function is called.

The Cython wrapper for the hyphenation shared library is very similar to the ctypes version, except that it needs its own directory and three tiny supporting files. If we are only interested in providing Python access to existing C and C++ libraries, ctypes alone is sufficient, although some programmers may find Cython (or CFFI) easier to use. However, Cython also offers another facility: the ability to write Cython—that is, Python with extentions—which can be compiled into fast-executing C. We'll look at this in the next subsection.

5.2.2. Writing Cython Modules for Greater Speed

Most of the time, Python code executes as fast as we need it to, or its speed is limited by external factors (e.g., network latency) that no amount of code tweaking can work around. However, for CPU-bound processing, it is possible to get the speed of compiled C code while using Python syntax plus Cython extensions.

Before embarking on any kind of optimization, it is essential to profile the code. Most programs spend most of their execution time in a small portion of their code, so, no matter how much we optimize, if the optimization isn't in that part of the code, all the effort is in vain. Profiling lets us see exactly where the bottlenecks are and makes it easy to target our optimizations to the code that really needs them. It also makes it possible to measure the effects of our optimizations by comparing the before and after profiles.

We noted in the Image module's case study (§3.12, 124 ◀) that the smooth scaling scale() method (131 ◀) wasn't very fast. In this subsection, we will try to optimize this method.

```
Scaling using Image.scale()...
        18875915 function calls in 21.587 seconds
  ncalls  tottime  percall  cumtime  percall filename:lineno(function)
       1    0.000    0.000   21.587   21.587 <string>:1(<module>)
       1    1.441    1.441   21.587   21.587 __init__.py:305(scale)
  786432    7.335    0.000   19.187    0.000 __init__.py:333(_mean)
 3145728    6.945    0.000    8.860    0.000 __init__.py:370(argb_for_color)
  786432    1.185    0.000    1.185    0.000 __init__.py:399(color_for_argb)
       1    0.000    0.000    0.000    0.000 __init__.py:461(<lambda>)
```

```
      1    0.000    0.000    0.002    0.002 __init__.py:479(create_array)
      1    0.000    0.000    0.000    0.000 __init__.py:75(__init__)
```

This is a profile of the method (excluding built-in functions that we can't optimize) as produced by the standard library's cProfile module. (See the example's benchmark_Scale.py program.) Over 21 seconds to scale a 2 048 × 1 536 (3 145 728 pixels) color photograph certainly isn't fast, and it is easy to see where the time is going: the _mean() method and the static argb_for_color() and color_for_argb() methods.

We want to get a true speed comparison with Cython, so as a first step we copied the scale() method and its helpers (_mean(), etc.) into the Scale/Slow.py module and turned them into functions. We then profiled the result.

```
Scaling using Scale.scale_slow()...
         9438727 function calls in 14.397 seconds
   ncalls  tottime  percall  cumtime  percall filename:lineno(function)
        1    0.000    0.000   14.396   14.396 <string>:1(<module>)
        1    1.358    1.358   14.396   14.396 Slow.py:18(scale)
   786432    6.573    0.000   12.109    0.000 Slow.py:46(_mean)
  3145728    3.071    0.000    3.071    0.000 Slow.py:69(_argb_for_color)
   786432    0.671    0.000    0.671    0.000 Slow.py:77(_color_for_argb)
```

Without the object-orientation overheads, the scale() function does half the calls (nine million versus eighteen million), yet only achieves a 1.5× speedup. Nonetheless, now that we have isolated the relevant functions, we are in a position to produce an optimized Cython version to see how it compares.

We put the Cython code in the Scale/Fast.pyx module and used cProfile to profile it scaling the same photograph as the previous two versions.

```
Scaling using Scale.scale_fast()...
         4 function calls in 0.114 seconds
   ncalls  tottime  percall  cumtime  percall filename:lineno(function)
        1    0.000    0.000    0.114    0.114 <string>:1(<module>)
        1    0.113    0.113    0.113    0.113 Scale.Fast.scale
```

The cProfile module can't analyze the Scale.Fast.scale() method, because it isn't Python: it has been compiled into C. But no matter, since it produces a 189× speedup! Of course, scaling a single image might not be representative, but tests on a wide range of images consistently produced speedups that were never less than 130× faster than the original method.

These impressive speedups were achieved as the result of many kinds of optimization, some of which are specific to the scale() function and its helpers, and some of which are more generally applicable. Here are the most important contributions to the Cython scale() function's improved performance:

- Copying the original Python file (e.g., Slow.py) to a Cython file (e.g., Fast.pyx) produced a 2× speedup.

- Changing all the private Python functions into Cython C functions produced an additional 3× speedup.

- Using the C libc library's round() function rather than the built-in Python round() function resulted in an additional 4× speedup.*

- Passing memory views rather than arrays produced an additional 3× speedup.

Further smaller speed improvements were achieved by using specific types for all variables, passing a struct rather than a Python object, making small functions inline, and doing some conventional optimizations such as precomputing offsets.

Now that we have seen the kind of difference Cython can make, let's review the faster code; that is, the Fast.pyx module, and in particular, the Cythonized versions of the scale() function and its helper functions _mean(), _argb_for_color() and _color_for_argb().

The original Image.scale() method was discussed earlier (131 ◄), although the function shown here is a Cython version of the Slow.py module's Scale.Slow. scale() function. Exactly the same applies to the _mean() function (132 ◄) and the _argb_for_color() function (133 ◄). The code in the methods and functions is almost identical. The only differences between them is that the methods access the pixel data via self and call other methods, while the functions pass the pixel data explicitly and call other functions.

We will begin with the Scale/Fast.pyx file's imports and supporting declarations.

```
from libc.math cimport round
import numpy
cimport numpy
cimport cython
```

We begin by importing the C libc library's round() function to replace the built-in Python round() function. We could, of course, have done cimport libc.math and then used libc.math.round() for the C function and round() for the Python function, if we wanted both. Then we import NumPy plus the numpy.pxd module supplied with Cython, which gives Cython access to NumPy at the C level. For

---

* These two functions are not always interchangeable, since they have different behavior. However, they behave the same as used in the scale() and _mean() functions.

the Cython `scale()` function we have decided to require NumPy, since this makes sense if we want fast array processing. We also import the Cython `cython.pxd` module for some of the decorators it provides.

```
_DTYPE = numpy.uint32
ctypedef numpy.uint32_t _DTYPE_t

cdef struct Argb:
    int alpha
    int red
    int green
    int blue

DEF MAX_COMPONENT = 0xFF
```

The first two lines here are used to create two types—the Python `_DTYPE` and the C `_DTYPE_t`—both of which are aliases for NumPy unsigned 32-bit integers. Then we create a C struct called `Argb`, which consists of four named integers. (This is the C equivalent of `Argb = collections.namedtuple("Argb", "alpha red green blue")`). We also create a C constant using a Cython `DEF` statement.

```
@cython.boundscheck(False)
def scale(_DTYPE_t[:] pixels, int width, int height, double ratio):
    assert 0 < ratio < 1
    cdef int rows = <int>round(height * ratio)
    cdef int columns = <int>round(width * ratio)
    cdef _DTYPE_t[:] newPixels = numpy.zeros(rows * columns, dtype=_DTYPE)
    cdef double yStep = height / rows
    cdef double xStep = width / columns
    cdef int index = 0
    cdef int row, column, y0, y1, x0, x1
    for row in range(rows):
        y0 = <int>round(row * yStep)
        y1 = <int>round(y0 + yStep)
        for column in range(columns):
            x0 = <int>round(column * xStep)
            x1 = <int>round(x0 + xStep)
            newPixels[index] = _mean(pixels, width, height, x0, y0, x1, y1)
            index += 1
    return columns, newPixels
```

The `scale()` function uses the same algorithm as `Image.scale()`, only it takes a one-dimensional array of pixels as its first argument, followed by the image's dimensions and the scaling ratio. We have switched off bounds checking, although doing so didn't improve performance in this case. The pixels array is passed as a memory view; this is more efficient than passing `numpy.ndarrays` and incurs no Python-level overhead. Of course, there are other optimizations possible for graphics programming—for example, ensuring that memory is aligned at specific byte boundaries—but our focus here is on Cython in general rather than graphics in particular.

As we mentioned earlier, the *<type>* syntax is used to cast one type to another in Cython. The creation of the variables is essentially the same as for the Image.scale() method, only here we use C data types (int for integers and double for floating-point numbers). We can still use our normal Python syntax; for example, for ... in loops.

```
@cython.cdivision(True)
@cython.boundscheck(False)
cdef _DTYPE_t _mean(_DTYPE_t[:] pixels, int width, int height, int x0,
        int y0, int x1, int y1):
    cdef int alphaTotal = 0
    cdef int redTotal = 0
    cdef int greenTotal = 0
    cdef int blueTotal = 0
    cdef int count = 0
    cdef int y, x, offset
    cdef Argb argb
    for y in range(y0, y1):
        if y >= height:
            break
        offset = y * width
        for x in range(x0, x1):
            if x >= width:
                break
            argb = _argb_for_color(pixels[offset + x])
            alphaTotal += argb.alpha
            redTotal += argb.red
            greenTotal += argb.green
            blueTotal += argb.blue
            count += 1
    cdef int a = <int>round(alphaTotal / count)
    cdef int r = <int>round(redTotal / count)
    cdef int g = <int>round(greenTotal / count)
    cdef int b = <int>round(blueTotal / count)
    return _color_for_argb(a, r, g, b)
```

The color components for each pixel in the scaled image are the average of the color components of the pixels in the original image that the pixel must represent. The original pixels are efficiently passed as a memory view, followed by the original image's dimensions and the corners of a rectangular region whose pixels' color components must be averaged.

Rather than performing the calculation $(y \times width) + x$ for every pixel, we compute the first part (as offset) once per row.

Incidentally, by using the @cython.cdivision decorator, we told Cython to use C's / operator rather than Python's, to make the function slightly faster.

```
cdef inline Argb _argb_for_color(_DTYPE_t color):
    return Argb((color >> 24) & MAX_COMPONENT,
                (color >> 16) & MAX_COMPONENT, (color >> 8) & MAX_COMPONENT,
                (color & MAX_COMPONENT))
```

This function is inlined, which means that instead of the overhead of a function call, its body will be inserted at the place it is called (in the _mean() function) to make it as fast as possible.

```
cdef inline _DTYPE_t _color_for_argb(int a, int r, int g, int b):
    return (((a & MAX_COMPONENT) << 24) | ((r & MAX_COMPONENT) << 16) |
            ((g & MAX_COMPONENT) << 8) | (b & MAX_COMPONENT))
```

This function is also inlined to improve performance, since it is called once per scaled pixel.

The Cython inline directive is a *request* that is normally honored only for small simple functions like those used here. Note, also, that although inlining improved performance in this example, sometimes it can degrade performance. This can happen if the inlined code uses up too much of the processor's cache. As always, we should profile before and after applying each optimization on the machine or machines we plan to deploy on so that we can make an informed decision about whether to keep the optimization.

Cython has far more features than were needed for this example and has extensive documentation. Cython's main disadvantage is that it requires a compiler and supporting tool chain on every platform that we wish to build our Cython modules on. But once the tools are in place, Cython can deliver incredible speedups for CPU-bound code.

5.3. Case Study: An Accelerated Image Package

In Chapter 3, we did a case study of the pure Python Image module (§3.12, 124 ◄). In this section, we will very briefly review the cyImage module, a Cython module that offers most of the functionality of the Image module but which executes much faster.

Table 5.1 *Cython image scaling speed comparisons*

Program	Concurrency	Cython	Secs	Speedup
imagescale-s.py	*None*	No	780	*Baseline*
imagescale-cy.py	*None*	Yes	88	8.86×
imagescale-m.py	4 processes in a process pool	No	206	3.79×
imagescale.py	4 processes in a process pool	Yes	23	33.91×

The two key differences between Image and cyImage are, first, that the former automatically imports whatever image-format-specific modules are available, whereas the latter has a fixed set of format-specific modules, and second, that cyImage requires NumPy, whereas Image will use NumPy if it is available and will fall back to array if it isn't.

Table 5.1 shows how using the Cython cyImage module compares with using the Python Image module in the image-scale programs. But why does using Cython only deliver an 8× speedup (per core), rather than the 130× speedup that the Cython scale() function delivers? Essentially, once we use Cython for scaling, the scaling takes almost no time at all, but the original images still have to be loaded and the scaled images saved. Cython doesn't deliver much speedup for file handling, because Python's file handling (since Python 3.1) is already done in fast C. So, we have changed the performance profile from one where scaling was a bottleneck to one where loading and saving are bottlenecks, and ones we can't do much about.

To create the cyImage module, the first step is to create a cyImage directory and copy the Image directory's modules into it. The second step is to rename those modules that we want to Cythonize: in this case, __init__.py to Image.pyx, Xbm.py to Xbm.pyx, and Xpm.py to Xpm.pyx. We also need to create a new __init__.py and a setup.py file.

Experimentation showed that replacing the body of the Image.Image.scale() method with the Scale.Fast.scale() function's code, and similarly Image.Image._mean() with Scale.Fast._mean(), resulted in a very disappointing speedup. The problem seems to be that Cython can speed up functions a lot more than methods. In view of this, we copied the Scale.Fast.pyx module into the cyImage directory and renamed it as _Scale.pyx. Then we deleted the Image.Image._mean() method and changed the Image.Image.scale() method so that it passes on all of its work to the _Scale.scale() function. This produced the 130× speedup we were expecting, although, of course, the overall speedup was much less, as noted earlier.

```
try:
    import cyImage as Image
```

```
except ImportError:
    import Image
```

Although cyImage isn't a complete replacement for Image (it has no PNG support and requires NumPy), for those cases where it is sufficient, we can use this import pattern to use it where possible.

```
distutils.core.setup(name="cyImage",
        include_dirs=[numpy.get_include()],
        ext_modules=Cython.Build.cythonize("*.pyx"))
```

This is the body of the cyImage/setup.py file, excluding the imports. It tells Cython where to find the NumPy header files and to build all the .pyx files it finds in the cyImage directory.

```
from cyImage.cyImage.Image import (Error, Image, argb_for_color,
        rgb_for_color, color_for_argb, color_for_rgb, color_for_name)
```

In the Image module, we put all the generic functionality into Image/__init__.py, but for cyImage, we have put this functionality into cyImage/Image.pyx and created this one-statement cyImage/__init__.py file. All this file does is import various compiled objects—an exception, a class, and some functions—and make them available directly as, say, cyImage.Image.from_file(), cyImage.color_for_name(), and so on. Because we use an as clause when importing, we end up being able to write Image.Image.from_file(), Image.Image.Image(), etc.

We won't review the .pyx files, since we have seen in the previous subsection how Python code can be turned into Cython code. However, we will review the imports used by the cyImage/Image.pyx file and the new cyImage.Image.scale() method.

```
import sys
from libc.math cimport round
from libc.stdlib cimport abs
import numpy
cimport numpy
cimport cython
import cyImage.cyImage.Xbm as Xbm
import cyImage.cyImage.Xpm as Xpm
import cyImage.cyImage._Scale as Scale
from cyImage.Globals import *
```

We have chosen to use the C round() and abs() functions rather than the Python versions. And rather than doing dynamic imports, as we did for the Image module, here we directly import the image-format-specific modules (i.e., cyImage/Xbm.pyx and cyImage/Xpm.pyx or, really, the shared C libraries that Cython compiles them into).

```
def scale(self, double ratio):
    assert 0 < ratio < 1
    cdef int columns
    cdef _DTYPE_t[:] pixels
    columns, pixels = Scale.scale(self.pixels, self.width, self.height,
            ratio)
    return self.from_data(columns, pixels)
```

This is the complete cyImage.Image.scale() method. It is tiny because it passes all the work onto the cyImage._Scale.scale() function (which is a copy of the Scale.Fast.scale() function we saw in the previous subsection; §5.2.2, 193 ◀.)

Using Cython isn't as convenient as using pure Python, so to justify the extra work, we should begin by profiling our Python code to see where the bottlenecks are. If the hotspots are for file I/O or due to network latency, Cython is unlikely to help much (and we could consider using concurrency). But if the hotspots are for CPU-bound code, we might achieve worthwhile speedups with Cython, so we should begin by installing Cython and setting up our compiler tool chain.

Having profiled and identified what we want to optimize, it is best to separate out the slow code into its own module and profile the program again to make sure we have correctly isolated the problem code. Next, we should copy and rename the module we want to Cythonize (i.e., from .py to .pyx) and create a suitable set-up.py file (and possibly a convenience __init__.py file). Again, we should profile, this time to see if Cython is able to produce the expected 2× speedup. Now we can go through repeated cycles of Cythonizing the code and profiling it: declaring types, using memory views, and replacing the bodies of slow methods with calls to Cythonized functions. After each optimization cycle, we can roll back useless changes and keep those that improve performance, until we achieve the level of performance we need or run out of optimizations to try.

Donald Knuth said, "We should forget about small efficiencies, say about 97% of the time: premature optimization is the root of all evil" ("Structured Programming with go to Statements", ACM Journal Computing Surveys Vol. 6, Nº 4, December 1974, p. 268). Furthermore, no amount of optimization will overcome the use of the wrong algorithm. But, if we have used the right algorithms, and profiling has revealed bottlenecks, ctypes and Cython are good examples of tools that can speed up CPU-bound processing.

Accessing functionality in libraries that use the C calling convention via ctypes or Cython allows us to write high-level Python programs that make use of fast, low-level code. Furthermore, we can write our own C or C++ code and access it using ctypes, Cython, or directly with the Python C interface. If we want to improve CPU-bound performance, using concurrency will, at best, give us speedups proportional to the number of cores. But using fast compiled C may produce $100\times$ speedups compared with pure Python. Cython gives us the best of both Python and C: Python's convenience and syntax with C's speed and access to C libraries.

6 High-Level Networking

The Python standard library has excellent support for networking all the way from low to high level. Low-level support is provided by modules such as `socket`, `ssl`, `asyncore`, and `asynchat`, and mid-level support by, for example, the `socketserver` module. Higher-level support is provided by the many modules that support various Internet protocols, including, most notably, the `http` and `urllib` modules.

There are also a number of third-party modules that support networking, including Pyro4 (Python remote objects; `packages.python.org/Pyro4`), PyZMQ (Python bindings for the C-based 0MQ library; `zeromq.github.com/pyzmq`), and Twisted (`twistedmatrix.com`). For those interested only in HTTP and HTTPS, the third-party `requests` package (`python-requests.org`) should be easy to use.

In this chapter, we will look at two modules that provide support for high-level networking: the `xmlrpc` module from the standard library (XML Remote Procedure Call) and the third-party RPyC module (Remote Python Call; `rpyc.sourceforge.net`). Both of these modules insulate us from a lot of low- and mid-level details, and are powerful yet convenient to use.

This chapter presents one server, and two clients, for both `xmlrpc` and RPyC. The servers and clients do essentially the same jobs, so that we can easily compare the two approaches. The servers are concerned with managing meter readings (e.g., for utility meters), and the clients are used by human meter readers to request meters to read and to provide readings or reasons why a reading could not be taken.

The most important difference between the examples is that the xmlrpc server is nonconcurrent, whereas the RPyC server is concurrent. As we will see, these implementation differences have a significant impact on how we manage the data for which the servers are responsible.

To keep the servers as simple as possible, we have separated out the management of meter readings into a separate module (the nonconcurrent Meter.py and the concurrency-supporting MeterMT.py). Another advantage of this separation is that it makes it easy to see how to replace the meter module with a custom module that manages quite different data, and therefore makes the clients and servers much easier to adapt for other purposes.

6.1. Writing XML-RPC Applications

Doing network communications using low-level protocols means that for each piece of data we want to pass, we must package up the data, send it, unpack it at the other end, and finally perform some operation in response to the sent data. This process can quickly become tedious and error-prone. One solution is to use a remote procedure call (RPC) library. This allows us to simply send a function name and arguments (e.g., strings, numbers, dates) and leaves the burden of packing, sending, unpacking, and performing the operation (i.e., calling the function) to the RPC library. A popular standardized RPC protocol is XML-RPC. Libraries that implement this protocol encode the data (i.e., function names and their arguments) in XML format and use HTTP as a transport mechanism.

Python's standard library includes the xmlrpc.server and xmlrpc.client modules, which provide support for the protocol. The protocol itself is programming-language neutral, so even if we write an XML-RPC server in Python, it will be accessible to XML-RPC clients written in any language that supports the protocol. It is also possible to write XML-RPC clients in Python that connect to XML-RPC servers written in other languages.

The xmlrpc module allows us to use some Python-specific extensions—for example, to pass Python objects—but doing so means that only Python clients and servers can be used. This section's example does not take advantage of this feature.

A lighter-weight alternative to XML-RPC is JSON-RPC. This provides the same broad functionality but uses a much leaner data format (i.e., it usually has far fewer bytes of overhead that need to be sent over the network). Python's library includes the json module for encoding and decoding Python data into or from JSON but does not provide JSON-RPC client or server modules. However, there are many third-party Python JSON-RPC modules available (en.wikipedia.org/wiki/JSON-RPC). Another alternative, for when we have only Python clients and servers, is to use RPyC, as we will see in the next section (§6.2, ➤ 219).

6.1.1. A Data Wrapper

The data that we want the clients and servers to handle is encapsulated by the `Meter.py` module. This module provides a `Manager` class that stores meter readings and provides methods for meter readers to login, acquire jobs, and submit results. This module could easily be substituted with another one to manage entirely different data.

```
class Manager:

    SessionId = 0
    UsernameForSessionId = {}
    ReadingForMeter = {}
```

The `SessionID` is used to provide every successful login with a unique session ID.

The class also keeps two static dictionaries: one with session ID keys and user-name values, the other with meter number keys and meter reading values.

None of this static data needs to be thread-safe, because the `xmlrpc` server is not concurrent. The `MeterMT.py` version of this module supports concurrency, and we will review how it differs from `Meter.py` in the next section's first subsection (§6.2.1, ➤ 220).

In a more realistic context, the data is likely to be stored in a DBM file or in a database, either of which could easily be substituted for the meter data dictionary used here.

```
    def login(self, username, password):
        name = name_for_credentials(username, password)
        if name is None:
            raise Error("Invalid username or password")
        Manager.SessionId += 1
        sessionId = Manager.SessionId
        Manager.UsernameForSessionId[sessionId] = username
        return sessionId, name
```

We want meter readers to login with a username and password before we allow them to acquire jobs or submit results.

If the username and password are correct, we return a unique session ID for the user and the user's real name (e.g., to display in the user interface). Each successful login is given a unique session ID and added to the `UsernameForSessionId` dictionary. All the other methods require a valid session ID.

```
_User = collections.namedtuple("User", "username sha256")
```

```
def name_for_credentials(username, password):
    sha = hashlib.sha256()
    sha.update(password.encode("utf-8"))
    user = _User(username, sha.hexdigest())
    return _Users.get(user)
```

When this function is called, it computes the SHA-256 hash of the given password, and if the username and the hash match an entry in the module's private _Users dictionary (not shown), it returns the corresponding actual name; otherwise, it returns None.

The _Users dictionary has _User keys consisting of a username (e.g., carol), an SHA-256 hash of the user's password, and real name values (e.g., "Carol Dent"). This means that no actual passwords are stored.*

```
def get_job(self, sessionId):
    self._username_for_sessionid(sessionId)
    while True: # Create fake meter
        kind = random.choice("GE")
        meter = "{}{}".format(kind, random.randint(40000,
                99999 if kind == "G" else 999999))
        if meter not in Manager.ReadingForMeter:
            Manager.ReadingForMeter[meter] = None
            return meter
```

Once the meter reader has logged in, they can call this method to get the number of a meter for them to read. The method begins by checking that the session ID is valid; if it isn't, the _username_for_sessionid() method will raise a Meter.Error exception.

We don't actually have a database of meters to read, so instead we create a fake meter whenever a meter reader asks for a job. We do this by creating a meter number (e.g., "E350718" or "G72168") and then inserting it into the ReadingForMeter dictionary with a reading of None as soon as we create a fake meter that isn't already in the dictionary.

```
def _username_for_sessionid(self, sessionId):
    try:
        return Manager.UsernameForSessionId[sessionId]
    except KeyError:
        raise Error("Invalid session ID")
```

---

* The approach used here is still not secure. To make it secure we would need to add a unique "salt" text to each password so that identical passwords didn't produce the same hash value. A better alternative is to use the third-party passlib package (code.google.com/p/passlib).

This method either returns the username for the given session ID or, in effect, converts a generic KeyError for an invalid session ID into a custom Meter.Error.

It is often better to use a custom exception rather than a built-in one, because then we can catch those exceptions we expect to get and not accidentally catch more generic ones that, had they not been caught, would have revealed errors in our code's logic.

```
def submit_reading(self, sessionId, meter, when, reading, reason=""):
    if isinstance(when, xmlrpc.client.DateTime):
        when = datetime.datetime.strptime(when.value,
            "%Y%m%dT%H:%M:%S")
    if (not isinstance(reading, int) or reading < 0) and not reason:
        raise Error("Invalid reading")
    if meter not in Manager.ReadingForMeter:
        raise Error("Invalid meter ID")
    username = self._username_for_sessionid(sessionId)
    reading = Reading(when, reading, reason, username)
    Manager.ReadingForMeter[meter] = reading
    return True
```

This method accepts a session ID, a meter number (e.g., "G72168"), the date and time when the reading took place, the reading value (a positive integer or -1 if no reading was obtained), and the reason why a reading couldn't be taken (which is a nonempty string for unsuccessful readings).

We can set the XML-RPC server to use built-in Python types, but this isn't done by default (and we haven't done it), because the XML-RPC protocol is language neutral. This means that our XML-RPC server could serve clients that are written in any language that supports XML-RPC, not just Python clients. The downside of not using Python types is that date/time objects get passed as xmlrpc.client.DateTimes rather than as datetime.datetimes, so we must convert these to datetime.datetimes. (An alternative would be to pass them as ISO-8601-format date/time strings.)

Once we have prepared and checked the data, we retrieve the username for the meter reader whose session ID was passed in, and use this to create a Meter.Reading object. This is simply a named tuple:

```
Reading = collections.namedtuple("Reading", "when reading reason username")
```

At the end, we set the meter's reading. We return True (rather than the default of None), since, by default, the xmlrpc.server module doesn't support None, and we want to keep our server language neutral. (RPyC can cope with any Python return value.)

```
    def get_status(self, sessionId):
        username = self._username_for_sessionid(sessionId)
        count = total = 0
        for reading in Manager.ReadingForMeter.values():
            if reading is not None:
                total += 1
                if reading.username == username:
                    count += 1
        return count, total
```

After a meter reader has submitted a reading, they might want to know what their status is; that is, how many readings they have made and the total number of readings the server has handled since it started. This method calculates these numbers and returns them.

```
    def _dump(file=sys.stdout):
        for meter, reading in sorted(Manager.ReadingForMeter.items()):
            if reading is not None:
                print("{}={}@{}[{}]{}".format(meter, reading.reading,
                        reading.when.isoformat()[:16], reading.reason,
                        reading.username), file=file)
```

This method is provided purely for debugging so that we can check that all the meter readings we have done were actually stored correctly.

The features that the Meter.Manager provides—a login() method, and methods to get and set data—are typical of a data-wrapping class that a server might use. It should be straightforward to replace this class with one for completely different data, while still using basically the same clients and servers shown in this chapter. The only caveat is that if we were to use concurrent servers, we must use locks or thread-safe classes for any shared data, as we will see later (§6.2.1, ➤ 220).

6.1.2. Writing XML-RPC Servers

Thanks to the xmlrpc.server module, writing custom XML-RPC servers is very easy. The code in this subsection is quoted from meterserver-rpc.py.

```
def main():
    host, port, notify = handle_commandline()
    manager, server = setup(host, port)
    print("Meter server startup at  {} on {}:{}{}".format(
            datetime.datetime.now().isoformat()[:19], host, port, PATH))
    try:
        if notify:
```

```
        with open(notify, "wb") as file:
            file.write(b"\n")
    server.serve_forever()
except KeyboardInterrupt:
    print("\rMeter server shutdown at {}".format(
        datetime.datetime.now().isoformat()[:19]))
    manager._dump()
```

This function gets the hostname and port number, creates a `Meter.Manager` and an `xmlrpc.server.SimpleXMLRPCServer`, and starts serving.

If the `notify` variable holds a filename, the server creates the file and writes a single newline to it. The notify filename is not used when the server is started manually, but as we will see later on (§6.1.3.2, ➤ 214), if the server is started by a GUI client, the client passes the server a notify filename. The GUI client then waits until the file has been created—at which point the client knows that the server is up and running—and then the client deletes the file and commences communication with the server.

The server can be stopped by entering Ctrl+C or by sending it an INT signal (e.g., kill -2 *pid* on Linux), which the Python interpreter transforms into a Keyboard-Interrupt. If the server is stopped in this way, we make the manager dump its readings for inspection. (This is the only reason this function needs access to the manager instance.)

```
HOST = "localhost"
PORT = 11002

def handle_commandline():
    parser = argparse.ArgumentParser(conflict_handler="resolve")
    parser.add_argument("-h", "--host", default=HOST,
        help="hostname [default %(default)s]")
    parser.add_argument("-p", "--port", default=PORT, type=int,
        help="port number [default %(default)d]")
    parser.add_argument("--notify", help="specify a notification file")
    args = parser.parse_args()
    return args.host, args.port, args.notify
```

This function is only quoted because it uses –h (and --host) as options for setting the hostname. By default, the `argparse` module reserves the -h (and --help) options to tell it to display the command-line help and then terminate. We want to take over the use of -h (but leave --help), and we do this by setting the argument parser's conflict handler.

Unfortunately, when `argparse` was ported to Python 3, the old Python 2–style % formatting was retained rather than being replaced with Python 3's `str.format()` braces. In view of this, when we want to include default values in help text, we must write %(default)*t* where *t* is the value's type (d for decimal integer, f for floating-point, s for string).

```
def setup(host, port):
    manager = Meter.Manager()
    server = xmlrpc.server.SimpleXMLRPCServer((host, port),
            requestHandler=RequestHandler, logRequests=False)
    server.register_introspection_functions()
    for method in (manager.login, manager.get_job, manager.submit_reading,
            manager.get_status):
        server.register_function(method)
    return manager, server
```

This function is used to create the data (i.e., meter) manager and the server. The resister_introspection_functions() method makes three introspection functions available to clients: system.listMethods(), system.methodHelp(), and system.methodSignature(). (These aren't used by the meter XML-RPC clients but might be needed for debugging more complex clients.) Each of the manager methods we want clients to have access to must be registered with the server, and this is easily accomplished using the register_function() method. (See the "Bound and Unbound Methods" sidebar, 63 ◄.)

```
PATH = "/meter"

class RequestHandler(xmlrpc.server.SimpleXMLRPCRequestHandler):
    rpc_paths = (PATH,)
```

The meter server doesn't need to do any special request handling, so we have created the most basic request handler possible: one that inherits xml-rpc.server.SimpleXMLRPCRequestHandler and that has a unique path to identify meter server requests.

Now that we have created a server, we can create clients to access it.

6.1.3. Writing XML-RPC Clients

In this subsection, we will review two different clients: one console based that assumes that the server is already running, and the other a GUI client that will use a running server or will start up its own server if there isn't one running already.

6.1.3.1. A Console XML-RPC Client

Before we dive into the code, let's look at a typical interactive console session. The meterserver-rpc.py server must have been started before this interaction took place.

```
$ ./meterclient-rpc.py
Username [carol]:
Password:
Welcome, Carol Dent, to Meter RPC
Reading for meter G5248: 5983
Accepted: you have read 1 out of 18 readings
Reading for meter G72168: 2980q
Invalid reading
Reading for meter G72168: 29801
Accepted: you have read 2 out of 21 readings
Reading for meter E445691:
Reason for meter E445691: Couldn't find the meter
Accepted: you have read 3 out of 26 readings
Reading for meter E432365: 87712
Accepted: you have read 4 out of 28 readings
Reading for meter G40447:
Reason for meter G40447:
$
```

User Carol starts up a meter client. She's prompted to enter her username or press Enter to accept the default (shown in square brackets), so she presses Enter. She is then prompted to enter her password, which she does without any echo. The server recognizes her and welcomes her giving her full name. The client then asks the server for a meter to read and prompts Carol to enter a reading. If she enters a number, it is passed to the server and will normally be accepted. If she makes a mistake (as she does with the second reading), or if the reading is invalid for some other reason, she is notified and prompted to enter the reading again. Whenever a reading (or reason) is accepted, she is told how many readings she has made this session and how many readings have been made in total this session (i.e., including the readings made by other people who are using the server at the same time). If she presses Enter without entering a reading, she is prompted to type in a reason why she can't give a reading. And if she doesn't enter a reading or a reason, the client terminates.

```
def main():
    host, port = handle_commandline()
    username, password = login()
    if username is not None:
        try:
            manager = xmlrpc.client.ServerProxy("http://{}:{}{}".format(
                    host, port, PATH))
            sessionId, name = manager.login(username, password)
            print("Welcome, {}, to Meter RPC".format(name))
            interact(manager, sessionId)
```

```
except xmlrpc.client.Fault as err:
    print(err)
except ConnectionError as err:
    print("Error: Is the meter server running? {}".format(err))
```

This function begins by getting the server's host name and port number (or their defaults) and then obtains the user's username and password. It then creates a proxy (manager) for the Meter.Manager instance used by the server. (We discussed the Proxy Pattern earlier; §2.7, 67 ◄.)

Once the proxy manager has been created, we use the proxy to login and then begin interacting with the server. If no server is running, we will get a ConnectionError exception (or a socket.error prior to Python 3.3).

```
def login():
    loginName = getpass.getuser()
    username = input("Username [{}]: ".format(loginName))
    if not username:
        username = loginName
    password = getpass.getpass()
    if not password:
        return None, None
    return username, password
```

The getpass module's getuser() function returns the username for the currently logged-in user, and we use this as the default username. The getpass() function prompts for a password and does not echo the reply. Both input() and get-pass.getpass() return strings without trailing newlines.

```
def interact(manager, sessionId):
    accepted = True
    while True:
        if accepted:
            meter = manager.get_job(sessionId)
            if not meter:
                print("All jobs done")
                break
        accepted, reading, reason = get_reading(meter)
        if not accepted:
            continue
        if (not reading or reading == -1) and not reason:
            break
        accepted = submit(manager, sessionId, meter, reading, reason)
```

If the login is successful, this function is called to handle the client–server interaction. This consists of repeatedly acquiring a job from the server (i.e., a meter to read), getting a reading or reason from the user, and submitting the data to the server, until the user enters neither a reading nor a reason.

```
def get_reading(meter):
    reading = input("Reading for meter {}: ".format(meter))
    if reading:
        try:
            return True, int(reading), ""
        except ValueError:
            print("Invalid reading")
            return False, 0, ""
    else:
        return True, -1, input("Reason for meter {}: ".format(meter))
```

This function must handle three cases: the user enters a valid (i.e., integer) reading, or the user enters an invalid reading, or the user doesn't enter a reading at all. If no reading is entered, the user either enters a reason or no reason (in the latter case signifying that they have finished).

```
def submit(manager, sessionId, meter, reading, reason):
    try:
        now = datetime.datetime.now()
        manager.submit_reading(sessionId, meter, now, reading, reason)
        count, total = manager.get_status(sessionId)
        print("Accepted: you have read {} out of {} readings".format(
                count, total))
        return True
    except (xmlrpc.client.Fault, ConnectionError) as err:
        print(err)
        return False
```

Whenever a reading or reason has been obtained, this function is used to submit it to the server via the proxied manager. Once the reading or reason has been submitted, the function asks for the status (i.e., how many readings has this user submitted; how many readings have been submitted in total since the server started).

The client code is longer than the server code but very straightforward. And since we are using XML-RPC, the client could be written in any language that supports the protocol. It is also possible to write clients that use different user interface technologies, such as Urwid (excess.org/urwid) for Unix console user interfaces or a GUI toolkit like Tkinter.

6.1.3.2. A GUI XML-RPC Client

Tkinter GUI programming is introduced in Chapter 7, so those unfamiliar with Tkinter might prefer to read that chapter first and then return here. In this subsubsection, we will focus on only those aspects of the GUI meter-rpc.pyw program that are concerned with interacting with the meter server. The program is shown in Figure 6.1.

 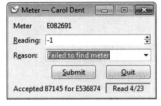

Figure 6.1 *The Meter XML-RPC GUI application's login and main windows on Windows*

```
class Window(ttk.Frame):

    def __init__(self, master):
        super().__init__(master, padding=PAD)
        self.serverPid = None
        self.create_variables()
        self.create_ui()
        self.statusText.set("Ready...")
        self.countsText.set("Read 0/0")
        self.master.after(100, self.login)
```

When the main window is created, we set a server PID (Process ID) of None and call the login() method 100 milliseconds after the main window has been constructed. This allows Tkinter time to paint the main window, and before the user has a chance to interact with it, an *application modal* login window is created. An application modal window is the only window that the user can interact with for a given application. This means that although the user can see the main window, they cannot use it until they have logged in and the modal login window has gone away.

```
class Result:

    def __init__(self):
        self.username = None
        self.password = None
        self.ok = False
```

This tiny class (from MeterLogin.py) is used to hold the results of the user's interaction with the modal login dialog window. By passing a reference to a

Result instance to the dialog, we can ensure that we are able to access what the user entered even after the dialog has been closed and deleted.

```
def login(self):
    result = MeterLogin.Result()
    dialog = MeterLogin.Window(self, result)
    if result.ok and self.connect(result.username, result.password):
        self.get_job()
    else:
        self.close()
```

This method creates a result object and then creates an application modal login dialog window. The MeterLogin.Window() call shows the login window and blocks until the window is closed. As long as this window is shown, the user cannot interact with any other application window, so they must either enter a username and password and click OK or cancel by clicking Cancel.

Once the user has clicked one of the buttons, the window is closed (and deleted). If the user clicked OK (which is only possible if they entered a nonempty user-name and a nonempty password), an attempt to connect to the server is made and the first job obtained. If the user canceled the login or the connection failed, the main window is closed (and deleted), and the application is terminated.

```
def connect(self, username, password):
    try:
        self.manager = xmlrpc.client.ServerProxy("http://{}:{}{}"
                .format(HOST, PORT, PATH))
        name = self.login_to_server(username, password)
        self.master.title("Meter \u2014 {}".format(name))
        return True
    except (ConnectionError, xmlrpc.client.Fault) as err:
        self.handle_error(err)
        return False
```

As soon as the user has entered their username and password, this method is called. It begins by creating a proxy to the server's Meter.Manager instance and then attempts to login. After this, it changes the application's title to the application's name, an em-dash (—, Unicode code point U+2014), and the user's name, and returns True.

If an error occurs, a message box is popped up with the error text and False is returned.

```
def login_to_server(self, username, password):
    try:
        self.sessionId, name = self.manager.login(username, password)
```

```
    except ConnectionError:
        self.start_server()
        self.sessionId, name = self.manager.login(username, password)
    return name
```

If a meter server is already running, the initial connection attempt will succeed and the session ID and user's name will be obtained. However, if the attempt to login fails due to a ConnectionError, the application assumes that the server isn't running and tries to start it, and then tries to login a second time. If the second attempt fails, the ConnectionError is propagated to the caller (self.login()), which catches it and presents the user with an error message box, after which the application terminates.

```
SERVER = os.path.join(os.path.dirname(os.path.realpath(__file__)),
        "meterserver-rpc.py")
```

This constant sets the server's name with its full path. It assumes that the server is in the same directory as the GUI client. Of course, it is more common for a client to be on one machine and a server on another. However, some applications are created in two separate parts—a server and a client—that are expected to be on the same machine.

The two-part application design is useful when we want to completely isolate an application's functionality from its user interface. This approach has the downsides that two executables must be supplied rather than one, and there is some networking overhead, but this shouldn't be noticeable by the user if the client and server are on the same machine. The upsides are that the client and server can be developed independently, and that it is much easier to port such applications to new platforms, since the server can be written using platform-independent code, and the porting work can focus almost entirely on the client. It also means that new user-interface technologies can be taken advantage of (e.g., a new GUI toolkit) purely by porting the client. Another potential benefit is for finer-grained security; for example, the server can be made to run with specific and limited permissions, while the client can be run with the user's permissions.

```
    def start_server(self):
        filename = os.path.join(tempfile.gettempdir(),
                "M{}.$$$".format(random.randint(1000, 9999)))
        self.serverPid = subprocess.Popen([sys.executable, SERVER,
                "--host", HOST, "--port", str(PORT), "--notify",
                filename]).pid
        print("Starting the server...")
        self.wait_for_server(filename)
```

The server is started using the subprocess.Popen() function. This particular usage means that the subprocess (i.e., the server) is started without blocking.

If we were executing a normal program (i.e., a subprocess) that we expected to terminate, we could wait for it to finish. But here we must start a server that won't terminate until our client does, so waiting isn't possible. Furthermore, we need to give the server a chance to start up, since we can't attempt to login until it is running. Our solution here is simple: we create a pseudo-random filename and start the server, passing the filename as its notify argument. We can then wait for the server to start up and create the notify file to let the client know that the server is ready.

```
def wait_for_server(self, filename):
    tries = 100
    while tries:
        if os.path.exists(filename):
            os.remove(filename)
            break
        time.sleep(0.1) # Give the server a chance to start
        tries -= 1
    else:
        self.handle_error("Failed to start the RPC Meter Server")
```

This method blocks (i.e., freezes) the user interface for up to ten seconds (100 tries × 0.1 seconds), although in practice the wait is almost always a fraction of a second. As soon as the server creates the notify file, the client deletes the file and resumes event processing; in this case, attempting to log the user in using the credentials they gave, and then showing the main window ready for them to enter meter readings. If the server fails to start, the while loop will finish without a break, and its else clause will be executed.

Polling is not ideal, especially in a GUI application, but since we want a cross-platform solution and the application cannot work without the server being available, this represents the simplest reasonable approach we can take.

```
def get_job(self):
    try:
        meter = self.manager.get_job(self.sessionId)
        if not meter:
            messagebox.showinfo("Meter \u2014 Finished",
                "All jobs done", parent=self)
            self.close()
        self.meter.set(meter)
        self.readingSpinbox.focus()
    except (xmlrpc.client.Fault, ConnectionError) as err:
        self.handle_error(err)
```

Once the login to the server has succeeded (with the server started by the
application, if necessary, as part of this process), this method is called to get the
first job. The self.meter variable is of type tkinter.StringVar and is associated
with the label that shows the meter number.

```
def submit(self, event=None):
    if self.submitButton.instate((tk.DISABLED,)):
        return
    meter = self.meter.get()
    reading = self.reading.get()
    reading = int(reading) if reading else -1
    reason = self.reason.get()
    if reading > -1 or (reading == -1 and reason and reason != "Read"):
        try:
            self.manager.submit_reading(self.sessionId, meter,
                    datetime.datetime.now(), reading, reason)
            self.after_submit(meter, reading, reason)
        except (xmlrpc.client.Fault, ConnectionError) as err:
            self.handle_error(err)
```

This method is called whenever the user clicks the Submit button—something
that the application allows only if the reading is nonzero or the reason
nonempty. The meter, reading (as an int), and reason are all obtained from the
user interface widgets and then submitted to the server via the proxied manager.
If the submitted reading is accepted, the after_submit() method is called; otherwise, the error is passed to the handle_error() method.

```
def after_submit(self, meter, reading, reason):
    count, total = self.manager.get_status(self.sessionId)
    self.statusText.set("Accepted {} for {}".format(
            reading if reading != -1 else reason, meter))
    self.countsText.set("Read {}/{}".format(count, total))
    self.reading.set(-1)
    self.reason.set("")
    self.get_job()
```

This method asks the proxied manager for the current status and updates the
status and counts labels. It also resets the reading and reason and asks the
manager for the next job.

```
def handle_error(self, err):
    if isinstance(err, xmlrpc.client.Fault):
        err = err.faultString
```

```
        messagebox.showinfo("Meter \u2014 Error",
                "{}\nIs the server still running?\n"
                "Try Quitting and restarting.".format(err), parent=self)
```

If an error occurs, this method is called. It displays the error in an application modal message box with a single OK button.

```
    def close(self, event=None):
        if self.serverPid is not None:
            print("Stopping the server...")
            os.kill(self.serverPid, signal.SIGINT)
            self.serverPid = None
        self.quit()
```

When the user closes the application, we check whether the application started the meter server itself or used an already running server. In the former case, the application cleanly terminates the server by sending it an interrupt (which Python will turn into a KeyboardInterrupt exception).

The os.kill() function sends a signal (one of the signal module's constants) to the program with the given process ID. The function is Unix-only for Python 3.1 but works on both Unix and Windows from Python 3.2.

The console client, meterclient-rpc.py, is around 100 lines. The GUI client, meter-rpc.pyw, is around 250 lines (plus about another 100 for the MeterLogin.py login dialog window). Both are easy to use and highly portable, and, thanks to Tkinter's theme support, the GUI client looks native on both OS X and Windows.

6.2. Writing RPyC Applications

If we are writing Python servers and Python clients, instead of using a verbose protocol like XML-RPC, we can use a Python-specific protocol. There are many packages that offer Python-to-Python remote procedure call, but for this section we will use RPyC (rpyc.sourceforge.net). This module offers two modes of use: the older "classic" and the newer "service-based". We will use the service-based approach.

By default, RPyC servers are concurrent, so we cannot use the nonconcurrent data wrapper (Meter.py) from the previous section (§6.1.1, 205 ◄). Instead, we will use a new MeterMT.py module. This introduces two new classes, ThreadSafe-Dict and _MeterDict, and has a modified Manager class that makes use of these dictionaries rather than standard dicts.

6.2.1. A Thread-Safe Data Wrapper

The `MeterMT` module contains a concurrency-supporting `Manager` class as well as two thread-safe dictionaries. We will begin by looking at the `Manager` class's static data and the methods where it differs from the original `Meter.Manager` class we saw in the previous section.

```
class Manager:

    SessionId = 0
    SessionIdLock = threading.Lock()
    UsernameForSessionId = ThreadSafeDict()
    ReadingForMeter = _MeterDict()
```

To support concurrency, the `MeterMT.Manager` class must use locks to serialize access to its static data. For session IDs we use a lock directly, but for the two dictionaries we use custom thread-safe dictionaries that we will review shortly.

```
    def login(self, username, password):
        name = name_for_credentials(username, password)
        if name is None:
            raise Error("Invalid username or password")
        with Manager.SessionIdLock:
            Manager.SessionId += 1
            sessionId = Manager.SessionId
        Manager.UsernameForSessionId[sessionId] = username
        return sessionId, name
```

This method differs from the original only in that we increment and assign the static session ID within the context of a lock. Without the lock, it would be possible for, say, thread *A* to increment the session ID, then for thread *B* to increment it, and then for threads *A* and *B* to both read the same double-incremented value, rather than each getting a unique session ID.

```
    def get_status(self, sessionId):
        username = self._username_for_sessionid(sessionId)
        return Manager.ReadingForMeter.status(username)
```

This method now passes almost all of its work onto a custom `_MeterDict.status()` method, which we will review further on.

```
    def get_job(self, sessionId):
        self._username_for_sessionid(sessionId)
        while True: # Create fake meter
            kind = random.choice("GE")
```

```
meter = "{}{}".format(kind, random.randint(40000,
    99999 if kind == "G" else 999999))
if Manager.ReadingForMeter.insert_if_missing(meter):
    return meter
```

It is the last couple of lines of this method that differ from before. We want to check if the fake meter is in the dictionary, and if it isn't, we want to insert it into the dictionary with an initial reading value of None. This will ensure that it cannot be reused. Before, we did the check and insertion as two separate statements, but we cannot do that in a concurrent context, because it is possible that one or more other threads will execute between the two statements. So, now, we pass on the work to a custom _MeterDict.insert_if_missing() method that returns whether the insertion took place.

```
def submit_reading(self, sessionId, meter, when, reading,
        reason=""):
    if (not isinstance(reading, int) or reading < 0) and not reason:
        raise Error("Invalid reading")
    if meter not in Manager.ReadingForMeter:
        raise Error("Invalid meter ID")
    username = self._username_for_sessionid(sessionId)
    reading = Reading(when, reading, reason, username)
    Manager.ReadingForMeter[meter] = reading
```

This is very similar to the XML-RPC version, only now we don't have to convert the when date/time value, and we don't need to return True, since an implicit return of None is perfectly acceptable to RPyC.

6.2.1.1. A Simple Thread-Safe Dictionary

If we are using CPython (the standard version of Python implemented in C), in theory, the GIL (Global Interpreter Lock) makes dicts seem thread-safe, because the Python interpreter can only execute on one thread at a time (no matter how many cores we have), so individual method calls execute as atomic actions. However, this doesn't help when we need to call two or more dict methods as a single atomic action. And in any case, we should not rely on this implementation detail; after all, other Python implementations (e.g., Jython and IronPython) don't have a GIL, so their dict methods cannot be assumed to execute atomically.

If we want a genuinely thread-safe dictionary, we must use a third-party one or create one ourselves. Creating one isn't difficult, since we can take an existing dict and provide access to it via our own thread-safe methods. In this subsection, we will review the ThreadSafeDict, a thread-safe dictionary that provides a subset of the dict interface that is sufficient to provide meter dictionaries.

```
class ThreadSafeDict:

    def __init__(self, *args, **kwargs):
        self._dict = dict(*args, **kwargs)
        self._lock = threading.Lock()
```

The ThreadSafeDict aggregates a dict and a threading.Lock. We didn't want to inherit dict, since we want to mediate all accesses to self._dict so that they are always serialized (i.e., so that only one thread can ever access the self._dict at a time).

```
    def copy(self):
        with self._lock:
            return self.__class__(**self._dict)
```

Python locks support the context manager protocol, so locking is simply a matter of using a with statement, confident that the lock will be released when it isn't needed, even in the face of exceptions.

The with self._lock statement will block if any other thread holds the lock and will only continue into the body of the block once the lock has been acquired; that is, when no other threads hold the lock. This is why it is important to do as little as possible as quickly as possible in the context of a lock. In this particular case, the operation is expensive, but there isn't any nice solution.

If a class implements a copy() method, the method is expected to return a copy of the instance it is called on. We could not return self._dict.copy(), since that produces a plain dict. Returning ThreadSafeDict(**self._dict) would have worked, except that it always returns a ThreadSafeDict, even from a subclass instance (unless the subclass reimplemented the copy() method). The code we have used here works both for ThreadSafeDicts and for subclasses. (See the "Sequence and Mapping Unpacking" sidebar, 13 ◄.)

```
    def get(self, key, default=None):
        with self._lock:
            return self._dict.get(key, default)
```

This method provides a faithful thread-safe implementation of the dict.get() method.

```
    def __getitem__(self, key):
        with self._lock:
            return self._dict[key]
```

This special method provides support for accessing dictionary values by key; that is, *value = d[key]*.

```
    def __setitem__(self, key, value):
        with self._lock:
            self._dict[key] = value
```

This special method provides support for inserting items into the dictionary or changing an existing item's value using the syntax, d[key] = value.

```
    def __delitem__(self, key):
        with self._lock:
            del self._dict[key]
```

Here is the special method that supports the del statement; that is, del d[key].

```
    def __contains__(self, key):
        with self._lock:
            return key in self._dict
```

This special method returns True if the dictionary has an item with the given key; otherwise, it returns False. It is used via the in keyword; for example, if k in d: ....

```
    def __len__(self):
        with self._lock:
            return len(self._dict)
```

This special method returns the number of items in the dictionary. It supports the built-in len() function; for example, count = len(d).

The ThreadSafeDict does not provide the dict methods clear(), fromkeys(), items(), keys(), pop(), popitem(), setdefault(), update(), and values(). Most of these methods should be straightforward to implement. However, for the methods that return views (e.g., items(), keys(), and values()) special care is required. The simplest and safest approach is not to implement them at all. An alternative is to have them return a copy of their data as a list (e.g., keys() could be implemented with a body of with self._lock: return list(self._dict.keys())). For large dictionaries, this could use a lot of memory, and, of course, such a method would block other threads from accessing the dictionary while it is executing.

Another approach to creating a thread-safe dictionary would be to create a plain dictionary in one thread. If we were careful to write to this dictionary only in the thread in which it was created (or to use a lock and only write to it in threads that held its lock), we could then provide read-only (i.e., thread-safe) views of this dictionary to other threads using the types.MappingProxyType class introduced in Python 3.3.

6.2.1.2. The Meter Dictionary Subclass

Rather than using a plain ThreadSafeDict for the meter readings dictionary (meter number keys, reading values), we have created a private _MeterDict subclass that adds two new methods.

```
class _MeterDict(ThreadSafeDict):

    def insert_if_missing(self, key, value=None):
        with self._lock:
            if key not in self._dict:
                self._dict[key] = value
                return True
        return False
```

This method inserts the given key and value into the dictionary and returns True, or, if the key (i.e., the fake meter number) is already in the dictionary, does nothing and returns False. This is to make sure that every job request is for a new and unique meter.

The code that the insert_if_missing() method executes is essentially:

```
if meter not in ReadingForMeter: # WRONG!
    ReadingForMeter[key] = None
```

The ReadingForMeter is a _MeterDict instance and so inherits all the Thread-SafeDict class's functionality. Even though the ReadingForMeter.__contains__() method (for in) and the ReadingForMeter.__setitem__() method (for []) are both thread-safe, the code shown here is *not* thread-safe. This is because a different thread could access the ReadingForMeter dictionary after the if statement but before the assignment. The solution is to execute both operations in the context of the same lock, and this is exactly what the insert_if_missing() method does.

```
    def status(self, username):
        count = total = 0
        with self._lock:
            for reading in self._dict.values():
                if reading is not None:
                    total += 1
                    if reading.username == username:
                        count += 1
        return count, total
```

This is a potentially expensive method, since it iterates over all the underlying dictionary's values within the context of a lock. An alternative would be to have just one statement inside the context—*values* = self._dict.values()—and to do the iteration afterwards (i.e., outside the context of the lock). Whether it is faster to copy the items inside a lock and then process the copied items without a lock, or to process the items inside a lock, depends on circumstances. The only way to know for sure, of course, is to profile both approaches in realistic contexts.

6.2.2. Writing RPyC Servers

We saw earlier that it is easy to create an XML-RPC server using the xmlr-pc.server module (§6.1.2, 208 ◄). It is just as easy—although different—to create an RPyC server.

```
import datetime
import threading
import rpyc
import sys
import MeterMT

PORT = 11003

Manager = MeterMT.Manager()
```

Here is the start of meterserver-rpyc.py. We import a couple of standard library modules, then the rpyc module, and then our thread-safe MeterMT module. We have set a fixed port number, although this could easily be changed by using a command-line option and the argparse module as we did for the XML-RPC version. And we have created a single instance of a MeterMT.Manager. This instance will be shared by the RPyC server's threads.

```
if __name__ == "__main__":
    import rpyc.utils.server
    print("Meter server startup at {}".format(
            datetime.datetime.now().isoformat()[:19]))
    server = rpyc.utils.server.ThreadedServer(MeterService, port=PORT)
    thread = threading.Thread(target=server.start)
    thread.start()
    try:
        if len(sys.argv) > 1: # Notify if called by a GUI client
            with open(sys.argv[1], "wb") as file:
                file.write(b"\n")
        thread.join()
    except KeyboardInterrupt:
        pass
    server.close()
    print("\rMeter server shutdown at {}".format(
            datetime.datetime.now().isoformat()[:19]))
    MeterMT.Manager._dump()
```

This is the end of the server program. We import the RPyC server module and announce the startup. Then we create an instance of a threaded server and pass it a `MeterService` class. The server will create instances of this class as needed; we will review the class in a moment.

Once the server has been created, we could then simply write `server.start()` and finish there. This would start the server and leave it to run "forever". However, we want the user to be able to stop the server with Ctrl+C (or an INT signal) and for the server to print out the meter readings when it is stopped.

To achieve this, we start the server in its own thread—from which it will create a thread pool to manage incoming connections—and then block waiting for the server's thread to finish (by using `thread.join()`). If the server is interrupted, we catch and ignore the exception and close the server. The `close()` call will block until every server thread has finished its current connection. Then we announce the server's shutdown and print the meter readings that were submitted to the server.

If the server is started by a GUI client, we expect the client to pass a notify filename as the server's sole argument. If a notify argument is present, we create the file and write a newline to it to notify the client that the server is up and running.

When using service mode, an RPyC server takes an `rpyc.Service` subclass that it can then use as a class factory to produce instances of the service. (Factories were discussed in Chapter 1; §1.1, 5 ◀, and §1.3, 17 ◀.) We have created the `MeterService` class as a thin wrapper around the `MeterMT.Manager` instance created at the start of the program.

```
class MeterService(rpyc.Service):

    def on_connect(self):
        pass

    def on_disconnect(self):
        pass
```

Whenever a connection is made to a service, the service's `on_connect()` method is called. And, similarly, when a connection finishes, the `on_disconnect()` method is called. We don't need to do anything in either of these cases, so we have created them as "do nothing" methods. It is perfectly acceptable not to implement these methods at all if they aren't needed; they are included here purely to show their signatures.

```
    exposed_login = Manager.login
    exposed_get_status = Manager.get_status
    exposed_get_job = Manager.get_job
```

A service can expose methods (or classes and other objects) to clients. Any class or method whose name begins with exposed_ is available for clients to access, and in the case of methods they can call the method with or without this prefix. For example, a meter RPyC client could call exposed_login() or login().

For the exposed_login(), exposed_get_status(), and exposed_get_job() methods, we simply set them to the corresponding methods in the program's meter-manager instance.

```
def exposed_submit_reading(self, sessionId, meter, when, reading,
        reason=""):
    when = datetime.datetime.strptime(str(when)[:19],
        "%Y-%m-%d %H:%M:%S")
    Manager.submit_reading(sessionId, meter, when, reading, reason)
```

For this method, we have provided a thin wrapper over the meter-manager method. The reason is that the when variable is passed as an RPyC netref-wrapped datetime.datetime rather than as a pure datetime.datetime. In most cases this wouldn't matter, but here we want to store actual datetime.datetimes in the meter dictionary rather than references to remote (i.e., client-side) date-time.datetimes. So, we convert the wrapped date/time to an ISO 8601 date/time string and parse that into a server-side datetime.datetime, which we then pass to the MeterMT.Manager.submit_reading() method.

The code shown in this subsection is the complete RPyC meter server and would be a few lines shorter if we dropped the on_connect() and on_disconnect() methods.

6.2.3. Writing RPyC Clients

Creating RPyC clients is very similar to creating XML-RPC clients, so in this subsection, we will only review the differences between the two kinds.

6.2.3.1. A Console RPyC Client

Just like the XML-RPC client, the RPyC client requires that the server is started and stopped separately and will only work when a server is running.

The code for the meterclient-rpyc.py program is almost the same as that for the meterclient-rpc.py client we saw earlier (§6.1.3.1, 210 ◀). Only the main() and submit() functions are different.

```
def main():
    username, password = login()
    if username is not None:
        try:
            service = rpyc.connect(HOST, PORT)
```

```
            manager = service.root
            sessionId, name = manager.login(username, password)
            print("Welcome, {}, to Meter RPYC".format(name))
            interact(manager, sessionId)
    except ConnectionError as err:
        print("Error: Is the meter server running? {}".format(err))
```

The first difference is that we have used a hard-coded hostname and port number. Naturally, we could easily make these configurable, as we did with the XML-RPC client. The second difference is that instead of creating a proxied manager and then connecting, we begin by connecting to a service-providing server. In this case, the server provides only one service (MeterService), and this we can use as a meter-manager proxy. All the other code—the meter-manager login, getting jobs, submitting readings, and getting status—uses the same code as before, with one exception: the submit() function catches different exceptions from those caught by the XML-RPC client.

Synchronizing hostnames and port numbers can be tedious, especially if a conflict forces us to use a different port number from the one we normally use. This problem can be avoided by using a registry server. This requires us to run the registry_server.py server that is supplied with RPyC somewhere on our network. RPyC servers automatically look for this server when they start up, and if they find it, they register their services with it. Then, instead of clients using rpyc.connect(*host, port*), they can use rpyc.connect_by_service(*service*); for example, rpyc.connect_by_service("Meter").

6.2.3.2. A GUI RPyC Client

The GUI RPyC client, meter-rpyc.pyw, is shown in Figure 6.2. In fact, the RPyC and XML-RPyC GUI clients are visually indistinguishable when run on the same platform.

Figure 6.2 *The Meter RPyC GUI application's login and main windows on OS X*

Creating a GUI RPyC client that uses Tkinter and will automatically use an existing meter server, or will start up a server if necessary, can be done with almost the same code as we used for the GUI XML-RPC client. In fact, the difference only amounts to a couple of changed methods, a different import, some slightly changed constants, and some different exceptions in except clauses.

```python
def connect(self, username, password):
    try:
        self.service = rpyc.connect(HOST, PORT)
    except ConnectionError:
        filename = os.path.join(tempfile.gettempdir(),
                "M{}.$$$".format(random.randint(1000, 9999)))
        self.serverPid = subprocess.Popen([sys.executable, SERVER,
                filename]).pid
        self.wait_for_server(filename)
        try:
            self.service = rpyc.connect(HOST, PORT)
        except ConnectionError:
            self.handle_error("Failed to start the RPYC Meter server")
            return False
    self.manager = self.service.root
    return self.login_to_server(username, password)
```

Once the login dialog window has been used to obtain the user's username and password, this method is called to connect to the server and log the user in with the meter manager.

If the connection fails, we assume that the server isn't running and try to start it, passing it a notify filename. The server is started without blocking (i.e., asynchronously), but we must wait until the server is running before trying to connect to it. The wait_for_server() method is almost identical to the one we saw earlier (217 ◄), except that this version raises a ConnectionError rather than calling handle_error() itself. If the connection is made, we acquire a proxied meter manager and try to log the user into the meter server.

```python
def login_to_server(self, username, password):
    try:
        self.sessionId, name = self.manager.login(username, password)
        self.master.title("Meter \u2014 {}".format(name))
        return True
    except rpyc.core.vinegar.GenericException as err:
        self.handle_error(err)
        return False
```

If the user's credentials are acceptable, we set the session ID and put their name in the application's title bar. If the login fails, we return False, and this will result in the application terminating (and terminating the server too, if the server was started by the GUI application).

None of the examples in this chapter use encryption, so eavesdroppers could potentially read the client–server network traffic. This may not matter at all for applications that don't transfer private data, or that execute both client and server on the same machine, or where clients and server are safely behind a firewall, or where encrypted network connections are used. But if encryption is required, it is perfectly possible to achieve. For XML-RPC, one approach is to use the third-party PyCrypto package (www.dlitz.net/software/pycrypto) to encrypt all data that is sent over the network. Another approach is to use Transport Layer Security ("secure sockets"), which is supported by Python's ssl module. For RPyC, it is much easier to achieve security, since support for it is built in. RPyC can use SSL with keys and certificates, or a much simpler SSH (Secure Shell) tunneling approach.

Python's excellent networking support covers everything from low to high level. The standard library includes modules for all the most popular high-level protocols, including FTP for file transfers; POP3, IMAP4, and SMTP for email; HTTP and HTTPS for web traffic; and, of course, TCP/IP and other low-level socket protocols. Python's mid-level socketserver module can be used as the basis for creating servers, although support for higher-level servers is also provided; for example, the smtpd module for creating email servers, the http.server module for web servers, and the xmlrpc.server module we saw in this chapter for XML-RPC servers.

Many third-party networking modules are also available, particularly for web frameworks that support Python's Web Server Gateway Interface (WSGI; see www.python.org/dev/peps/pep-3333). For more about third-party Python web frameworks see wiki.python.org/moin/WebFrameworks, and for more about web servers see wiki.python.org/moin/WebServers.

7 Graphical User Interfaces with Tkinter

Well-designed graphical user interface (GUI) applications can present users with the most attractive, innovative, and easy-to-use interfaces. And the more sophisticated the application, the more it can benefit from a custom GUI, especially if the GUI includes application-specific custom widgets.* By comparison, web applications can be very confusing, with the browser's menus and toolbars in addition to the web application's widgets. And until the HTML5 canvas is widely available, web applications have very limited means of presenting custom widgets. Furthermore, web applications cannot compete with native applications for performance.

Smartphone users are increasingly able to interact with their apps using voice control, but for desktops, laptops, and tablets, the choices are still primarily between conventional GUI applications controlled by mouse and keyboard or voice, and touch-controlled applications. At the time of this writing, almost every touch-controlled device uses proprietary libraries and requires the use of specific languages and tools. Fortunately, the third-party, open-source Kivy library (kivy.org) is designed to provide Python support for developing cross-platform, touch-based applications to address this problem. Of course, this doesn't change the fact that most touch-based interfaces are designed for machines with limited processing power and small screens, and which may allow the user to see only one application at a time.

---

* Windows GUI programmers often use the terms "control", "container", or "form" when describing a GUI object. In this book, we use the generic term *widget*, adopted from Unix GUI programming.

231

Desktop and power users want to take full advantage of their big screens and powerful processors, and this is still best done with conventional GUI applications. Furthermore, voice control—as provided by modern versions of Windows, for example—is designed to work with existing GUI applications. And just as Python command-line programs can be used cross-platform, so can Python GUI programs, providing we use an appropriate GUI toolkit. There are several such toolkits to choose from. Here is a brief overview of the four main ones, all of which have been ported to Python 3 and work at the very least on Linux, OS X, and Windows, with native look and feel.

- **PyGtk and PyGObject:** PyGtk (www.pygtk.org) is stable and successful. However, development ceased in 2011 in favor of a successor technology called PyGObject (live. gnome.org/PyGObject). Unfortunately, at the time of this writing, PyGObject cannot be considered cross-platform, since all the development effort appears to be confined to Unix-based systems.

- **PyQt4 and PySide:** PyQt4 (www.riverbankcomputing.co.uk) provides Pythonic bindings for the Qt 4 GUI application development framework (qt-project.org). PySide (www.pyside.org) is a more recent project that is highly compatible with PyQt4 and has a more liberal license. PyQt4 is probably the most stable and mature cross-platform Python GUI toolkit available.* (Both PyQt and PySide are expected to have versions that support Qt 5 in 2013.)

- **Tkinter:** Tkinter provides bindings to the Tcl/Tk GUI toolkit (www.tcl.tk). Python 3 is normally supplied with Tcl/Tk 8.5, although this should change to Tcl/ Tk 8.6 with Python 3.4 or a later Python version. Unlike the other toolkits mentioned here, Tkinter is very basic, with no built-in support for toolbars, dock windows, or status bars (although all of these can be created). Also, while the other toolkits automatically work with many platform-specific features—such as OS X's universal menu bar—Tkinter (at least with Tcl/Tk 8.5) requires programmers to account for many platform differences themselves. Tkinter's chief virtues are that it is supplied with Python as standard, and that it is a very small package compared to the other toolkits.

- **wxPython:** wxPython (www.wxpython.org) provides bindings to the wxWidgets toolkit (www.wxwidgets.org). Although wxPython has been around for many years, a significant rewrite has been undertaken for the port to Python 3, and the results should be available by the time this book is published.

Except for PyGObject, the toolkits listed above provide all that is necessary to create cross-platform GUI applications with Python. If we care about only a

---

* Disclosure: the author was once Qt's documentation manager and has written a book about PyQt4 programming: *Rapid GUI Programming with Python and Qt* (see the Selected Bibliography, ➤ 287).

specific platform, there are almost certainly Python bindings available to the platform-specific GUI libraries (see `wiki.python.org/moin/GuiProgramming`), or we can use a platform-specific Python interpreter such as Jython or IronPython. If we want to do 3D graphics, we can usually do so within one of the GUI toolkits. Alternatively, we can use PyGame (`www.pygame.org`), or, if our needs are simpler, we can use one of the Python OpenGL bindings directly—as we will see in the next chapter.

Since Tkinter is supplied as standard, we can create GUI applications that we can easily deploy (even bundling Python and Tcl/Tk with the application itself if necessary; see, for example, `cx-freeze.sourceforge.net`). Such applications are more attractive and easier to use than command-line programs and are often more acceptable to users, particularly on OS X and Windows.

This chapter presents three example applications: a tiny "hello world" application, a small currency converter, and the more substantial Gravitate game. Gravitate can be thought of as a TileFall/SameGame variant where the tiles gravitate to the center to fill empty space rather than falling and shifting left. The Gravitate application illustrates how to create a main-window–style Tkinter application with some of the modern accoutrements, such as menus, dialogs, and a status bar. We will review a couple of Gravitate's dialogs in §7.2.2 (➤ 244), and we will review Gravitate's main-window infrastructure in §7.3 (➤ 253).

7.1. Introduction to Tkinter

GUI programming is no more difficult than any other specialized kind of programming and has the potential reward of producing applications that look professional and that people enjoy using.

Figure 7.1 *The dialog-style Hello application on Linux, OS X, and Windows*

Note, though, that the subject of GUI programming is so substantive that we cannot explore it in any real depth in a single chapter; it would need at least an entire book for that. What we can do, however, is review some of the key aspects of writing GUI programs and, in particular, how to fill some of the gaps in Tkinter's facilities. First, though, we will begin with the classic "hello world" program, in this case `hello.pyw`, shown running in Figure 7.1.

```
import tkinter as tk
import tkinter.ttk as ttk
```

```
class Window(ttk.Frame):

    def __init__(self, master=None):
        super().__init__(master) # Creates self.master
        helloLabel = ttk.Label(self, text="Hello Tkinter!")
        quitButton = ttk.Button(self, text="Quit", command=self.quit)
        helloLabel.pack()
        quitButton.pack()
        self.pack()

window = Window() # Implicitly creates tk.Tk object
window.master.title("Hello")
window.master.mainloop()
```

The code quoted above is the entire hello.pyw application's code. Many Tkinter programmers import all the Tkinter names (e.g., from tkinter import *), but we prefer to use namespaces (albeit the shortened ones, tk and ttk) so that we are clear about where everything comes from. (Incidentally, the ttk module is a wrapper around the official Ttk "Tile" Tcl/Tk extension.) We could have simply done the first import and used a tkinter.Frame rather than tkinter.ttk.Frame, and so on, but the tkinter.ttk versions provide support for themes, so using these is preferable, especially on OS X and Windows.

Most of the plain tkinter widgets also have themed tkinter.ttk versions. The plain and themed widgets don't always have the same interfaces, and there are some contexts where only a plain widget can be used, so it is important to read the documentation. (We recommend the documentation at www.tcl.tk for those who can understand Tcl/Tk code; otherwise, we recommend www.tkdocs.com, which shows examples in Python and some other languages, and also infohost.nmt.edu/tcc/help/pubs/tkinter/web, which provides a useful Tkinter tutorial/reference.) There are also several tkinter.ttk-themed widgets for which there are no plain equivalents; for example, tkinter.ttk.Combobox, tkinter.ttk.Notebook, and tkinter.ttk.Treeview.

The style of GUI programming we use in this book is to create one class per window, normally in its own module. For a top-level window (i.e., an application's main window), it is usual to inherit from tkinter.Toplevel or tkinter.ttk.Frame, as we have done here. Tkinter maintains an ownership hierarchy of parent and child widgets (sometimes called masters and slaves). By and large we don't have to worry about this, so long as we call the built-in super() function in the __init__() method of any class we create that inherits a widget.

Creating most GUI applications follows a standard pattern: create one or more window classes, one of which is the application's main window. For each window class, create the window's variables (there are none in hello.pyw), create the widgets, lay out the widgets, and specify methods to be called in response to events (e.g., mouse clicks, key presses, timeouts). In this case, we associate the user clicking the quitButton with the inherited tkinter.ttk.Frame.quit() method that will close the window, and since this is the application's only top-level window, this will then cleanly terminate the application. Once all the window classes are ready, the final step is to create an application object (done implicitly in this example) and start off the GUI event loop. The event loop was illustrated in an earlier chapter (Figure 4.8; 167 ◀).

Naturally, most GUI applications are much longer and more complicated than hello.pyw. However, their window classes normally follow the same pattern as described here, only they usually create far more widgets and associate far more events.

It is common in most modern GUI toolkits to use layouts rather than hard-coded sizes and positions for widgets. This makes it possible for widgets to automatically expand or shrink to most neatly accommodate their contents (e.g., a label or button's text), even if the contents change, while keeping their position relative to all the other widgets. Using layouts also saves programmers from having to do lots of tedious calculations.

Tkinter provides three layout managers: place (hard-coded positions; rarely used), pack (position widgets around a notional central cavity), and grid (arrange widgets in a grid of rows and columns; the most popular). In this example, we packed the label and the button one after the other and then packed the entire window. Packing is fine for very simple windows like this one, but grid is the easiest to use, as we will see in later examples.

GUI applications fall into two broad camps: dialog style and main-window style. The former are windows that have no menus or toolbars, instead being controlled through buttons, comboboxes, and the like. Using dialog style is ideal for applications that need only a simple user interface, such as small utilities, media players, and some games. Main-window–style applications usually have menus and toolbars above a central area, and a status bar at the bottom. They may also have dock windows. Main windows are ideal for more complex applications and often have menu options or toolbar buttons that result in dialogs being popped up. We will look at both kinds of application, starting with dialog style, since almost everything we learn about them also applies to the dialogs used by main-window–style applications.

7.2. Creating Dialogs with Tkinter

Dialogs have four possible modalities and varying levels of intelligence. Here is a brief summary of the modalities, after which we discuss intelligence.

- **Global Modal:** A global modal window is one that blocks the entire user interface—including all other applications—and only allows interactions with itself. Users cannot switch applications or do anything except interact with the window. The two common use cases are the dialog for logging into a computer at start up and the dialog for unlocking a password-protected screensaver. Application programmers should never use global modal windows because a bug could result in the entire machine becoming unusable.

- **Application Modal:** Application modal windows prevent users from interacting with any other window in the application. But users can still context switch to other applications. Modal windows are easier to program than modeless windows, since the user can't change the application's state behind the programmer's back. However, some users find them inconvenient.

- **Window Modal:** Window modal windows are very similar to application modal windows, except that rather than preventing interaction with any other application window, they prevent interaction with any other application window in the same window hierarchy. This is useful, for example, if the user opens two top-level document windows, since we wouldn't want their use of a dialog in one of those windows to prevent them from interacting with the other window.

- **Modeless:** Modeless dialogs do not block interaction with any other window either in their application or any other application. Modeless dialogs are potentially much more challenging for programmers to create than modal dialogs. This is because a modeless dialog must be able to cope with the user interacting with other application windows and possibly changing the state that the modeless dialog depends on.

Global modal windows are said to have *global grab* in Tcl/Tk terminology. Application and window modal windows (commonly simply called "modal windows") are said to have *local grab*. In Tkinter on OS X, some modal windows appear as sheets.

A dumb dialog is typically one that presents some widgets to the user and provides what the user entered back to the application. Such dialogs have no application-specific knowledge. A typical example is an application-login dialog that just accepts a username and password that it then passes to the application. (We saw an example of such a dialog being used in the previous chapter; §6.1.3.2, 214 ◄. The code is in MeterLogin.py.)

A smart dialog is one that embodies some level of knowledge of the application and may even be passed references to application variables or data structures so that it can work directly on the application's data.

Modal dialogs can be dumb or smart, or somewhere on the continuum between. A fairly smart modal dialog is typically one that understands enough about the application to provide validation, not just per data item it presents for editing, but for combinations of data items. For example, a reasonably intelligent dialog for entering a start and end date would not accept an end date that was earlier than the start date.

Modeless dialogs are almost always smart. They typically come in two flavors: apply/close and live. Apply/close dialogs allow users to interact with widgets and then click an Apply button to see the results in the application's main window. Live dialogs apply changes as the user interacts with the dialog's widgets; these are quite common on OS X. Smarter modeless dialogs offer undo/redo or a Default button (to reset the widgets to the application's default values) and maybe a Revert button (to reset the widgets to the values they held when the dialog was first invoked). Modeless dialogs can be dumb if they just provide information, such as a Help dialog. These typically just have a Close button.

Modeless dialogs are particularly useful when changing colors, fonts, formats, or templates, since they allow us to see the effects of each change and to then make another change, and another. Using a modal dialog in such cases means that we must open the dialog, do our changes, accept the dialog, and then repeat this cycle for every change until we were happy with the results.

A dialog-style application's main window is essentially a modeless dialog. Main-window–style applications usually have both modal and modeless dialogs that pop up in response to the user choosing particular menu options or clicking particular toolbar buttons.

7.2.1. Creating a Dialog-Style Application

In this subsection, we will review a very simple, yet useful, dialog-style application that does currency conversions. The source code is in the `currency` directory, and the application is shown in Figure 7.2.

Figure 7.2 *The dialog-style Currency application on OS X and Windows*

The application has two comboboxes listing currency names (and currency identifiers), a spinbox for entering an amount, and a label that shows the value of the amount converted from the top currency to the bottom currency.

The application's code is distributed over three Python files: `currency.pyw`, which is the program we execute; `Main.py`, which provides the `Main.Window` class; and `Rates.py`, which provides the `Rates.get()` function that was discussed in an earlier chapter (§1.5, 26 ◀). In addition, there are two icons, `currency/images/icon_16x16.gif` and `currency/images/icon_32x32.gif`, which provide icons for the application on Linux and Windows.

Python GUI applications can use the standard `.py` extension, but on OS X and Windows the `.pyw` extension is often associated with a different Python interpreter (e.g., `pythonw.exe` rather than `python.exe`). This interpreter allows the application to be run without starting up a console window, and so is much nicer for users. For programmers, though, it is best to execute Python GUI applications from inside a console using the standard Python interpreter, since this will allow any `sys.stdout` and `sys.stderr` output to be visible as an aid to debugging.

7.2.1.1. The Currency Application's main() Function

Especially for large programs, it is best to have a very small "executable" module and for all the rest of the code to be in separate .py module files (no matter how big or small they are). On fast modern machines this may appear to make no difference the first time the program is run, but on that first run all the .py module files (except for the "executable" one) are byte-compiled into .pyc files. The second and subsequent times the program is run, Python will use the .pyc files (except where a .py file has changed), so startup times will be faster than the first time.

The currency application's executable `currency.pyw` file contains one small function, `main()`.

```
def main():
    application = tk.Tk()
    application.title("Currency")
    TkUtil.set_application_icons(application, os.path.join(
            os.path.dirname(os.path.realpath(__file__)), "images"))
    Main.Window(application)
    application.mainloop()
```

The function begins by creating the Tkinter "application object". This is really a normally invisible top-level window that serves as the application's ultimate parent (or master or root) widget. In the `hello.pyw` application, we implicitly let Tkinter create this for us, but it is normally best to create it ourselves so that we can then apply application-wide settings. Here, for example, we set the application's title to "Currency".

The book's examples are supplied with the `TkUtil` module, which includes some built-in convenience functions to support Tkinter programming, plus some modules that we will discuss as we encounter them. Here, we use the `TkUtil.set_application_icons()` function.

With the title and icons set (although the icons are ignored on OS X), we create an instance of the application's main window, passing it the application object as parent (or master), and then start the GUI event loop. The application will terminate when the event loop terminates; for example, if we call `tkinter.Tk.quit()`.

```
def set_application_icons(application, path):
    icon32 = tk.PhotoImage(file=os.path.join(path, "icon_32x32.gif"))
    icon16 = tk.PhotoImage(file=os.path.join(path, "icon_16x16.gif"))
    application.tk.call("wm", "iconphoto", application, "-default", icon32,
        icon16)
```

For completeness, here is the TkUtil.set_application_icons() function. The tk.PhotoImage class can load a pixmap image in PGM, PPM, or GIF format. (Support for PNG format is expected to be added in Tcl/Tk 8.6.) Having created the two images, we call the tkinter.Tk.tk.call() function and in effect send it a Tcl/Tk command. Going this low-level should be avoided if possible, but is sometimes necessary where Tkinter doesn't bind the functionality we need.

7.2.1.2. The Currency Application's Main.Window Class

The currency application's main window follows the pattern we described earlier, and this pattern is clearly visible in the calls made in the class's __init__() method. All this subsubsection's code is quoted from currency/Main.py.

```
class Window(ttk.Frame):

    def __init__(self, master=None):
        super().__init__(master, padding=2)
        self.create_variables()
        self.create_widgets()
        self.create_layout()
        self.create_bindings()
        self.currencyFromCombobox.focus()
        self.after(10, self.get_rates)
```

It is essential to call the built-in super() function when we initialize a class that inherits a widget. Here, we not only pass in the master (i.e., the tk.Tk "application object" from the application's main() function), but also a padding value of 2 pixels. This padding provides a margin between the application window's inner border and the widgets laid out inside it.

Next, we create the window's (i.e., the application's) variables and widgets, and lay out the widgets. Then, we create the event bindings, after which we give the keyboard focus to the top combobox ready for the user to change the initial currency. Finally, we call the inherited Tkinter after() method, which takes a time in milliseconds and a callable that it will call after at least that many milliseconds have passed.

Since we download the rates from the Internet, they might take several seconds to arrive. But we want to ensure that the application is visible straight away (otherwise the user might think it didn't start and may try to start it again). So, we defer getting the rates until the application has had enough time to display itself.

```
def create_variables(self):
    self.currencyFrom = tk.StringVar()
    self.currencyTo = tk.StringVar()
    self.amount = tk.StringVar()
    self.rates = {}
```

The `tkinter.StringVars` are variables that hold strings and that can be associated with widgets. Thus, when a `StringVar`'s string is changed, that change is automatically reflected in any associated widget, and vice versa. We could have made the `self.amount` a `tkinter.IntVar`, but since Tcl/Tk operates almost entirely in terms of strings internally, it is often more convenient to use strings when working with it, even for numbers. The `rates` is a `dict` with currency name keys and conversion rate values.

```
Spinbox = ttk.Spinbox if hasattr(ttk, "Spinbox") else tk.Spinbox
```

The `tkinter.ttk.Spinbox` widget was not added to Python 3's Tkinter but will hopefully arrive with Python 3.4. This snippet of code allows us to take advantage of it if it is available, with the fallback of a non-themed spinbox. Their interfaces are not the same, so care must be taken to use only those features that are common to both.

```
def create_widgets(self):
    self.currencyFromCombobox = ttk.Combobox(self,
            textvariable=self.currencyFrom)
    self.currencyToCombobox = ttk.Combobox(self,
            textvariable=self.currencyTo)
    self.amountSpinbox = Spinbox(self, textvariable=self.amount,
            from_=1.0, to=10e6, validate="all", format="%0.2f",
            width=8)
    self.amountSpinbox.config(validatecommand=(
            self.amountSpinbox.register(self.validate), "%P"))
    self.resultLabel = ttk.Label(self)
```

Every widget should be created with a parent (or master), except for the `tk.Tk` object, which is usually the window or frame that the widget will be laid out inside. Here, we create two comboboxes and associate each one with its own `StringVar`.

We also create a spinbox, also associated with a `StringVar`, with a minimum and maximum set. The spinbox's `width` is in characters; the `format` uses old-style Python 2 % formatting (equivalent to a `str.format()` format string of `"{:0.2f}"`); and the `validate` argument says to validate whenever the spinbox's value is changed, whether by the user entering numbers or using the spin buttons. Once the spinbox has been created, we register a validation callable. This callable will be called with an argument that corresponds to the given format (`"%P"`); this is a Tcl/Tk format string, not a Python one. Incidentally, the spinbox's value is automatically set to its minimum (`from_`) value (in this case, 1.0) if no other value is explicitly set.

Finally, we create the label that will display the calculated amount. We don't give it any initial text.

```
def validate(self, number):
    return TkUtil.validate_spinbox_float(self.amountSpinbox, number)
```

This is the validation callable we registered with the spinbox. In this context, the Tcl/Tk `"%P"` format signifies the spinbox's text. So, whenever the spinbox's value is changed, this method is called with the spinbox's text. The actual validation is passed on to a generic convenience function in the `TkUtil` module.

```
def validate_spinbox_float(spinbox, number=None):
    if number is None:
        number = spinbox.get()
    if number == "":
        return True
    try:
        x = float(number)
        if float(spinbox.cget("from")) <= x <= float(spinbox.cget("to")):
            return True
    except ValueError:
        pass
    return False
```

This function expects to be passed a spinbox and a number value (as a string or None). If no value is passed, the function gets the spinbox's text itself. It returns True (i.e., "valid") for an empty spinbox to allow the user to delete the spinbox's value and start typing a new number from scratch. Otherwise, it tries to convert the text into a floating-point number and checks that it is in the spinbox's range.

All Tkinter widgets have a `config()` method that takes one or more *key=value* arguments to set widget attributes, and a `cget()` method that takes a *key* argument and returns the associated attribute value. They also have a `configure()` method that is just an alias for `config()`.

```
def create_layout(self):
    padWE = dict(sticky=(tk.W, tk.E), padx="0.5m", pady="0.5m")
    self.currencyFromCombobox.grid(row=0, column=0, **padWE)
```

```
self.amountSpinbox.grid(row=0, column=1, **padWE)
self.currencyToCombobox.grid(row=1, column=0, **padWE)
self.resultLabel.grid(row=1, column=1, **padWE)
self.grid(row=0, column=0, sticky=(tk.N, tk.S, tk.E, tk.W))
self.columnconfigure(0, weight=2)
self.columnconfigure(1, weight=1)
self.master.columnconfigure(0, weight=1)
self.master.rowconfigure(0, weight=1)
self.master.minsize(150, 40)
```

This method creates the layout shown in Figure 7.3. Each widget is put in a specific grid position and made "sticky" in the West and East directions, meaning that it will stretch or shrink horizontally as the window is resized but will not change height. The widgets are also padded by 0.5 mm (millimeters) in the x and y directions, so each widget is surrounded by 0.5 mm of empty space. (See the "Sequence and Mapping Unpacking" sidebar, 13 ◄.)

(0, 0) currencyFromCombobox	(0, 1) amountSpinbox
(1, 0) currencyToCombobox	(1, 1) resultLabel

Figure 7.3 *The Currency application's main window's layout*

Once the widgets have been laid out, the window itself is laid out in a grid consisting of a single cell that will shrink or stretch in all directions (North, South, East, West). Then, the columns are configured with weights: these are stretch factors. So, in this case, if the window is expanded horizontally, for every extra pixel of width given to the spinbox and label, the comboboxes will get an extra two pixels of width. Nonzero weights are also given to the window's single grid cell itself; this makes the window's contents resizable. And, finally, the window is given a sensible minimum size; otherwise, the user would be able to shrink it down to almost nothing.

```
def create_bindings(self):
    self.currencyFromCombobox.bind("<<ComboboxSelected>>",
            self.calculate)
    self.currencyToCombobox.bind("<<ComboboxSelected>>",
            self.calculate)
    self.amountSpinbox.bind("<Return>", self.calculate)
    self.master.bind("<Escape>", lambda event: self.quit())
```

This method is used to bind events to actions. Here, we are concerned with two kinds of events: "virtual events", which are custom events that some widgets produce, and "real events", which represent things happening in the user interface, such as a key press or the window being resized. Virtual events are signified by giving their name in double angle brackets, and real events by giving their name in single angle brackets.

Whenever a combobox's selected value changes, it adds a <<ComboboxSelected>> virtual event to the event loop's queue of events. For both comboboxes, we have chosen to bind this event to a self.calculate() method that will recalculate the currency conversion. For the spinbox, we only force a recalculation if the user presses Enter or Return. And if the user presses Esc, we terminate the application by calling the inherited tkinter.ttk.Frame.quit() method.

```
def calculate(self, event=None):
    fromCurrency = self.currencyFrom.get()
    toCurrency = self.currencyTo.get()
    amount = self.amount.get()
    if fromCurrency and toCurrency and amount:
        amount = ((self.rates[fromCurrency] / self.rates[toCurrency]) *
            float(amount))
        self.resultLabel.config(text="{:,.2f}".format(amount))
```

This method obtains the two currencies to be used and the amount to convert and then performs the conversion. At the end, it sets the result label's text to the converted amount using commas as a thousands separator, and showing two digits after the decimal point.

```
def get_rates(self):
    try:
        self.rates = Rates.get()
        self.populate_comboboxes()
    except urllib.error.URLError as err:
        messagebox.showerror("Currency \u2014 Error", str(err),
            parent=self)
        self.quit()
```

This method is called using a timer to give the window a chance to paint itself. It gets a dictionary of rates (currency name keys, conversion factor values) and populates the comboboxes accordingly. If the rates could not be obtained, an error message box is popped up, and after the user closes the message box (e.g., by clicking OK), the application is terminated.

The tkinter.messagebox.showerror() function takes a window-title text, a message text, and optionally a parent (which if given, the message box will center itself over). Since Python 3 files use UTF-8 encoding, we could have used a literal em dash (—), but the book's monospaced font doesn't have this character, so we have used the Unicode escape instead.

```
def populate_comboboxes(self):
    currencies = sorted(self.rates.keys())
    for combobox in (self.currencyFromCombobox,
                     self.currencyToCombobox):
        combobox.state(("readonly",))
        combobox.config(values=currencies)
    TkUtil.set_combobox_item(self.currencyFromCombobox, "USD", True)
    TkUtil.set_combobox_item(self.currencyToCombobox, "GBP", True)
    self.calculate()
```

This method populates the comboboxes with the currency names in alphabetical order. The comboboxes are set to be read-only. We then attempt to set the top spinbox's currency to U.S. dollars and the bottom one's to British Pounds. Finally, we call self.calculate() to set an initial conversion value.

Every Tkinter themed widget has a state() method for setting one or more states and an instate() method for checking whether the widget is in a particular state. The most commonly used states are "disabled", "readonly", and "selected".

```
def set_combobox_item(combobox, text, fuzzy=False):
    for index, value in enumerate(combobox.cget("values")):
        if (fuzzy and text in value) or (value == text):
            combobox.current(index)
            return
    combobox.current(0 if len(combobox.cget("values")) else -1)
```

This generic function is in the TkUtil module. It attempts to set the given combobox's value to the entry that has the given text—or to the entry that contains the given text if fuzzy is True.

This simple but useful currency application is around 200 lines of code (not including standard library modules or the book's TkUtil module). It is quite common for small GUI utilities to need a lot more code than their command-line equivalents, but the disparity rapidly diminishes with more complex and sophisticated applications.

7.2.2. Creating Application Dialogs

Creating stand-alone dialog-style applications is straightforward and convenient for small utilities, media players, and for some games. But for more complex applications, it is usual to have a main window and supporting dialogs. In this subsection, we will see how to create a modal dialog and a modeless dialog.

There is no difference between modal and modeless dialogs when it comes to widgets, layouts, and bindings. However, whereas modal dialogs typically assign what the user entered to variables, modeless dialogs normally call application methods or change application data in response to user interactions. Furthermore, modal dialogs block when they are invoked, whereas modeless dialogs don't, and our code must account for this important difference.

7.2.2.1. Creating Modal Dialogs

In this subsubsection, we will review the Gravitate application's Preferences dialog. The dialog's code is in `gravitate/Preferences.py`, and the dialog is shown in Figure 7.4.

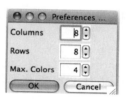 

Figure 7.4 *The Gravitate application's modal Preferences dialog on OS X and Windows*

On Linux and Windows, when the user clicks Gravitate's File→Preferences menu option, the `Main.Window.preferences()` method is invoked, and this causes the modal Preferences dialog to appear. On OS X the user must click the application menu's Preferences option or press ⌘, in accordance with OS X conventions. (Unfortunately, though, we must handle both these cases ourselves, as we will see in §7.3.2.1, ➤ 258.)

```
def preferences(self):
    Preferences.Window(self, self.board)
    self.master.focus()
```

This is the main-window method that invokes the Preferences dialog. The dialog is a smart dialog, so rather than pass it some values and then, if the user clicks OK, update the application's state, we pass it an application object directly—in this case the `self.board` of type `Board`, a `tkinter.Canvas` subclass for showing 2D graphics.

The method creates a new Preferences dialog window. This call results in the dialog being shown and blocks (since the dialog is modal) until the user clicks OK or Cancel. We don't have to do any further work here, because the dialog itself is smart enough to update the `Board` object if the user clicks OK. After the dialog is closed, all we do is make sure that the main window has the keyboard focus.

Tkinter comes with the `tkinter.simpledialog` module that provides a couple of base classes for creating custom dialogs, and some ready-made convenience functions for popping up dialogs to get single values from the user, such as `tkinter.simpledialog.askfloat()`. The ready-made dialogs provide some built-in hooks to make it as easy as possible to inherit them and to customize them with our own widgets. However, at the time of this writing, they hadn't been updated in a long time and didn't use the themed widgets. In view of this, the book's examples come with a TkUtil/Dialog.py module that provides a base class for themed custom dialogs and that works in a similar way to the tkinter.simpledialog.Dialog, and which also provides some convenience functions, such as TkUtil.Dialog.get_float().

All the book's dialogs use the TkUtil module rather than tkinter.simpledialog, so as to take advantage of the themed widgets that give Tkinter a native look and feel on OS X and Windows.

```
class Window(TkUtil.Dialog.Dialog):

    def __init__(self, master, board):
        self.board = board
        super().__init__(master, "Preferences \u2014 {}".format(APPNAME),
                TkUtil.Dialog.OK_BUTTON|TkUtil.Dialog.CANCEL_BUTTON)
```

The dialog takes a parent (master) and a Board instance. This instance will be used to provide the initial values for the dialog's widgets, and if the user clicks OK, will be given the widget values that the user has set before the dialog destroys itself. The APPNAME constant (not shown) holds the string "Gravitate".

Classes that inherit TkUtil.Dialog.Dialog must provide a body() method that will create the dialog's widgets but not its buttons: the base class does that. It should also provide an apply() method that will be called only if the user accepts the dialog (i.e., clicks OK or Yes, depending on which "accept" button has been specified). It is also possible to create an initialize() method and a validate() method, but they aren't needed for this example.

```
    def body(self, master):
        self.create_variables()
        self.create_widgets(master)
        self.create_layout()
        self.create_bindings()
        return self.frame, self.columnsSpinbox
```

This method must create the dialog's variables, lay out the dialog's widgets, and provide event bindings (excluding the buttons and their bindings). It must return either the widget that contains all the widgets we have created (typically a frame), or that widget plus the widget to which the initial keyboard focus should be given. Here, we return the frame where we have put all of our widgets and the first spinbox as the initial keyboard focus widget.

```
    def create_variables(self):
        self.columns = tk.StringVar()
```

```
        self.columns.set(self.board.columns)
        self.rows = tk.StringVar()
        self.rows.set(self.board.rows)
        self.maxColors = tk.StringVar()
        self.maxColors.set(self.board.maxColors)
```

This dialog is very simple, since it uses only labels and spinboxes. For every spinbox, we create a `tkinter.StringVar` to associate with it and initialize the StringVar's value with the corresponding value in the passed in Board instance. It might seem more natural to use `tkinter.IntVars`, but internally Tcl/Tk really uses only strings, so StringVars are often a better choice.

```
    def create_widgets(self, master):
        self.frame = ttk.Frame(master)
        self.columnsLabel = TkUtil.Label(self.frame, text="Columns",
                underline=2)
        self.columnsSpinbox = Spinbox(self.frame,
                textvariable=self.columns, from_=Board.MIN_COLUMNS,
                to=Board.MAX_COLUMNS, width=3, justify=tk.RIGHT,
                validate="all")
        self.columnsSpinbox.config(validatecommand=(
            self.columnsSpinbox.register(self.validate_int),
                "columnsSpinbox", "%P"))
        ...
```

This method is used to create the widgets. We begin by creating an outer frame that we can return as the parent (i.e., containing) widget for all the other widgets we create. The frame's parent must be the one given it by the dialog; all the other widgets we create must have the frame (or a child of the frame) as their parent.

We have shown the code only for the columns widgets, since the rows and maximum colors code is structurally identical. In each case, we create a label and a spinbox, and each spinbox is associated with its corresponding `StringVar`. The `width` attribute is the number of characters wide the spinbox should be.

Incidentally, to avoid the inconvenience of having to write, say, `underline=-1` if `TkUtil.mac()` `else 0` when creating the labels, we have used `TkUtil.Labels` instead of `tkinter.ttk.Labels`.

```
class Label(ttk.Label):

    def __init__(self, *args, **kwargs):
        super().__init__(*args, **kwargs)
        if mac():
            self.config(underline=-1)
```

(0, 0) columnsLabel	(0, 1) columnsSpinbox
(1, 0) rowsLabel	(1, 1) rowsSpinbox
(2, 0) maxColorsLabel	(2, 1) maxColorsSpinbox

Figure 7.5 *The Gravitate application's Preferences dialog's body's layout*

This tiny class allows us to set the underlined letter to indicate a keyboard shortcut and not have to worry about whether the code is executed on OS X, since in that case the underlining will have been disabled by setting a value of –1. The TkUtil/__init__.py module also has Button, Checkbutton, and Radiobutton classes, all with the same __init__() method as the one shown here.

```
def validate_int(self, spinboxName, number):
    return TkUtil.validate_spinbox_int(getattr(self, spinboxName),
        number)
```

We discussed how to validate spinboxes and the TkUtil.validate_spinbox_float() function earlier (241 ◀). The only difference between the validate_int() method used here and the validate() method used earlier (apart from their names and that we do integer validation here) is that here, we parameterize by the spinbox to validate, whereas the earlier example used a specific spinbox.

The registered validation function was given two strings: the first the name of the relevant spinbox and the second a Tcl/Tk format string. These are passed to the validation function when validation takes place, and Tcl/Tk parses them. In the case of the spinbox name, Tcl/Tk does nothing, but it replaces the "%P" with the string value of the spinbox. The TkUtil.validate_spinbox_int() function requires a spinbox widget and a string value as its arguments. So, here, we use the built-in getattr() function, passing it the dialog (self) and the name of the attribute we want (spinboxName), and getting back a reference to the relevant spinbox widget.

```
def create_layout(self):
    padW = dict(sticky=tk.W, padx=PAD, pady=PAD)
    padWE = dict(sticky=(tk.W, tk.E), padx=PAD, pady=PAD)
    self.columnsLabel.grid(row=0, column=0, **padW)
    self.columnsSpinbox.grid(row=0, column=1, **padWE)
    self.rowsLabel.grid(row=1, column=0, **padW)
    self.rowsSpinbox.grid(row=1, column=1, **padWE)
    self.maxColorsLabel.grid(row=2, column=0, **padW)
    self.maxColorsSpinbox.grid(row=2, column=1, **padWE)
```

This method creates the layout illustrated in Figure 7.5. It is very simple, because it grids all the labels to align left (sticky=tk.W, i.e., West) and all the spinboxes to fill all the available horizontal space, while padding all the widgets with 0.75 mm (the PAD constant, not shown) of space. (See the "Sequence and Mapping Unpacking" sidebar, 13 ◀.)

```
def create_bindings(self):
    if not TkUtil.mac():
        self.bind("<Alt-l>", lambda *args: self.columnsSpinbox.focus())
        self.bind("<Alt-r>", lambda *args: self.rowsSpinbox.focus())
        self.bind("<Alt-m>",
                lambda *args: self.maxColorsSpinbox.focus())
```

For non-OS X platforms, we want to provide users with the ability to navigate between the spinboxes and click the buttons using keyboard shortcuts. For example, if the user presses Alt+R, the rows spinbox will be given the keyboard focus. We don't have to do this for the buttons, since the base class takes care of them.

```
def apply(self):
    columns = int(self.columns.get())
    rows = int(self.rows.get())
    maxColors = int(self.maxColors.get())
    newGame = (columns != self.board.columns or
            rows != self.board.rows or
            maxColors != self.board.maxColors)
    if newGame:
        self.board.columns = columns
        self.board.rows = rows
        self.board.maxColors = maxColors
        self.board.new_game()
```

This method is called only if the user clicks the dialog's "accept" button (OK or Yes). We retrieve the StringVar values and convert them to ints (which should always succeed). Then we assign them to the Board instance's corresponding attributes. If any of the values has changed, we start a new game, so as to account for the change.

In large, complex applications it might require quite a lot of navigation—clicking menu options and invoking dialogs within dialogs—before we reach a dialog we want to test. To make testing easier, it is often helpful to add an if __name__ == "__main__": statement at the end of a module that contains a window class, and to put in it code that will invoke the dialog for testing purposes. Here is the code inside such a statement for the gravitate/Preferences.py module.

```
def close(event):
    application.quit()
application = tk.Tk()
```

```
        scoreText = tk.StringVar()
        board = Board.Board(application, print, scoreText)
        window = Window(application, board)
        application.bind("<Escape>", close)
        board.bind("<Escape>", close)
        application.mainloop()
        print(board.columns, board.rows, board.maxColors)
```

We begin by creating a tiny function that will terminate the application. Then we create the normally hidden (but visible in this case) tk.Tk object that serves as the application's ultimate parent. We bind the Esc key to the close() function so that the user can easily close the window.

The Board instance is normally passed to the dialog by the calling main window, but since we are executing the dialog stand-alone here, we must create such an instance ourselves.

Next, we create the dialog, which will block until the user clicks OK or Cancel. Of course, the dialog only actually appears once the event loop begins. And once the dialog has been closed, we print out the values of the Board attributes that the dialog can change. If the user clicked OK, these should reflect any changes the user made in the dialog; otherwise, they should all have their original values.

7.2.2.2. Creating Modeless Dialogs

In this subsection, we will review the Gravitate application's modeless Help dialog, shown in Figure 7.6.

As mentioned earlier, for widgets, layouts, and event bindings, there are no differences between modal and modeless dialogs. What makes the two kinds distinct is that when a modeless dialog is shown it does not block (whereas a modal one does), so the caller (e.g., the main window) continues to execute its event loop and can be interacted with. We will begin by looking at the code that invokes the dialog, and then at the dialog's code.

```
    def help(self, event=None):
        if self.helpDialog is None:
            self.helpDialog = Help.Window(self)
        else:
            self.helpDialog.deiconify()
```

This is the Main.Window.help() method. The Main.Window keeps an instance variable (self.helpDialog) that is set to None in the __init__() method (not shown). The first time the user invokes the Help dialog, the dialog is created and passed the main window as its parent. The act of creating the widget causes it to pop up over the main window, but because the dialog is modeless, the main window's

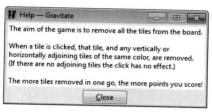

Figure 7.6 *The Gravitate application's modeless Help dialog on Windows*

event loop resumes, and the user can interact with both the dialog and the main window.

On the second and subsequent times that the user invokes the Help dialog, we already have a reference to it, so we merely show it again (using tkinter.Toplevel.deiconify()). This works because when the user closes the dialog, instead of destroying itself, the dialog merely hides. Creating, showing, and hiding a dialog the first time it is used, and then showing and hiding it on subsequent uses, is much faster than creating, showing, and then destroying it every time it is needed. Also, hiding a dialog preserves its state between uses.

```
class Window(tk.Toplevel):

    def __init__(self, master):
        super().__init__(master)
        self.withdraw()
        self.title("Help \u2014 {}".format(APPNAME))
        self.create_ui()
        self.reposition()
        self.resizable(False, False)
        self.deiconify()
        if self.winfo_viewable():
            self.transient(master)
        self.wait_visibility()
```

Modeless dialogs usually inherit tkinter.ttk.Frame or tkinter.Toplevel, as we have done here. The dialog takes a parent (master). The tkinter.Toplevel.withdraw() call immediately hides the window (before the user even sees it) to ensure that there is no flickering while the window is being created.

Next, we set the window's title to "Help — Gravitate" and then create the dialog's widgets. Since the help text is so short, we have set the dialog to be nonresizable and leave Tkinter to make it just the right size to show the help text and the Close button. If we had lots of help text, we could have used a tkinter.Text subclass with scrollbars and made the dialog resizable.

Once all the widgets have been created and laid out, we call tkinter.Toplevel.deiconify() to show the window. If the window is viewable (i.e., shown by the system's window manager)—as it should be—we notify Tkinter that this window is transient in relation to its parent. This notification provides a hint to the window system that the transient window might soon go away to help optimize repainting what is revealed when it is hidden or destroyed.

The tkinter.Toplevel.wait_visibility() call at the end blocks (for too short a time for the user to notice) until the window is visible. By default, tkinter.Toplevel windows are modeless, but if we add two extra statements after the last one, we can make the window modal. These statements are self.grab_set() and self.wait_window(self). The first statement restricts the application's focus ("grab" in Tk/Tcl terminology) to this window, thus making it modal. The second statement blocks until the window is closed. We didn't see either of these commands when we discussed modal dialogs, because it is a standard pattern to create a modal dialog by inheriting tkinter.simpledialog.Dialog (or in this book, TkUtil.Dialog), both of which have these two statements.

The user can now interact with this window, with the application's main window, and with any of the application's other modeless windows that happen to be visible.

```
    def create_ui(self):
        self.helpLabel = ttk.Label(self, text=_TEXT, background="white")
        self.closeButton = TkUtil.Button(self, text="Close", underline=0)
        self.helpLabel.pack(anchor=tk.N, expand=True, fill=tk.BOTH,
                padx=PAD, pady=PAD)
        self.closeButton.pack(anchor=tk.S)
        self.protocol("WM_DELETE_WINDOW", self.close)
        if not TkUtil.mac():
            self.bind("<Alt-c>", self.close)
        self.bind("<Escape>", self.close)
        self.bind("<Expose>", self.reposition)
```

The window's user interface is so simple that we have created it all in this one method. First, we create the label to show the help text (in the _TEXT constant, not shown) and then the Close button. We have used a TkUtil.Button (derived from tkinter.ttk.Button) so that the underline is correctly ignored on OS X. (We saw a TkUtil.Label subclass that is almost identical to TkUtil.Button earlier; 247 ◀.)

With only two widgets, it makes sense to use the simplest layout manager, so, here, we pack the label to the top of the window, set it to be able to grow in both directions, and pack the button at the bottom.

If we aren't on OS X, we add a keyboard accelerator of Alt+C for the Close button, and on all platforms we bind Esc to close the window.

Since the modeless dialog window is hidden and shown rather than destroyed and recreated, it is possible that the user shows the help window, then closes (i.e., hides) it, then moves the main window, and then shows the help window again. It is perfectly reasonable to leave the help window wherever it was first shown (or wherever the user last moved it). However, since the help text is so short, it seems to make more sense to reposition it every time it is shown. This is achieved by binding the <Expose> event (which occurs whenever a window must repaint itself) to a custom reposition() method.

```
def reposition(self, event=None):
    if self.master is not None:
        self.geometry("+{}+{}".format(self.master.winfo_rootx() + 50,
            self.master.winfo_rooty() + 50))
```

This method moves the window to the same position as its master (i.e., the main window), but offset 50 pixels right and down.

In theory, we don't need to call this method explicitly in the __init__() method, but by doing so, we ensure that the window is correctly positioned before it is shown. This avoids the window suddenly jumping into position after it first appears, since when it is shown, it is already in the right place.

```
def close(self, event=None):
    self.withdraw()
```

If the dialog window is closed—whether by the user pressing Esc or Alt+C, clicking the Close button, or clicking the × close button—this method is called. The method simply hides the window rather than destroying it. The window can be shown again by calling tkinter.Toplevel.deiconify() on it.

7.3. Creating Main-Window Applications with Tkinter

In this section, we will study how to create those aspects of the Gravitate main-window–style application that are most generic. The application is shown in Figure 7.7 (➤ 254), and the game is described in the "Gravitate" sidebar (➤ 254). The user interface has some of the standard elements that users would expect, such as a menu bar, a central widget, a status bar, and dialogs. Tkinter provides support for menus out of the box, but we must create the central widget and status bar ourselves. It should be straightforward to adapt the Gravitate application's code to create other main-window–style applications, by changing the widget in the central area and changing the menus and status bar, but keeping the same overall infrastructure.

Gravitate consists of seven Python files and nine icon images. The application's "executable" is gravitate/gravitate.pyw, and the main window is in gravitate/Main.py. These are supported by three dialog windows: gravitate/About.py, which we won't cover; gravitate/Help.py, which we covered in the previous section (§7.2.2.2, 250 ◄); and gravitate/Preferences.py, which we covered earlier (§7.2.2.1, 245 ◄). The main window's central area is occupied by a Board from gravitate/Board.py, a subclass of tkinter.Canvas (and which we don't have the space to cover).

Figure 7.7 *The Gravitate application on Windows and OS X*

Gravitate

The aim of the game is to remove all the tiles from the board. When a tile is clicked, that tile and any vertically or horizontally adjoining tiles of the same color are removed. (If there are no adjoining tiles the click has no effect.) The more tiles removed in one go, the more points are scored.

Gravitate's logic is a similar to Tile Fall or the Same Game. The key difference between Gravitate and the other two is that when tiles are removed in Tile Fall or the Same Game, tiles fall down and shift left to fill any gaps, whereas with Gravitate, tiles "gravitate" toward the center of the board.

The book's examples include three versions of Gravitate. The first version is in directory gravitate and is described in this section. The second version is in directory gravitate2: this has the same game logic as the first version, and in addition features a hidable/showable toolbar and a more sophisticated Preferences dialog that provides additional options, such as a choice of tile shapes and a zoom factor to show larger or smaller tiles. Also, gravitate2 remembers the high score between sessions and can be played using the keyboard as well as the mouse, navigating with the arrow keys and removing by pressing the spacebar. The third version is three-dimensional and is covered in Chapter 8 (§8.2, ➤ 272). There's also an online version at www.qtrac.eu/gravitate.html.

```
def main():
    application = tk.Tk()
    application.withdraw()
    application.title(APPNAME)
    application.option_add("*tearOff", False)
    TkUtil.set_application_icons(application, os.path.join(
            os.path.dirname(os.path.realpath(__file__)), "images"))
    window = Main.Window(application)
    application.protocol("WM_DELETE_WINDOW", window.close)
    application.deiconify()
    application.mainloop()
```

This is the gravitate/gravitate.pyw file's main() function. It creates the normally hidden top-level tkinter.Tk object and then immediately hides the application to avoid flicker while the main window is being created. By default, Tkinter has tear-off menus (a throwback to the ancient Motif GUI); we switch the feature off, since no modern GUI uses them. Next, we set the application's icons using a function we discussed earlier (239 ◀). Then, we create the application's main window, and we tell Tkinter that if the application's ✕ close button is clicked, it must call the Main.Window.close() method. Finally, we show the application (or rather, add an event to the event loop to schedule it to be shown) and then start off the application's event loop. At this point the application will appear.

7.3.1. Creating a Main Window

Tkinter main windows are, in principle, no different from dialogs. In practice, though, main windows normally have a menu bar and a status bar, often have toolbars, and sometimes have dock windows. They also usually have one central widget—a text editor, a table (e.g., for a spreadsheet), or a graphic (e.g., for a game or simulation or visualization). For Gravitate, we have a menu bar, a graphics central widget, and a status bar.

```
class Window(ttk.Frame):

    def __init__(self, master):
        super().__init__(master, padding=PAD)
        self.create_variables()
        self.create_images()
        self.create_ui()
```

The Gravitate Main.Window class derives from tkinter.ttk.Frame and passes on most of its work to the base class and to three helper methods.

```
    def create_variables(self):
        self.images = {}
```

```
self.statusText = tk.StringVar()
self.scoreText = tk.StringVar()
self.helpDialog = None
```

The status bar's transient text messages are stored in self.statusText, and the permanent score (and high score) indicator's text is stored in self.scoreText. The Help dialog is initially set to None; this was discussed earlier (§7.2.2.2, 250 ◄).

It is very common for GUI applications to display icons beside menu options, and icons are essential for toolbar buttons. For the Gravitate game, we have put all the icon images in the gravitate/images subdirectory and have defined a set of constants for their names (e.g., the NEW constant is set to the "New" string). When the Main.Window is created, it calls a custom create_images() method to load all the necessary images as the values of the self.images dictionary. It is essential that we keep references to images loaded by Tkinter; otherwise, they will be garbage collected (and disappear).

```
def create_images(self):
    imagePath = os.path.join(os.path.dirname(
            os.path.realpath(__file__)), "images")
    for name in (NEW, CLOSE, PREFERENCES, HELP, ABOUT):
        self.images[name] = tk.PhotoImage(
                file=os.path.join(imagePath, name + "_16x16.gif"))
```

We have chosen to use 16×16 pixel images in menus, so for each action constant (NEW, CLOSE, and so on), we load the appropriate images.

The built-in __file__ constant holds the filename including its path. We use os.path.realpath() to get the absolute path and eliminate ".." components and symbolic links, then we extract just the directory portion (i.e., dropping the filename) and combine this with "images" to get the path to the application's images subdirectory.

```
def create_ui(self):
    self.create_board()
    self.create_menubar()
    self.create_statusbar()
    self.create_bindings()
    self.master.resizable(False, False)
```

Thanks to our ruthless approach to refactoring, this method hands off its work to helper methods. And then, when the user interface is complete, it sets the window to be nonresizable. After all, it doesn't make sense for the user to resize when the tiles are a fixed size. (The Gravitate 2 application also doesn't allow user resizing, but it does allow users to change the tile size and resizes the window accordingly on the user's behalf.)

```
def create_board(self):
    self.board = Board.Board(self.master, self.set_status_text,
            self.scoreText)
    self.board.update_score()
    self.board.pack(fill=tk.BOTH, expand=True)
```

This method creates a Board instance (a tkinter.Canvas subclass) and passes it the self.set_status_text() method so that it can display transient messages in the main window's status bar, and the self.scoreText so that it can update the score (and high score).

Once the board has been created, we call its update_score() method to get "0 (0)" displayed in the permanent score indicator. We also pack the board into the main window, telling it to expand in both directions.

```
def create_bindings(self):
    modifier = TkUtil.key_modifier()
    self.master.bind("<{}-n>".format(modifier), self.board.new_game)
    self.master.bind("<{}-q>".format(modifier), self.close)
    self.master.bind("<F1>", self.help)
```

Here, we provide three keyboard shortcuts: Ctrl+N (or ⌘N) to start a new game, Ctrl+Q (or ⌘Q) to quit, and F1 to pop up (or show, if hidden), the modeless help window. The TkUtil.key_modifier() method returns the platform-appropriate shortcut modifier name ("Control" or "Command").

7.3.2. Creating Menus

Tkinter shows menus beneath window title bars on Linux and Windows, as is traditional. But on OS X, Tkinter integrates menus into the single OS X menu at the top of the screen. However, as we will see, we must help Tkinter with this integration.

Menus and submenus are instances of tkinter.Menu. One menu must be created as a top-level window's menu bar (e.g., as the main window's menu bar), and all the other menus as children of the menu bar menu.

```
def create_menubar(self):
    self.menubar = tk.Menu(self.master)
    self.master.config(menu=self.menubar)
    self.create_file_menu()
    self.create_help_menu()
```

Here, we create a new empty menu as the child of the window and set the window's menu attribute (i.e., its menu bar) to be this menu (self.menubar). We

then add submenus to the menu bar; in this case, just two, both of which we will
review in the following subsubsections.

7.3.2.1. Creating a File Menu

Most main-window–style applications have a file menu with options to create a
new document, open an existing document, save the current document, and quit
the application. However, for games, many of these options aren't needed, so
for the Gravitate application we only provide a couple of them, as can be seen in
Figure 7.8.

```
def create_file_menu(self):
    modifier = TkUtil.menu_modifier()
    fileMenu = tk.Menu(self.menubar, name="apple")
    fileMenu.add_command(label=NEW, underline=0,
            command=self.board.new_game, compound=tk.LEFT,
            image=self.images[NEW], accelerator=modifier + "+N")
    if TkUtil.mac():
        self.master.createcommand("exit", self.close)
        self.master.createcommand("::tk::mac::ShowPreferences",
                self.preferences)
    else:
        fileMenu.add_separator()
        fileMenu.add_command(label=PREFERENCES + ELLIPSIS, underline=0,
                command=self.preferences,
                image=self.images[PREFERENCES], compound=tk.LEFT)
        fileMenu.add_separator()
        fileMenu.add_command(label="Quit", underline=0,
                command=self.close, compound=tk.LEFT,
                image=self.images[CLOSE],
                accelerator=modifier + "+Q")
    self.menubar.add_cascade(label="File", underline=0,
            menu=fileMenu)
```

This method is used to create the file menu. Constants are written in all upper-
case, and unless shown otherwise, hold strings of the same name; for example,
NEW is a constant holding the string "New".

The method begins by getting the modifier to use for keyboard accelerators (⌘
on OS X, Ctrl on Linux and Windows). Then it creates the file menu as a child
of the window's menu bar. The name given to this menu ("apple") tells Tkinter
that on OS X, this menu should be integrated with (i.e., *is*) the application's
application menu; it is ignored on other platforms.

Menu options are added using the tkinter.Menu.add_command(), tkinter.Menu
.add_checkbutton(), and tkinter.Menu.add_radiobutton() methods, although we

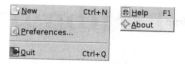

Figure 7.8 *The Gravitate application's menus on Linux*

use only the first of these for Gravitate. Separators are added with tkinter .add_separator(). The underline attribute is ignored on OS X, and on Windows, underlines are only visible if set to be so or if the Alt key is held down. For each menu option, we specify its label text, its underline, the command to execute when the menu option is invoked, and the menu's icon (the image attribute). The compound attribute says how to handle icons and text: tk.LEFT means show both, with the icon on the left. We also set an accelerator key; for example, for File→New, the user can press Ctrl+N on Linux and Windows, or ⌘N on OS X.

On OS X, the current application's Preferences and Quit menu options are shown in the application menu (to the right of the apple menu, after which comes the application's file menu). To integrate with OS X, we use the tkinter.Tk.create-command() method to associate the Tcl/Tk ::tk::mac::ShowPreferences and exit commands with Gravitate's corresponding methods. For other platforms, we add both Preferences and Quit as normal menu options.

Once the file menu has been fully populated, we add it as a cascade (i.e., submenu) of the menu bar.

```
def menu_modifier():
    return "Command" if mac() else "Ctrl"
```

This tiny function from TkUtil/__init__.py is used for the text in menus. The word "Command" is treated specially on OS X and appears as the ⌘ symbol.

7.3.2.2. Creating a Help Menu

The application's help menu has only two options: Help and About. However, OS X handles both of these differently from Linux and Windows, so our code must account for the differences.

```
def create_help_menu(self):
    helpMenu = tk.Menu(self.menubar, name="help")
    if TkUtil.mac():
        self.master.createcommand("tkAboutDialog", self.about)
        self.master.createcommand("::tk::mac::ShowHelp", self.help)
    else:
        helpMenu.add_command(label=HELP, underline=0,
                command=self.help, image=self.images[HELP],
                compound=tk.LEFT, accelerator="F1")
```

```
helpMenu.add_command(label=ABOUT, underline=0,
            command=self.about, image=self.images[ABOUT],
            compound=tk.LEFT)
self.menubar.add_cascade(label=HELP, underline=0,
            menu=helpMenu)
```

We begin by creating the help menu with a name of "help". The name is ignored on Linux and Windows but ensures that, on OS X, the menu is properly integrated with the system's help menu. If we are on an OS X system, we use the tkinter.Tk.createcommand() method to associate the Tcl/Tk tkAboutDialog and ::tk::mac::ShowHelp commands with the appropriate Gravitate methods. On other platforms, we create the Help and About menu options in the conventional way.

7.3.3. Creating a Status Bar with Indicators

The Gravitate application has a typical status bar that shows transient text messages on the left and has a permanent status indicator on the right. Figure 7.7 (254 ◀) shows the status indicator and (in the left-hand screenshot) a transient message.

```
def create_statusbar(self):
    statusBar = ttk.Frame(self.master)
    statusLabel = ttk.Label(statusBar, textvariable=self.statusText)
    statusLabel.grid(column=0, row=0, sticky=(tk.W, tk.E))
    scoreLabel = ttk.Label(statusBar, textvariable=self.scoreText,
            relief=tk.SUNKEN)
    scoreLabel.grid(column=1, row=0)
    statusBar.columnconfigure(0, weight=1)
    statusBar.pack(side=tk.BOTTOM, fill=tk.X)
    self.set_status_text("Click a tile or click File→New for a new "
            "game")
```

To create a status bar, we begin by creating a frame. Then we add a label and associate the label with the self.statusText (of type StringVar). We can now set the status text by setting the self.statusText's text, although in practice we will call a method instead. We also add one permanent status indicator: a label that displays the score (and high score) and that is associated with the self.scoreText.

We grid the two labels inside the status bar frame and make the statusLabel (for showing transient messages) occupy as much of the width as is available. We pack the status bar frame itself at the bottom of the main window and make it stretch horizontally to occupy the full width of the window. At the end, we set an initial transient message using a custom set_status_text() method.

```
def set_status_text(self, text):
    self.statusText.set(text)
    self.master.after(SHOW_TIME, lambda: self.statusText.set(""))
```

This method sets the text of the `self.statusText` to the given text (which could be empty) and then clears the text after `SHOW_TIME` milliseconds (5 seconds in this example).

Although we have put only labels into the status bar, there is no reason why we couldn't add other widgets—comboboxes, spinboxes, or buttons, for example.

There has been only enough space in this chapter to show some basic Tkinter use. Since Python adopted Tcl/Tk 8.5 (the first version to use theming), Tkinter has become much more attractive, as it now supports the native look and feel on OS X and Windows. Tkinter contains some very powerful and flexible widgets, most notably the `tkinter.Text` widget, which can be used for editing and presenting styled and formatted text, and the `tkinter.Canvas` widget, for 2D graphics (and used by Gravitate and Gravitate 2). Three other very useful widgets are `tkinter.ttk.Treeview`, for showing tables or trees of items, `tkinter.ttk.Notebook`, for showing tabs (used in Gravitate 2's Preferences dialog), and `tkinter.ttk.Panedwindow`, for providing splitters.

Although Tkinter doesn't provide some of the high-level features that other GUI toolkits provide, as we have seen, it is straightforward to create status bars with transient message areas and permanent status indicators. Tkinter's menus are more sophisticated than were needed in this chapter, supporting submenus, subsubmenus, and so on, as well as checkable (checkbox- and radiobutton-style) menu options. And it is also quite straightforward to create context menus.

In terms of modern features that we might want, the most obviously missing are toolbars. These are pretty easy to create, although it does take some care to make them hidable and showable, and to make them automatically lay themselves out to account for window resizing. Another modern feature that many applications benefit from is dock windows. It is possible to create dock windows that can be hidden or shown, dragged from one dock area to another, and even floated free.

The book's examples include two applications that are not covered in this chapter due to lack of space: `texteditor` and `texteditor2`, the latter shown in Figure 7.9 (➤ 262). Both applications demonstrate how to implement showable/hidable toolbars that automatically lay themselves out, submenus, checkbox- and radiobutton-style menu options, context menus, and a recent files list. They both also have an extension dialog, shown in Figure 7.10 (➤ 262). They also show how to use the `tkinter.Text` widget and how to interact with the clipboard. In addition, `texteditor2` illustrates how to implement dock windows (although floating them free doesn't work correctly on OS X).

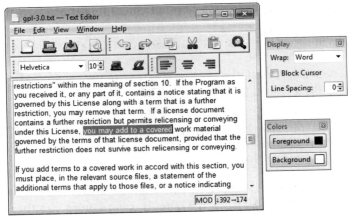

Figure 7.9 *The Text Editor 2 application on Windows*

Figure 7.10 *The Text Editor applications' extension dialog on Windows*

Clearly, Tkinter requires more effort to provide fundamental infrastructure than most other GUI toolkits. However, Tkinter does not impose many limitations, and if we create the necessary infrastructure (e.g., for toolbars and dock windows) with enough care, we can reuse the infrastructure in all of our applications. Tkinter is very stable and comes standard with Python, so it is ideal for creating easy-to-deploy GUI applications.

8
OpenGL 3D Graphics

Many modern applications, such as design tools, data visualization tools, games —and, of course, screensavers—use 3D graphics. All of the Python GUI toolkits mentioned in the previous chapter provide support for 3D graphics, either directly or through add-ons. The 3D support is almost invariably in the form of an interface to the system's OpenGL libraries.

There are also many 3D Python graphics packages that provide high-level interfaces to simplify OpenGL programming. Some examples of these include the Python Computer Graphics Kit (cgkit.sourceforge.net), OpenCASCADE (github.com/tenko/occmodel), and VPython (www.vpython.org).

It is also possible to access OpenGL more directly. The two main packages that provide this functionality are PyOpenGL (pyopengl.sourceforge.net) and pyglet (www.pyglet.org). Both faithfully wrap the OpenGL libraries, which makes it very easy to translate examples in C (OpenGL's native language and used in OpenGL textbooks) into Python. Both packages can be used to create stand-alone 3D programs, in the case of PyOpenGL by using its wrapper for the OpenGL GLUT GUI library, and in the case of pyglet through its own event handling and top-level window support.

For stand-alone 3D programs, it is probably best to use an existing GUI toolkit in conjunction with PyOpenGL (which can interoperate with Tkinter, PyQt, PySide, and wxPython, among others) or, where a simpler GUI is sufficient, pyglet.

There are many versions of OpenGL, and there are two quite different ways of using it. The traditional approach (called "direct mode") works everywhere and for all versions: it involves calling OpenGL functions that are executed immediately. A more modern approach, available since version 2.0, is to set up the scene using the traditional approach and then write OpenGL programs in the OpenGL Shading Language (a kind of specialized version of the C language). Such programs are then sent (as plain text) to the GPU, which compiles and executes them. This approach can produce much faster programs and is much more versatile than the traditional approach, but it isn't as widely supported.

In this chapter, we will review one PyOpenGL program and two pyglet programs, which between them illustrate many fundamental aspects of 3D OpenGL programming. We will use the traditional approach throughout, since it is much easier to see how to do 3D graphics through using function calls than having to learn the OpenGL Shading Language, and, in any case, our primary concern is with Python programming. This chapter assumes prior knowledge of OpenGL programming, so most of the OpenGL calls shown in this chapter are not explained. Readers unfamiliar with OpenGL might find the *OpenGL SuperBible* mentioned in the Selected Bibliography (➤ 286) to be a useful starting point.

One important point to note is an OpenGL naming convention. Many OpenGL function names end with a number followed by one or more letters. The number is the number of arguments and the letters the arguments' type. For example, the glColor3f() function is used to set the current color using three floating-point arguments—red, green, and blue, each in the in the range 0.0 to 1.0—whereas the glColor4ub() function is used to set the color using four unsigned byte arguments—red, green, blue, alpha (transparency), each in the range 0 to 255. Naturally, in Python, we can normally use numbers of any type and rely on the conversions being done automatically.

Three-dimensional scenes are usually projected onto two-dimensional surfaces (e.g., the computer screen) in one of two ways: orthographically or with perspective. Orthographic projection preserves object sizes and is usually preferred for computer-aided design tools. Perspective projections show objects larger when they are near the viewer and smaller when they are further away. This can produce more realistic effects, particularly when showing landscapes. Both projections are used for games. In the chapter's first section we will create a scene that uses perspective, and in the second section we will create a scene that uses an orthographic projection.

8.1. A Perspective Scene

In this section, we will create the Cylinder programs shown in Figure 8.1. Both programs show three colored axes and a lighted hollow cylinder. The PyOpenGL version (shown on the left) is the purest in terms of adherence to the OpenGL interfaces, while the pyglet version (shown on the right) is perhaps slightly easier to program and is a tiny bit more efficient.

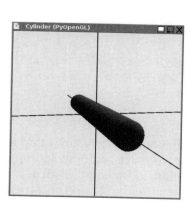

Figure 8.1 *The Cylinder programs on Linux and Windows*

Most of the code is the same in both programs, and some of those methods that differ do so only in their names. In view of this, we will review the full PyOpenGL version in the first subsection, and only those things that are different in the pyglet version will be shown in the second subsection. We will see plenty more pyglet code further on (§8.2, ➤ 272).

8.1.1. Creating a Cylinder with PyOpenGL

The cylinder1.pyw program creates a simple scene that the user can rotate independently about the x and y axes. And when the window containing the scene is resized, the scene is scaled to fit.

```
from OpenGL.GL import *
from OpenGL.GLU import *
from OpenGL.GLUT import *
```

The program makes use of the OpenGL GL (core library), GLU (utility library), and GLUT (windowing toolkit). It is normally best practice to avoid importing using the from *module* import * syntax, but for PyOpenGL it seems reasonable, because all the imported names begin with a prefix of gl, glu, glut, or GL, and so they are easy to identify and unlikely to cause conflicts.

```
SIZE = 400
ANGLE_INCREMENT = 5

def main():
    glutInit(sys.argv)
    glutInitWindowSize(SIZE, SIZE)
```

```
window = glutCreateWindow(b"Cylinder (PyOpenGL)")
glutInitDisplayString(b"double=1 rgb=1 samples=4 depth=16")
scene = Scene(window)
glutDisplayFunc(scene.display)
glutReshapeFunc(scene.reshape)
glutKeyboardFunc(scene.keyboard)
glutSpecialFunc(scene.special)
glutMainLoop()
```

The GLUT library provides the event handling and top-level windows that a GUI toolkit normally supplies. To use this library, we must begin by calling glut-Init() and passing it the program's command-line arguments; it will apply and remove any that it recognizes. We can then, optionally, set an initial window size (as we do here). Next, we create a window and give it an initial title. The call to glutInitDisplayString() is used to set some of the OpenGL context's parameters—in this case, to turn on double-buffering, to use the RGBA (red, green, blue, alpha) color model, to turn on antialiasing support, and to set a depth buffer with 16 bits of precision. (See the PyOpenGL documentation for a list of all the options and their meanings.)

The OpenGL interfaces use 8-bit strings (normally ASCII-encoded). One way to pass such strings is to use the str.encode() method, which returns a bytes encoded with the given encoding—for example, "title".encode("ascii"), which returns b'title'—but here we have used bytes literals directly.

The Scene is a custom class that we will use to render OpenGL graphics onto the window. Once the scene is created, we register some of its methods as GLUT call-back functions; that is, functions that OpenGL will call in response to particular events. We register the Scene.display() method, which will be called whenever the window is shown (i.e., for the first time and whenever revealed if it is uncovered). We also register the Scene.reshape() method, which is called whenever the window is resized; the Scene.keyboard() method, which is called when the user presses a key (excluding certain keys); and the Scene.special() method, which is called when the user presses a key not handled by the registered keyboard function.

With the window created and the callback functions registered, we start off the GLUT event loop: This will run until the program is terminated.

```
class Scene:

    def __init__(self, window):
        self.window = window
        self.xAngle = 0
        self.yAngle = 0
        self._initialize_gl()
```

We begin the Scene class by keeping a reference to the OpenGL window and setting the x and y axes angles to zero. We defer all the OpenGL-specific initialization to a separate function that we call at the end.

```python
def _initialize_gl(self):
    glClearColor(195/255, 248/255, 248/255, 1)
    glEnable(GL_DEPTH_TEST)
    glEnable(GL_POINT_SMOOTH)
    glHint(GL_POINT_SMOOTH_HINT, GL_NICEST)
    glEnable(GL_LINE_SMOOTH)
    glHint(GL_LINE_SMOOTH_HINT, GL_NICEST)
    glEnable(GL_COLOR_MATERIAL)
    glEnable(GL_LIGHTING)
    glEnable(GL_LIGHT0)
    glLightfv(GL_LIGHT0, GL_POSITION, vector(0.5, 0.5, 1, 0))
    glLightfv(GL_LIGHT0, GL_SPECULAR, vector(0.5, 0.5, 1, 1))
    glLightfv(GL_LIGHT0, GL_DIFFUSE, vector(1, 1, 1, 1))
    glMaterialf(GL_FRONT_AND_BACK, GL_SHININESS, 50)
    glMaterialfv(GL_FRONT_AND_BACK, GL_SPECULAR, vector(1, 1, 1, 1))
    glColorMaterial(GL_FRONT_AND_BACK, GL_AMBIENT_AND_DIFFUSE)
```

This method is called just once to set up the OpenGL context. We begin by setting the clear color (i.e., the background color) to a shade of light blue. Then we enable various OpenGL features, of which the most important is creating a light. The presence of this light is why the cylinder isn't of a uniform color. We also make the cylinder's basic (unlit) color depend on calls to the glColor...() functions; for example, having enabled the GL_COLOR_MATERIAL option, setting the current color to red with, say, glColor3ub(255, 0, 0) will also affect the material color (in this case the cylinder's color).

```python
def vector(*args):
    return (GLfloat * len(args))(*args)
```

This helper function is used to create an OpenGL array of floating-point values (each of type GLfloat).

```python
def display(self):
    glClear(GL_COLOR_BUFFER_BIT|GL_DEPTH_BUFFER_BIT)
    glMatrixMode(GL_MODELVIEW)
    glPushMatrix()
    glTranslatef(0, 0, -600)
    glRotatef(self.xAngle, 1, 0, 0)
    glRotatef(self.yAngle, 0, 1, 0)
    self._draw_axes()
```

```
        self._draw_cylinder()
        glPopMatrix()
```

This method is called when the scene's window is first shown and whenever the scene is revealed (e.g., if a covering window is moved or closed). It moves the scene back (along the *z* axis) so that we are viewing it from in front, and rotates it in the *x* and *y* axes depending on the user's interaction. (Initially, these rotations are of zero degrees.) Once the scene has been translated and rotated, we draw the axes and then the cylinder itself.

```
    def _draw_axes(self):
        glBegin(GL_LINES)
        glColor3f(1, 0, 0)         # x-axis
        glVertex3f(-1000, 0, 0)
        glVertex3f(1000, 0, 0)
        glColor3f(0, 0, 1)         # y-axis
        glVertex3f(0, -1000, 0)
        glVertex3f(0, 1000, 0)
        glColor3f(1, 0, 1)         # z-axis
        glVertex3f(0, 0, -1000)
        glVertex3f(0, 0, 1000)
        glEnd()
```

A *vertex* is the OpenGL term for a point in three-dimensional space. Each axis is drawn the same way: we set the axis's color and then give its start and end vertices. The glColor3f() and glVertex3f() functions each require three floating-point arguments, but we have used ints and left Python to do the conversions.

```
    def _draw_cylinder(self):
        glPushMatrix()
        try:
            glTranslatef(0, 0, -200)
            cylinder = gluNewQuadric()
            gluQuadricNormals(cylinder, GLU_SMOOTH)
            glColor3ub(48, 200, 48)
            gluCylinder(cylinder, 25, 25, 400, 24, 24)
        finally:
            gluDeleteQuadric(cylinder)
        glPopMatrix()
```

The GLU utility library has built-in support for creating some basic 3D shapes, including cylinders. We begin by moving our starting point further back along the *z* axis. Then we create a "quadric", an object that can be used to render various 3D shapes. We set the color using three unsigned bytes (i.e., red, green, blue values in the range 0 to 255). The gluCylinder() call takes the generic quadric, the cylinder's radii at each end (in this case they are the same), the cylinder's height, and then two granularity factors (where higher values produce smoother results that are more expensive to process). And at the end, we explicitly delete the quadric rather than rely on Python's garbage collection to minimize our resource usage.

```python
def reshape(self, width, height):
    width = width if width else 1
    height = height if height else 1
    aspectRatio = width / height
    glViewport(0, 0, width, height)
    glMatrixMode(GL_PROJECTION)
    glLoadIdentity()
    gluPerspective(35.0, aspectRatio, 1.0, 1000.0)
    glMatrixMode(GL_MODELVIEW)
    glLoadIdentity()
```

This method is called whenever the scene's window is resized. Almost all of the burden is passed on to the gluPerspective() function. And, in fact, the code shown here should serve as a sensible starting point for any scene that uses a perspective projection.

```python
def keyboard(self, key, x, y):
    if key == b"\x1B": # Escape
        glutDestroyWindow(self.window)
```

If the user presses a key (excluding a function key, an arrow key, Page Up, Page Down, Home, End, or Insert), this method (registered with glutKeyboardFunc()) is called. Here, we check to see if the Esc key was pressed, and if so, we delete the window, and since there are no other windows, this terminates the program.

```python
def special(self, key, x, y):
    if key == GLUT_KEY_UP:
        self.xAngle -= ANGLE_INCREMENT
    elif key == GLUT_KEY_DOWN:
        self.xAngle += ANGLE_INCREMENT
    elif key == GLUT_KEY_LEFT:
        self.yAngle -= ANGLE_INCREMENT
    elif key == GLUT_KEY_RIGHT:
        self.yAngle += ANGLE_INCREMENT
    glutPostRedisplay()
```

This method was registered with the glutSpecialFunc() function and is called whenever the user presses a function key, an arrow key, Page Up, Page Down, Home, End, or Insert. Here, we only respond to arrow keys. If an arrow key is pressed, we increment or decrement the *x*- or *y*-axis angle and tell the GLUT toolkit to redraw the window. This will result in the callable registered with the glutDisplayFunc() being called—in this example, the Scene.display() method.

We have now seen the complete code for the PyOpenGL cylinder1.pyw program. Those familiar with OpenGL should feel immediately at home, since the OpenGL calls are almost all the same as in C.

8.1.2. Creating a Cylinder with pyglet

Structurally, the pyglet version (cylinder2.pyw) is very similar to the PyOpenGL version. The key difference is that pyglet provides its own event-handling and window-creation interface, so we don't need to use GLUT calls.

```
def main():
    caption = "Cylinder (pyglet)"
    width = height = SIZE
    resizable = True
    try:
        config = Config(sample_buffers=1, samples=4, depth_size=16,
                double_buffer=True)
        window = Window(width, height, caption=caption, config=config,
                resizable=resizable)
    except pyglet.window.NoSuchConfigException:
        window = Window(width, height, caption=caption,
                resizable=resizable)
    path = os.path.realpath(os.path.dirname(__file__))
    icon16 = pyglet.image.load(os.path.join(path, "cylinder_16x16.png"))
    icon32 = pyglet.image.load(os.path.join(path, "cylinder_32x32.png"))
    window.set_icon(icon16, icon32)
    pyglet.app.run()
```

Rather than passing the OpenGL context configuration as a bytes string, pyglet supports using a pyglet.gl.Config object to specify our requirements. Here, we begin by creating our preferred configuration and then creating our own custom Window (a pyglet.window.Window subclass), based on the configuration; if this fails, we fall back to creating the window with a default configuration.

One nice feature of pyglet is that it supports setting the application's icon, which typically appears in the corner of the title bar and in task switchers. Once the window has been created and the icons set, we start off the pyglet event loop.

```
class Window(pyglet.window.Window):

    def __init__(self, *args, **kwargs):
        super().__init__(*args, **kwargs)
```

```
        self.set_minimum_size(200, 200)
        self.xAngle = 0
        self.yAngle = 0
        self._initialize_gl()
        self._z_axis_list = pyglet.graphics.vertex_list(2,
                ("v3i", (0, 0, -1000, 0, 0, 1000)),
                ("c3B", (255, 0, 255) * 2)) # one color per vertex
```

This method is similar to the equivalent Scene method we reviewed in the previous subsection. One difference is that, here, we have set a minimum size for the window. As we will see in a moment, pyglet can draw lines in three different ways. The third way is to draw a preexisting list of vertex–color pairs, and here we create such a list. The function that creates the list takes the number of vertex–color pairs followed by a sequence of that number of pairs. Each pair consists of a string format and a sequence. In this case, the first pair's string format means "vertices specified by three integer coordinates", so, here, two vertices are given. The second pair's string format means "colors specified by three unsigned bytes"; here, two colors are given (both the same), one for each vertex.

We do not show the _initialize_gl(), on_draw(), on_resize(), or _draw_cylinder() methods. The _initialize_gl() method is very similar to the one used in cylinder1.pyw. Furthermore, the body of the on_draw() method that pyglet calls automatically to display pyglet.window.Window subclasses is identical to the body of the cylinder1.pyw program's Scene.display() method. Similarly, the on_resize() method that is called to handle resizing has the same body as the previous program's Scene.reshape() method. Both programs' _draw_cylinder() methods (Scene._draw_cylinder() and Window._draw_cylinder()) are identical.

```
    def _draw_axes(self):
        glBegin(GL_LINES)
        glColor3f(1, 0, 0)                      # x-axis (traditional-style)
        glVertex3f(-1000, 0, 0)
        glVertex3f(1000, 0, 0)
        glEnd()
        pyglet.graphics.draw(2, GL_LINES, # y-axis (pyglet-style "live")
                ("v3i", (0, -1000, 0, 0, 1000, 0)),
                ("c3B", (0, 0, 255) * 2))
        self._z_axis_list.draw(GL_LINES)  # z-axis (efficient pyglet-style)
```

We have drawn each axis using a different technique to show some of the options available. The *x* axis is drawn using traditional OpenGL function calls in exactly the same way as for the PyOpenGL version of the program. The *y* axis is drawn by telling pyglet to draw lines between 2 points (it could be any number, of course), and for which we provide the corresponding vertices and colors. Especially for large numbers of lines, this should be a bit more efficient than the traditional approach. The *z* axis is drawn in the most efficient way possible: here we take a preexisting list of vertex–color pairs stored as a `pyglet.graphics.vertex_list` and tell it to draw itself as lines between the vertices.

```
def on_text_motion(self, motion): # Rotate about the x or y axis
    if motion == pyglet.window.key.MOTION_UP:
        self.xAngle -= ANGLE_INCREMENT
    elif motion == pyglet.window.key.MOTION_DOWN:
        self.xAngle += ANGLE_INCREMENT
    elif motion == pyglet.window.key.MOTION_LEFT:
        self.yAngle -= ANGLE_INCREMENT
    elif motion == pyglet.window.key.MOTION_RIGHT:
        self.yAngle += ANGLE_INCREMENT
```

If the user presses an arrow key, this method is called (provided we define it). Here, we do the same work as we did in the previous example's `special()` method, only now we use `pyglet`-specific constants rather than GLUT constants for the keys.

We have not provided an `on_key_press()` method (which would be called for other key presses), because `pyglet`'s default implementation closes the window (and hence terminates the program) if Esc is pressed, which is the behavior we want.

The two cylinder programs are both around 140 lines. However, if we use `pyglet.graphics.vertex_lists` and other `pyglet` extensions, we gain both convenience—particularly for event and window handling—and efficiency.

8.2. An Orthographic Game

In Chapter 7, we showed the code for a 2D Gravitate game, although we omitted the code that draws the tiles. In fact, each tile was produced by drawing a square surrounded by four isosceles trapezoids positioned above, below, left, and right. The above and left trapezoids were drawn in a lighter shade of the square's color and the below and right in a darker shade; this resulted in a 3D-look. (See Figure 7.7, 254 ◄, and the "Gravitate" sidebar, 254 ◄.)

In this section, we will review most of the code for the Gravitate 3D game shown in Figure 8.2. This program uses spheres rather than tiles and arranges the spheres with gaps in between so that the user can see into the three-dimensional structure as they rotate the scene about the *x* and *y* axes. We will focus on the GUI and 3D code, omitting some of the low-level details that implement the game's logic. The complete source code is in `gravitate3d.pyw`.

The program's `main()` function (not shown) is almost identical to the one in `cylinder2.pyw`, the only differences being the name of the caption and the names of the icon images.

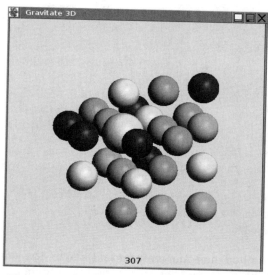

Figure 8.2 *The Gravitate 3D program on Linux*

```
BOARD_SIZE = 4 # Must be > 1.
ANGLE_INCREMENT = 5
RADIUS_FACTOR = 10
DELAY = 0.5 # seconds
MIN_COLORS = 4
MAX_COLORS = min(len(COLORS), MIN_COLORS)
```

Here are some of the constants that the program uses. The BOARD_SIZE is the number of spheres in each axis; when set to 4, this produces a $4 \times 4 \times 4$ board of 64 spheres. The ANGLE_INCREMENT set to 5 means that when the user presses an arrow key, the scene will be rotated in steps of 5°. The DELAY is the time to wait between deleting the sphere (and all its adjoining spheres of the same color, as well as *their* adjoining spheres of the same color) that the user has selected and clicked, and moving any spheres toward the center to fill any gaps. The COLORS (not shown) is a list of 3-tuples of integers (each in the range 0 to 255), each representing a color.

When the user clicks an unselected sphere, it is selected (and any selected sphere deselected), and this is shown by drawing the sphere with a radius that is RADIUS_FACTOR bigger than the radius normally used. When a selected sphere is clicked, that sphere and any spheres of the same color adjoining it (at 90°, not diagonally), and any adjoining them, and so on, are deleted—providing at least two spheres are deleted. Otherwise, the sphere is simply unselected.

```
class Window(pyglet.window.Window):

    def __init__(self, *args, **kwargs):
        super().__init__(*args, **kwargs)
        self.set_minimum_size(200, 200)
        self.xAngle = 10
        self.yAngle = -15
        self.minColors = MIN_COLORS
        self.maxColors = MAX_COLORS
        self.delay = DELAY
        self.board_size = BOARD_SIZE
        self._initialize_gl()
        self.label = pyglet.text.Label("", bold=True, font_size=11,
                anchor_x="center")
        self._new_game()
```

This __init__() method has more statements than the equivalent cylinder-
program methods, because we need to set the colors, delay, and board size. We
also start the program off with some initial rotation, so that the user can see
straight away that the game is three dimensional.

One particularly useful feature offered by pyglet is text labels. Here, we create
an empty label centered at the bottom of the scene. We will use this to show
messages and the current score.

The call to the custom _initialize_gl() method (not shown, but similar to the
one we saw before) sets up the background and a light. With everything set up
in terms of the program's logic and OpenGL, we start a new game.

```
    def _new_game(self):
        self.score = 0
        self.gameOver = False
        self.selected = None
        self.selecting = False
        self.label.text = ("Click to Select • Click again to Delete • "
                "Arrows to Rotate")
        random.shuffle(COLORS)
        colors = COLORS[:self.maxColors]
        self.board = []
        for x in range(self.board_size):
            self.board.append([])
            for y in range(self.board_size):
                self.board[x].append([])
                for z in range(self.board_size):
                    color = random.choice(colors)
                    self.board[x][y].append(SceneObject(color))
```

This method creates a board where each sphere has a random color chosen from the COLORS list and where there are at most self.maxColors colors in use. The board is represented by a list of lists of lists of SceneObjects. Each of these objects has a color (the sphere color passed to the constructor) and a selection color (automatically generated and used for selecting, explained later; §8.2.2, ➤ 277).

Since we changed the label text, pyglet will redraw the scene (by calling our on_draw() method), and the new game will be visible and waiting for user interaction.

8.2.1. Drawing the Board Scene

When a scene is shown for the first time or revealed when a covering window is closed or moved, pyglet calls the on_draw() method. And when a scene is resized (i.e., when its window is resized), pyglet calls the on_resize() method.

```
def on_resize(self, width, height):
    size = min(self.width, self.height) / 2
    height = height if height else 1
    width = width if width else 1
    glViewport(0, 0, width, height)
    glMatrixMode(GL_PROJECTION)
    glLoadIdentity()
    if width <= height:
        glOrtho(-size, size, -size * height / width,
                size * height / width, -size, size)
    else:
        glOrtho(-size * width / height, size * width / height,
                -size, size, -size, size)
    glMatrixMode(GL_MODELVIEW)
    glLoadIdentity()
```

We have used an orthographic projection for Gravitate 3D. The code shown here should work as is for any orthographic scene. (So, if we were using PyOpenGL, we would call this method reshape() and register it with the glutReshapeFunc() function.)

```
def on_draw(self):
    diameter = min(self.width, self.height) / (self.board_size * 1.5)
    radius = diameter / 2
    offset = radius - ((diameter * self.board_size) / 2)
    radius = max(RADIUS_FACTOR, radius - RADIUS_FACTOR)
    glClear(GL_COLOR_BUFFER_BIT|GL_DEPTH_BUFFER_BIT)
    glMatrixMode(GL_MODELVIEW)
```

```
    glPushMatrix()
    glRotatef(self.xAngle, 1, 0, 0)
    glRotatef(self.yAngle, 0, 1, 0)
    with Selecting(self.selecting):
        self._draw_spheres(offset, radius, diameter)
    glPopMatrix()
    if self.label.text:
        self.label.y = (-self.height // 2) + 10
        self.label.draw()
```

This is pyglet's equivalent to a PyOpenGL display() method registered with the glutDisplayFunc() function. We want the board to fill as much of the window's space as possible while allowing for it to be rotated without any spheres being clipped. We also need to compute an offset to ensure that the board is correctly centered.

Once the preliminaries have been taken care of, we rotate the scene (e.g., if the user has pressed any arrow keys), and then we draw the spheres in the context of a custom Selecting context manager. This context manager ensures that certain settings are turned on or off depending on whether the scene is being drawn to be seen by the user or is in effect being drawn out of sight for the purpose of detecting which sphere the user has clicked. (Selecting is discussed in the following subsection; §8.2.2, ➤ 277.)

If the label has any text, we make sure that the label's *y* position is at the bottom of the window—since the window might have been resized—and then tell the label to draw itself (i.e., to draw its text).

```
    def _draw_spheres(self, offset, radius, diameter):
        try:
            sphere = gluNewQuadric()
            gluQuadricNormals(sphere, GLU_SMOOTH)
            for x, y, z in itertools.product(range(self.board_size),
                    repeat=3):
                sceneObject = self.board[x][y][z]
                if self.selecting:
                    color = sceneObject.selectColor
                else:
                    color = sceneObject.color
                if color is not None:
                    self._draw_sphere(sphere, x, y, z, offset, radius,
                            diameter, color)
        finally:
            gluDeleteQuadric(sphere)
```

Quadrics can be used to draw spheres as well as cylinders, although, in this case, we must draw many spheres (up to 64) rather than just one cylinder. We can use the same quadric to draw every sphere, though.

Rather than writing for x in range(self.board.size): for y in range(self.board.size): for z in range(self.board.size): to produce an *x*, *y*, *z* triple for every sphere in the board list of lists of lists, we have achieved the same thing using a single for loop in conjunction with the itertools.product() function.

For each triple, we retrieve the corresponding scene object (whose colors will be None if it has been deleted) and set the color to the selection color, if we are drawing to see which sphere has been clicked, or to the sphere's color, if we are drawing for the user to see. If the color is not None we draw the particular sphere.

```
def _draw_sphere(self, sphere, x, y, z, offset, radius, diameter,
        color):
    if self.selected == (x, y, z):
        radius += RADIUS_FACTOR
    glPushMatrix()
    x = offset + (x * diameter)
    y = offset + (y * diameter)
    z = offset + (z * diameter)
    glTranslatef(x, y, z)
    glColor3ub(*color)
    gluSphere(sphere, radius, 24, 24)
    glPopMatrix()
```

This method is used to draw each sphere offset into its correct position in the 3D grid of spheres. If the sphere is selected we draw it with an increased radius. The last two arguments to gluSphere() are two granularity factors (where higher values produce smoother results that are more expensive to process).

8.2.2. Handling Scene Object Selection

Selecting an object in a three-dimensional space that is displayed on a two-dimensional surface is not easy! Various techniques have been developed over the years, but the one that seems to be the most reliable and widely used is the one we have used for Gravitate 3D.

The technique works as follows. When the user clicks the scene, the scene is redrawn in an off-screen buffer not visible to the user, with every object drawn with a unique color. The color of the pixel at the click position is then read from the buffer and used to identify the unique scene object associated with that color. For this to succeed, we must draw the scene with no antialiasing, no lighting, and no textures, so that each object is drawn in its unique color with no additional color processing.

We will begin by looking at the SceneObject that each sphere is represented by, and then we will review the Selecting context manager.

```
class SceneObject:

    __SelectColor = 0

    def __init__(self, color):
        self.color = color
        SceneObject.__SelectColor += 1
        self.selectColor = SceneObject.__SelectColor
```

We give each scene object its display color (self.color), which need not be unique, and a unique select color. The private static __SelectColor is an integer that is incremented for every new scene object; it is used to give each object a unique select color.

```
    @property
    def selectColor(self):
        return self.__selectColor
```

This property returns the scene object's select color, which is either None (e.g., for a deleted object) or a 3-tuple of color integers (each in the range 0 to 255).

```
    @selectColor.setter
    def selectColor(self, value):
        if value is None or isinstance(value, tuple):
            self.__selectColor = value
        else:
            parts = []
            for _ in range(3):
                value, y = divmod(value, 256)
                parts.append(y)
            self.__selectColor = tuple(parts)
```

This select-color setter accepts the given value if it is None or a tuple; otherwise, it computes a unique color tuple based on the unique integer value it is given. The first scene object is passed a value of 1, and so its color is (1, 0, 0). The second is passed 2, so its color is (2, 0, 0), and so on up to the 255th, whose color is (255, 0, 0). The 256th color is (0, 1, 0), the 257th is (1, 1, 0), and the 258th (2, 1, 0), and so on. This system can cope with over sixteen million unique objects, which should be enough for most situations.

```
SELECTING_ENUMS = (GL_ALPHA_TEST, GL_DEPTH_TEST, GL_DITHER,
        GL_LIGHT0, GL_LIGHTING, GL_MULTISAMPLE, GL_TEXTURE_1D,
        GL_TEXTURE_2D, GL_TEXTURE_3D)
```

We need to turn antialiasing, lighting, textures, and anything else that changes an object's color on or off depending on whether we are drawing for the user to see or off-screen for the purpose of detecting which object the user has clicked. These are the OpenGL enums that affect object color in the Gravitate 3D program.

```
class Selecting:

    def __init__(self, selecting):
        self.selecting = selecting
```

The Selecting context manager remembers whether the spheres drawn in its context (276 ◀) are for the user or for clicked-object detection; that is, for selecting.

```
    def __enter__(self):
        if self.selecting:
            for enum in SELECTING_ENUMS:
                glDisable(enum)
            glShadeModel(GL_FLAT)
```

When the context manager is entered, if the drawing is for selecting, we disable all the color-changing aspects of OpenGL's state and switch to a flat shading model.

```
    def __exit__(self, exc_type, exc_value, traceback):
        if self.selecting:
            for enum in SELECTING_ENUMS:
                glEnable(enum)
            glShadeModel(GL_SMOOTH)
```

When the context manager is exited when we are drawing for selecting, we reenable all the color-changing aspects of the OpenGL state and switch back to a smooth shading model.

It is easy to see how the selecting works by making two changes to the source code. First, change the += 1 in the SceneObject.__init__() method to += 500. Second, comment out the self.selecting = False statement in the Window. on_mouse_press() method (that we will review in the next subsection). Now run the program and click any sphere: the scene will be redrawn to show the normally off-screen selecting scene but in all other respects will work normally.

8.2.3. Handling User Interaction

The Gravitate 3D game is mostly mouse driven. However, the arrow keys are used to provide a means of rotating the board, and other keys are used to start a new game and to quit.

```
def on_mouse_press(self, x, y, button, modifiers):
    if self.gameOver:
        self._new_game()
        return
    self.selecting = True
    self.on_draw()
    self.selecting = False
    selectColor = (GLubyte * 3)()
    glReadPixels(x, y, 1, 1, GL_RGB, GL_UNSIGNED_BYTE, selectColor)
    selectColor = tuple([component for component in selectColor])
    self._clicked(selectColor)
```

This method is called by pyglet whenever the user clicks a mouse button (providing we have defined the method). If the game has finished, we take this click to mean start a new game. Otherwise, we assume that the user is clicking a sphere. We set selecting to True and redraw the scene (this happens off-screen, so the user doesn't notice), then we reset selecting to False.

The glReadPixels() function is used to read the colors of one or more pixels; in this case, we use it to read the off-screen pixel in the position that the user clicked and retrieve its RGB value as three unsigned bytes (each in the range 0 to 255). Then we put these bytes into a 3-tuple of integers so that we can compare it with each sphere's unique select color.

Note that our glReadPixels() call assumes a coordinate system whose *y* origin is bottom-left (which it is in pyglet). If the coordinate system has a top-left *y* origin, two extra statements are needed: viewport = (GLint * 4)(); glGetInte-gerv(GL_VIEWPORT, viewport), and the y in the glReadPixels() call must be replaced with viewport[3] – y.

```
def _clicked(self, selectColor):
    for x, y, z in itertools.product(range(self.board_size), repeat=3):
        if selectColor == self.board[x][y][z].selectColor:
            if (x, y, z) == self.selected:
                self._delete() # Second click deletes
            else:
                self.selected = (x, y, z)
            return
```

We call this method whenever the user clicks, except when the click results in a new game being started. We use the `itertools.product()` function to produce every x, y, z triple for the board and compare the scene object at each coordinate triple's select color with the color of the clicked pixel. If we get a match, we have uniquely identified the scene object that the user has clicked. If this object is already selected, then the user is clicking it for a second time, so we attempt to delete it and its adjoining spheres of the same color. Otherwise, the object is being clicked to select it (and any previously selected scene object will be unselected).

```python
def _delete(self):
    x, y, z = self.selected
    self.selected = None
    color = self.board[x][y][z].color
    if not self._is_legal(x, y, z, color):
        return
    self._delete_adjoining(x, y, z, color)
    self.label.text = "{:,}".format(self.score)
    pyglet.clock.schedule_once(self._close_up, self.delay)
```

This method is used to delete the clicked sphere and its adjoining spheres of the same color (and *their* adjoining spheres of the same color). We begin by unselecting the selected sphere, and then we check to see if the deletion is legal (i.e., there is at least one suitable adjoining sphere). If the deletion is legal, we perform the deletion using the `_delete_adjoining()` method and its helper methods (none of which are shown). Then, we update the label to show the newly increased score and schedule a call to the `self._close_up()` method (not shown) after half a second. This allows the user to see which spheres have been deleted before any gaps are filled by spheres gravitating toward the center. (A more sophisticated alternative would be to animate the closing up by moving the spheres one or a few pixels at a time to their new positions.)

```python
def on_key_press(self, symbol, modifiers):
    if (symbol == pyglet.window.key.ESCAPE or
        ((modifiers & pyglet.window.key.MOD_CTRL or
          modifiers & pyglet.window.key.MOD_COMMAND) and
         symbol == pyglet.window.key.Q)):
        pyglet.app.exit()
    elif ((modifiers & pyglet.window.key.MOD_CTRL or
           modifiers & pyglet.window.key.MOD_COMMAND) and
          symbol == pyglet.window.key.N):
        self._new_game()
```

```
elif (symbol in {pyglet.window.key.DELETE, pyglet.window.key.SPACE,
                    pyglet.window.key.BACKSPACE} and
        self.selected is not None):
    self._delete()
```

The user can terminate the program by clicking the ✕ close button, but we also allow them to do so by clicking Esc or Ctrl+Q (or ⌘Q). The user can start a new game when the existing game has finished simply by clicking, or they can start a new game at any time by clicking Ctrl+N (or ⌘N). We also allow the user to delete the selected sphere (and its adjoining spheres) either by clicking it a second time or by pressing Del, Space, or Backspace.

The Window also has an on_text_motion() method that handles the arrow keys and rotates the scene about the *x* or *y* axis. The method isn't shown here, because it is identical to the one we saw earlier (§8.1.2, 270 ◀).

This completes our coverage of the Gravitate 3D game. The only methods we have omitted are those concerned with the details of the game's logic, in particular the methods that handle the deletion of adjoining spheres (by setting their color and select colors to None), and those that handle the moving of the spheres toward the center.

Creating 3D scenes programmatically can be quite challenging, especially since the traditional OpenGL interfaces are entirely procedural (i.e., based on functions) rather than object oriented. Nonetheless, thanks to PyOpenGL and pyglet, it is straightforward to port OpenGL C code directly into Python and to use the complete OpenGL interfaces. Furthermore, pyglet in particular provides convenient support for event handling and window creation, while PyOpenGL provides integration with many GUI toolkits, including Tkinter.

Epilogue

This book has explained many valuable techniques and introduced several useful libraries. And through doing so, the book has hopefully provided ideas and inspiration for producing better programs using Python 3 (www.python.org).

Python continues to grow in popularity and use across application domains and across continents. Python is an ideal first language with its support for procedural, object-oriented, and functional-style programming, and its clear, lightweight, and consistent syntax. Yet, Python is also a superb language for professional use (as, for example, Google has demonstrated over many years). This is particularly due to Python's support for rapid development and for the production of highly maintainable code, as well as its ease of access to powerful functionality written in C or other compiled languages that support the C calling conventions.

There are no dead ends in Python programming: there is always more to learn and further to go. So, while Python can comfortably meet the needs of novice programmers, it has the advanced features and intellectual depth to satisfy even the most demanding experts. Not only is the Python language open in the sense of licensing and the availability of its source code, but it is also open with regards to introspection, right down to the byte code if we want it. And, of course, Python itself is open to those who want to contribute to it (docs.python.org/devguide).

There are probably many thousands of computer languages in existence—although only a few dozen languages are very widely used—and nowadays, Python is certainly among the most popular. As a computer scientist who has used many different languages over the decades, I would often get frustrated with the languages that my employers required me to use. And I suspect like many other computer scientists, I kept thinking about creating a better language; one that would have none of the problems and inconveniences of the languages I was used to, and one that would incorporate all the best features of the languages I'd learned or knew about. Over the years, I came to realize that every time I dreamed up an ideal language, it turned out to be Python, albeit with a few unpythonic features—constants, optional typing, and access control (private attributes). So now I don't dream of creating my ideal programming language —I use it instead. Thank you, Guido van Rossum and all the other Python contributors, past and present, for giving the world a programming language and ecosystem that is incredibly powerful and useful, that works pretty well everywhere, and that's a pleasure to use.

B Selected Bibliography

C++ Concurrency in Action: Practical Multithreading

Anthony Williams (Manning Publications, Co., 2012, ISBN-13: 978-1-933988-77-1)

This challenging book covers concurrency in C++ but is valuable because it describes many of the problems and pitfalls that can afflict concurrent programs (regardless of language) and explains how to avoid them.

Clean Code: A Handbook of Agile Software Craftsmanship

Robert C. Martin (Prentice Hall, 2009, ISBN-13: 978-0-13-235088-4)

This book addresses many of the "tactical" issues in programming: good naming, function design, refactoring, and similar. The book has many ideas that should help any programmer improve their coding style and make their programs more maintainable. (The book's examples are in Java.)

Code Complete: A Practical Handbook of Software Construction, Second Edition

Steve McConnell (Microsoft Press, 2004, ISBN-13: 978-0-7356-1967-8)

This book shows how to build solid software, going beyond the language specifics into the realms of ideas, principles, and practices. The book is packed with examples that will make any programmer think more deeply about their programming.

Design Patterns: Elements of Reusable Object-Oriented Software

Erich Gamma, Richard Helm, Ralph Johnson, and John Vlissides (Addison-Wesley, 1995, ISBN-13: 978-0-201-63361-0)

This is one of the most influential programming books of modern times. The design patterns are fascinating and of great practical use in everyday programming. (The book's examples are mostly in C++.)

Domain-Driven Design: Tackling Complexity in the Heart of Software

Eric Evans (Addison-Wesley, 2004, ISBN-13: 978-0-321-12521-7)

This is a very interesting book on software design, particularly useful for large, multiperson projects. At heart it is about creating and refining domain models that represent what the system is designed to do, and about creating a ubiquitous language through which all those involved with the system—not just software engineers—can communicate their ideas.

Don't Make Me Think!: A Common Sense Approach to Web Usability, Second Edition
Steve Krug (New Riders, 2006, ISBN-13: 978-0-321-34475-5)

This is a short and practical book on web usability based on research and experience. Applying the easy-to-understand ideas in this book will improve any web site of any size.

GUI Bloopers 2.0: Common User Interface Design Don'ts and Dos
Jeff Johnson (Morgan Kaufmann, 2008, ISBN-13: 978-0-12-370643-0)

Don't be put off by the slightly whimsical title; this is a serious book that every GUI programmer should read. You won't agree with every single suggestion, but you will think more carefully and with more insight about user interface design after reading this book.

Java Concurrency in Practice
Brian Goetz, et. al. (Addison-Wesley, 2006, ISBN-13: 978-0-321-34960-6)

This book provides excellent coverage of concurrency in Java. The book contains many tips on concurrent programming that are applicable to any language.

The Little Manual of API Design
Jasmin Blanchette (Trolltech/Nokia, 2008)

This very short manual (available for free from www21.in.tum.de/~blanchet/api-design.pdf) provides ideas and insight into the design of APIs and draws most of its examples from the Qt toolkit.

Mastering Regular Expressions, Third Edition
Jeffrey E.F. Friedl (O'Reilly Media, 2006, ISBN-13: 978-0-596-52812-6)

This is the standard text on regular expressions. It is written in an accessible manner with lots of fully explained and practical examples.

OpenGL® SuperBible: Comprehensive Tutorial and Reference, Fourth Edition
Richard S. Wright, Jr., Benjamin Lipchak, and Nicholas Haemel (Addison-Wesley, 2007, ISBN-13: 978-0-321-49882-3)

This is a good introduction to 3D graphics using OpenGL, suitable for programmers without prior 3D graphics experience. The examples are written in C++, but the OpenGL APIs are pretty faithfully reproduced in pyglet and other Python OpenGL bindings, so the book's examples can be used without too much adaptation.

Programming in Python 3: A Complete Introduction to the Python Language, Second Edition

Mark Summerfield (Addison-Wesley, 2010, ISBN-13: 978-0-321-68056-3)

This book teaches Python 3 programming to people who can program in any other conventional procedural or object-oriented language (including Python 2, of course).

Python Cookbook, Third Edition

David Beazley and Brian K. Jones (O'Reilly Media, 2013, ISBN-13: 978-1-4493-4037-7)

This book is full of interesting and practical ideas covering all aspects of Python 3 programming. It is an excellent companion to *Python in Practice*.

Rapid GUI Programming with Python and Qt: The Definitive Guide to PyQt Programming

Mark Summerfield (Prentice Hall, 2008, ISBN-13: 978-0-13-235418-9)

This book teaches GUI programming using Python 2 and the Qt 4 toolkit. Python 3 versions of the examples are available from the author's website, and almost all of the text applies to PySide as well as to PyQt.

Security in Computing, Fourth Edition

Charles P. Pfleeger and Shari Lawrence Pfleeger (Prentice Hall, 2007, ISBN-13: 978-0-13-239077-4)

This book provides interesting, useful, and practical coverage of the broad range of computer security issues. It explains how attacks can be made and how to protect against them.

Tcl and the Tk Toolkit, Second Edition

John K. Ousterhout and Ken Jones (Addison-Wesley, 2010, ISBN-13: 978-0-321-33633-0)

This is the standard text on Tcl/Tk 8.5. Tcl is an unconventional, almost syntax-free language, but this book is useful to learn how to read the Tcl/Tk documentation, since this is often necessary when writing Python/Tkinter applications.

Index

Symbols

♞ black chess knight character, 21

!= not equal operator, 48

& bitwise and operator, 133

() call, generator, and tuple operator, 22; *see also* __call__()

* multiplication and sequence unpacking operator, 13, 26, 30–31, 43, 49, 70, 109

** mapping unpacking operator, 13, 222, 241–242, 248

< less than operator, 48; *see also* __lt__()

<= less than or equal operator, 48

== equal operator, 48; *see also* __eq__()

> greater than operator, 48

>= greater than or equal operator, 48

>> bitwise right shift operator, 133

@ at symbol, 48, 52; *see also* decorator

A

abc (module), 30–32, 35
    ABCMeta (type); *see* top-level entry
    abstractmethod(), 12–14, 42, 120
    abstractproperty(), 42

ABCMeta (type; abc module), 12–14, 30–32, 35, 42, 120

abs() (built-in), 130

abspath() (os.path module), 146

abstractmethod() (abc module), 12–14, 42, 120

abstractproperty() (abc module), 42

adding properties, 57–58

after() (tkinter module), 214, 239, 261

all() (built-in), 31, 36

antialiasing, 266

append() (list type), 43, 102, 274

application
    design, 216
    dialog-style, 237–244
    main-window–style, 253–261
    modal, 214, 236–237

argparse (module), 145–146, 157, 209

arguments
    keyword and positional, 13, 50, 51–52
    maximum, 134

array (module), 124; *see also* numpy module

Array (type; multiprocessing module), 144, 154

as_completed() (concurrent.futures module), 153–154

assert (statement), 30, 37, 55, 69, 82, 127, 131

AssertionError (exception), 30

ast (module)
    literal_eval(), 88

asynchronous I/O, 142

atexit (module)
    register(), 67, 187, 193

Atom format, 159

atomic operations, 143

AttributeError (exception), 56, 103, 113

P

Mark Summerfield

Mark is a computer science graduate with many years experience working in the software industry, primarily as a programmer and documenter. Mark owns Qtrac Ltd. (www.qtrac.eu), where he works as an independent author, editor, consultant, and trainer, specializing in the C++, Go, and Python languages, and the Qt, PyQt, and PySide libraries.

Other books by Mark Summerfield include

- *Programming in Go* (2012, ISBN-13: 978-0-321-77463-7)
- *Advanced Qt Programming* (2011, ISBN-13: 978-0-321-63590-7)
- *Programming in Python 3* (First Edition, 2009, ISBN-13: 978-0-13-712929-4; Second Edition, 2010, ISBN-13: 978-0-321-68056-3)
- *Rapid GUI Programming with Python and Qt* (2008, ISBN-13: 978-0-13-235418-9)

Other books by Jasmin Blanchette and Mark Summerfield include

- *C++ GUI Programming with Qt 4* (First Edition, 2006, ISBN-13: 978-0-13-187249-3; Second Edition, 2008, ISBN-13: 978-0-13-235416-5)
- *C++ GUI Programming with Qt 3* (2004, ISBN-13: 978-0-13-124072-8)

Production

The text was written using the *gvim* editor. The typesetting—including all the diagrams—was done using the *lout* typesetting language. All of the code snippets were automatically extracted directly from the example programs and from test programs using custom tools. The index was compiled by the author. The text and source code was version-controlled using *Mercurial*. The monospaced code font was derived from a condensed version of DejaVu Mono and modified using *FontForge*. The book was previewed using *evince* and *gv,* and converted to PDF by *Ghostscript.* The cover was provided by the publisher. Note that only English print editions are definitive; *ebook* versions and translations are not under the author's control and may introduce errors.

All the editing and processing was done on Debian Linux systems. All the book's examples have been tested with Python 3.3 (and, where possible, Python 3.2 and Python 3.1) on Linux, OS X (in most cases), and Windows (in most cases). The examples are available from the book's web site, www.qtrac.eu/pipbook.html, and should work with all future Python 3.*x* versions.

Python
in Practice
Create Better Programs Using
Concurrency, Libraries, and Patterns

Mark Summerfield

Foreword by Doug Hellmann,
Senior Developer, DreamHost

Developer's Library

Safari.
Books Online

FREE
Online Edition

Your purchase of **Python in Practice** includes access to a free online edition for 45 days through the Safari Books Online subscription service. Nearly every Addison-Wesley Professional book is available online through Safari Books Online, along with over thousands of books and videos from publishers such as Cisco Press, Exam Cram, IBM Press, O'Reilly Media, Prentice Hall, Que, Sams, and VMware Press.

Safari Books Online is a digital library providing searchable, on-demand access to thousands of technology, digital media, and professional development books and videos from leading publishers. With one monthly or yearly subscription price, you get unlimited access to learning tools and information on topics including mobile app and software development, tips and tricks on using your favorite gadgets, networking, project management, graphic design, and much more.

Activate your FREE Online Edition at
informit.com/safarifree

STEP 1:   Enter the coupon code: DSVHDDB.

STEP 2:   New Safari users, complete the brief registration form.
Safari subscribers, just log in.

If you have difficulty registering on Safari or accessing the online edition,
please e-mail customer-service@safaribooksonline.com